In search of the virtual class

This book presents a vision of what education and training could become as information technology develops. The argument is simple. To prepare people for life in an information society they need to be taught with the technology of an information society. But what does this mean? The authors examine the nature of education as a communication system, applying their findings to the classroom to discover why the good old classroom system has been around for four thousand years. Their answer is that it's a remarkably powerful communication system, which explains why attempts to use communications technology for education (educational television, computer-assisted instruction, correspondence education) have failed to replace it. Examining today's attempts to use telecommunications for telelearning, the authors suggest that a genuine revolution in education may at last be in the making. There is a cluster of new technologies currently being developed, including virtual reality, nanotechnology and artificial intelligence which, when they combine with fibre optics, will cause a technological revolution to rival the industrial upheavals of the nineteenth century. From this, a serious alternative and/or complement to the conventional class will emerge – the virtual class.

The authors are currently involved in research which seeks to implement a virtual class by the year 2001. **Professor John Tiffin** holds the David Beattie Chair of Communications at Victoria University of Wellington, New Zealand. He has worked as a teacher and television producer in Britain, America, Africa and Latin America, and for seven years was senior specialist in educational technology in the multi-national project in educational technology of the Organisation of American States. **Dr Lalita Rajasingham** is Chairperson and Senior Lecturer in the Department of Communications Studies at Victoria University of Wellington. She has worked in radio and television in Malaysia, Britain, Australia and New Zealand. Since 1971 she has been Consultant with the Asia-Pacific Institute of Broadcasting Development and has conducted in-country courses in broadcasting in Pakistan, Fiji, Malaysia, the Philippines and Sri Lanka.

'Our world faces serious problems – population explosion, environmental pollution, energy shortage. . . . Global thinking and global action are the only ways forward. The virtual classroom . . . will play an important role in making these possible.'

Dr Nobuyoshi Terashima, President, Advanced
Telecommunications Research, Japan

'This timely book adds a valuable international perspective to distance learning.'

Patrick S. Portway, Founder and Executive Director,
United States Distance Learning Association

'This is a book to be read, discussed and acted upon by all those with an interest in education. *In Search of the Virtual Class* stirs the mind. It should do more: it should bestir us to action.'

Vijay Menon, Secretary General of the Asian Mass
Communication Research and Information Centre

'This book provides an extensive and indepth critical analysis of the design, application and evaluation of information technology for education and training . . . and a comprehensive base for studying the convergence of mainstream and distance education.'

Santosh Panda, Director of Research, Association of Indian Universities

In search of the virtual class

Education in an information society

John Tiffin and Lalita Rajasingham

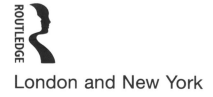

London and New York

First published 1995
by Routledge
11 New Fetter Lane, London EC4P 4EE

Simultaneously published in the USA and Canada
by Routledge
29 West 35th Street, New York, NY 10001

Reprinted 1995

© 1995 John Tiffin and Lalita Rajasingham

Typeset in Garamond by J&L Composition Ltd, Filey, North Yorkshire
Printed and bound in Great Britain by Biddles Ltd, Guildford and King's Lynn

British Library Cataloguing in Publication Data
A catalogue record for this book is available from the British Library

Library of Congress Cataloguing in Publication Data
A catalogue record for this book is available from the Library of Congress

ISBN 0-415-11556-6 (hbk)
ISBN 0-415-12483-2 (pbk)

Dedication

This book is dedicated to the country that adopted us.
First country to give the vote to women.
First country to make university education universally available.
First country to develop a national telelearning network.
First country to see the light of the new day.
New Zealand,
Aotearoa,
Land of the Long White Cloud.

Contents

List of figures and tables   ix
Foreword   xi
Acknowledgements   xvii

1 The vision   1
New schools for a new society   1
The choice   2
Televirtuality   3
Balancing conventional learning and telelearning   3
The virtual class today   5
The virtual class tomorrow   6
The search   8
The vision   13

2 Education is communication   19
What is education?   22
What is communication?   26
What kind of communication system is needed for education?   39

3 In a class of its own   48
The eras of education   48
The home as a communication system for education   49
The workplace as an educational system   52
The classroom as a communication system for education   57
The fractal levels in the classroom   64
Classrooms in tertiary education   66
Control in the classroom   68
Classrooms as the integrators of education   70

4 The writing on the wall   71
There's trouble at school   71
The size of the problem   73
Problems of space   74

Problems of storage   76
Problems of time   77
Problems of teacher-to-learner ratios   79
Failure to adapt   80
Removing the fences   84

5 Roads to the virtual class   87
The road to Damascus: correspondence education   88
The road to Puebla: educational television (ETV)   90
The road through Silicon Valley: computers applied to learning   97

6 Telelearning in cyberspace   102
Tracks to superhighways   102
Synchronous teleconferencing   107
Asynchronous teleservices for telelearning   115
The emerging pattern   116
Design for a multi-level telelearning system   118
Cyberspace   124

7 Virtual reality   126
Internal and external generation of virtual reality   129
Virtual reality generators   131
The evolution of computer-generated virtual reality   133
Telepresence in televirtual realities   139

8 The virtual class   142
Level 1: The autonomous learner   143
Level 2: Learner and teacher   148
Level 3: The small group   155
Level 4: The large institution   157

9 Think global   161
Telecommunications versus transport   161
The global educational utility   163
The commercialisation of education   164
Economies of scale   166
Teachers and the virtual class   168
The flow of new knowledge   169
Tectonic shift   170

10 Act local   172
Fractal levels   183
Notes   188
Bibliography   192
Index   198

Figures and tables

FIGURES

1.1	The experiment	4
1.2	ATR system for teleconferencing with virtual reality	8
2.1	How a communication system functions	21
2.2	Shannon's model of a communication system	27
2.3	A half duplex dyad	28
2.4	Full duplex dyad	28
2.5	Star and ring network	28
2.6	The interconnectibility of networks	29
2.7	Kinds of communication storage	32
2.8	Communication processing	33
2.9	A sundial	33
2.10	A person's brain is a complex communications-processing device	34
2.11	A computer is a communications-processing device	35
2.12	The fractal dimension in communications	36
2.13	The levels in communications studies	39
2.14	The education system as a communications system	46
3.1	Fractal levels in a family educational network	51
3.2	The new apprentice	53
3.3	Fractal levels in apprentice training	55
3.4	Patterns of communication in classrooms, 1	60
3.5	Patterns of communication in classrooms, 2	60
3.6	Patterns of communication in classrooms, 3	61
3.7	Triadic relationship between learner, teacher and problem solving	62
3.8	Patterns of communication in classrooms, 4	63
3.9	Fractal levels in conventional classroom education	65
3.10	Lecture theatre	67
3.11	Seminar room	68
3.12	Office used for tutorial	69
4.1	The end of an era	72

5.1   Interactive television   95
5.2   Basic CAI model   98
5.3   Basic CMI model   100
6.1   GEO networks   105
6.2   LEO networks   106
6.3   Audioconferencing   108
6.4   Videoconferencing   111
6.5   Audiographic conferencing   114
6.6   Design for a telelearning system   119
7.1   The technological convergence behind computer-generated
      virtual reality   128
7.2   Jean-Léon Gérome, *The Bath*   132
7.3   The child in toy-generated virtual reality   133
7.4   The changing nature of proximity   140
8.1   A platform in front of the castle at Elsinore   147
8.2   A computer-based instructional engine   149
10.1 Suntech City   181

TABLES

4.1   Salient characteristics of education   85
10.1 Fractal levels in the educational systems of industrial and
      information societies   184

Foreword

by Reidar Roll

Secretary General of the International Council for Distance Education

In the mid-1990s we are living in a period of dramatic historical and technological change, which has been characterised as a profound civilisation change. For one who is working in distance education it is clearer than ever that the world is in the midst of an equally profound change in the whole learning paradigm.

A dramatic revolution is going on in the communication and technology sectors. The developments in digitalisation and fibre optics technologies are rapidly taking us into the information society of the future, where practically any kind of information and services will be available everywhere, and our ability to communicate across the planet will be immense. It is still difficult for most of us fully to grasp the changes it will bring in society as we know it today: how we spend and organise our lives, our work and leisure time; how we learn, manufacture, provide services; how we fight wars; how it will affect the relationship between the haves and have-nots in the world; how it will affect culture and language.

In the world of the future computer-generated virtual reality classroom of John Tiffin and Lalita Rajasingham, the education environment as we know it today, how we provide and organise education, and the way we learn, will have changed dramatically in pace with new realities and new learning needs. We are already well into this process of change as we see distance and conventional education blending more and more in many countries. As conventional education changes, distance education will change as well.

Some countries are in a period of re-examining their education system, while others, also in the western world, seem to be discovering more slowly the changes that the coming of the information society will bring to their education system. There is real danger in this, because it may mean that the formal education systems may be so slow in changing that their capacity to provide the kind of educational services society and its citizens need will be seriously diminished. It will be those schools, universities and education systems that are able to change in pace with new realities that will be more valuable, and that will succeed in providing their services to the vast education market of tomorrow. Maybe this market will see a *rapprochement* of parts of the education system and the corporate world of telecommunications and producers of hardware and software for the education market, leaving politicians behind for a while?

Professor John Tiffin and Dr Lalita Rajasingham of Victoria University in New Zealand have provided us with a wonderful book that challenges our imagination and ability to grasp fully the change of which we are all a part, as we move towards the information society of the coming decades. Their scenarios of the future computer-generated virtual reality makes me want to jump into the future and be a student again!

I hope that the book will be widely read and studied not only by those who are working in open and distance learning at the cutting edge of educational development today, but also by educators in the traditional system, planners, civil servants and politicians, and by those in the South and the North who are responsible for providing the means for human resources development in the Third World. The gap in knowledge, competence and basic skills may become even wider between those who have access to the wonderworld of educational opportunity of computer-generated virtual reality and those who have not, between those who can pay for the service and those who cannot. There is a challenge here to the nations and intergovernmental organisations of the world. Let us hope they see it in time.

In many nations around the world there are growing demands for access to education, while at the same time the recession affecting many countries has repercussions on government spending in the education sector, restricting not only the numbers of students who can be admitted into tertiary education but also the quality of learning materials and what goes on in the classroom.

As the next decade unfolds, it will be the institutions in the education systems which can master the processes of change that will be more central and valuable to our societies. It is not only the advances in information technology that will accelerate the changes that are badly needed in the education sector. In many places there is scepticism in political circles as to whether the education sector is using its resources effectively, whether it is productive. In the period ahead many argue, and I think it is true, that we are unlikely to see large increases in spending on education in many countries, primarily because there is a shortage of money, and the education sector faces fierce competition for resources from other sectors, such as the social sector and the environment. In this scenario, the education sector is likely to be looking at its productivity.

However, the transformation of teaching by means of new advances in educational technology will perhaps be even more fruitful in this process. In large parts of the conventional university systems this was until recently a somewhat abstract concept, in the sense that not much really changed in the daily life of universities as we know it, except in distance education institutions. On the other hand, there is a growing experience in many dual mode elementary and secondary schools and universities in countries such as New Zealand, the United States and Australia, of the use of computers and telecommunication tools and applications in the daily learning process. In these environments the role of the teacher is changing from that of the talker in the classroom to the coach to students learning from technology. We are also beginning to see really interesting cases of how distance teaching schools work together with others (for example, secondary schools) to provide additional learning resources and interactive communication to classrooms.

As the technology develops, discussion of change will become more realistic. In the past, distance teaching took place in designated institutions in many countries – single-mode distance-teaching institutions, or open universities and schools whose role was not yet fully accepted. But we are now finding, all over the world, that the traditional universities are adapting these concepts. The trend is accelerating at an ever brisker pace.

Single-mode distance teaching institutions will find fierce competition from the traditional system on their doorsteps, and will need to change in order to have a role to play at all in the future. If open universities become fixed and unchanging, we will only have two styles of obsolete universities, each with its own outmoded approach.

It is more likely, given today's budget pressures, and the incentives to change, that both single-mode and traditional universities and schools, will evolve to resemble each other.

Another theme in current discussions among politicians is the quality of the education that students are gaining. We are not only talking about better-educated citizens, but differently educated citizens, where reasoning skills, creativity and international understanding, and the ability to understand and value different cultures, will be important and necessary skills in the labour market, as the labour market as well as the market place becomes more international with increasing international competition for jobs as well as for markets for services and commodities.

This is just as much a challenge to single-mode or open schools and universities as to the traditional ones. Open schools and universities are going to need to focus just as sharply on how they provide interaction among students as on how they deliver the course at a distance. They need to focus most sharply on the student support services if the students are going to acquire the skills and abilities that are needed in tomorrow's work place, where the ability to interact with others, not only from one's own culture, will be important assets in the international competition for jobs.

Moreover, in traditional systems, at school as well as university level, we are likely to experience the need for massive re-training of teachers to adapt to new goals and roles.

We are in the midst of a transformation in our societies. That transformation means that we are going to be more international and competitive, both in the labour market and in the education and training sector. It is going to be dangerous to be stuck in old, outmoded ways of doing things. This is true not only for powerful corporations and military organisations, but also for powerful distance teaching universities as well as for traditional ones. How we manufacture and how we provide services to the citizens of our societies in future will change how we educate.

The advances in communications technologies and services, in equipment and software applications for use in education in a new technological environment, will make the move of the traditional schools and universities into technology much more feasible and dynamic. In this scenario, distance teaching universities, some of them very large organisations, can no longer see themselves as remarkably successful forerunners, and as such immune to changes. They also will need to change, because to stand still is increasingly to be left behind.

To educate is to communicate, by spoken and written language, by image, symbols, sound and body language. Over the next twenty to thirty years, the transformation of our societies into information societies will make it necessary for the education systems of our societies to adapt to a new educational environment in the information society. This process of change will be extremely hard for many, as were the changes brought about by the industrial revolution. Educators, corporations, researchers and politicians could make this process of change less painful to our societies if timely and competent partnerships were formed between them at national, regional and global levels.

This is why the International Council for Distance Education focuses so sharply on this process of change and partnership building, to make it more likely that educational institutions and networks, in both traditional and single-mode distance teaching institutions, cooperate not only among themselves, but with representatives of the major players in the information transformation of the world.

The establishment of global partnerships is being called for in many of today's most important international declarations among the governments of the world, and in their strategies for economic recovery and development. Education and training plays an important role in these declarations and policies.

I would like to recall the first lines of the preamble of Agenda 21, the Programme of Action from the Rio Conference on Environment and Development:

Humanity stands at a defining moment in history. We are confronted with a perpetuation of disparities between and within nations, a worsening of poverty, hunger, ill health and illiteracy, and the continuing deterioration of the ecosystems on which we depend for our well-being. However, integration of environment and development concerns and greater attention to them will lead to the fulfilment of basic needs, improving living standards for all, better protected and managed eco-systems and a safer, more prosperous future. No nation can achieve this on its own; but together we can – in a global partnership for sustainable development.

If ever there was a time for international partnerships, that time is here and now. The Earth is on the threshold of a new century, a new millennium. Many industrialised countries are experiencing the deepest recession since the Second World War. High unemployment rates, unprecedented since the Great Depression, waste their most valuable resource. For the govern-ments and intergovernmental organisations of western countries, resump-tion of non-inflationary, sustainable and job-creating growth is a pressing priority.

Many governments call for increased competition among suppliers of educational services. In their strategies for renewal, governments see that intensified regional and global cooperation as essential. I believe that this is equally important to education if it is to improve its productivity and competitiveness, and in the longer run emerge from its present crises better equipped, prepared and able to handle the enormous educational needs of our societies and peoples.

In the world of education, global partnerships are developing rapidly. The new electronic superhighways will make such partnerships ever more feasible and effective.

However, there are the dangers of new cultural imperialism and of the export of educational programmes on the communication highways that are out of place in the cultural and linguistic setting of countries to which they are being exported. This may give rise to new international conflicts unless we are careful. We can already see the eagerness of some huge educational operations to find new markets overseas without caring too much about the problems they cause. Again, international cooperation is needed to avoid conflicts and to set the necessary parameters for successful international delivery of educational programmes. And it is necessary to advance the partnerships that can successfully develop educational services that respect the cultural parameters within which nations wish to see their citizens educated. For surely, the people of Norway or Zimbabwe do not contemplate becoming British! Nor do their governments. To the contrary. The political trend today is not towards globalisation of cultures; it is strongly in the direction of ethnic and cultural identity and the protection of national cultures. The importance the peoples of Europe now give to the subsidiarity principle in the Maastricht Treaty of the European Union is a message to us as educators to avoid cultural adventures. They will not work today.

   Partnerships, if they are successful, create greater strength. They could also lead the way towards the development of global educational utilities or consortia 'that make education available as international value-added services to anyone, anywhere who can afford them', to quote Tiffin and Rajasingham. It is in global partnerships among peers from different sectors and cultures – which, for instance, ICDE is developing between educational institutions, researchers, governments and corporations – that I see the hope that we will master the changes that will surely come along the lines described in this wonderful book by Professor John Tiffin and Dr Lalita Rajasingham.

   When I met them in Wellington in May 1994, they called such partner-ships the common meeting ground that we need now. And on this meeting ground, Tiffin and Rajasingham have promised to play a part. We are indebted to them for that.

Oslo
12 August 1994

Acknowledgements

In a footnote in *The Pilgrim's Progress*, John Bunyan writes, 'The blessedness of savoury experimental conversation with fellow pilgrims cannot be too highly praised.' The present book is the product of several years of research and discourse undertaken with many people whose insights helped us envisage the future of education.

To fellow pilgrims at international conferences, gratitude for sharing your collective world view. We would like to thank the members of the Network College of Communication in the Pacific for acting as a sounding board – in particular, Jan Walls, Director of the David Lam Centre for International Communication at Simon Fraser University, Canada; Jitraporn Sudhivora-seth, Deputy Dean of Research and Foreign Affairs at the Faculty of Communication Arts, Chulalongkorn University, Thailand; Vijay Menon, Director of the Asian Mass Communications Information Centre, Singapore; Ely Gomez, Director of the Institute of Development Communication, University of the Philippines at Los Baños; Kenji Saga, Vice-President for International Affairs, Asia University, Tokyo, Japan; and Nobuyoshi Terashima, President of ATR Communication Systems Research Laboratories, Japan. It was the opportunity to examine the developmental work at ATR Laboratories and discussions with Dr Terashima that convinced us of the technical feasibility of the virtual class.

John Tiffin would also like to express his gratitude for a fellowship from the East-West Center that enabled him to do research for the book at Hawaii and for the advice and encouragement he received there from Syed Rahim and Meheroo Jussawalla.

High praise for 'savoury conversations' must be addressed to Professor Somasundram Puvi-Rajasingham of Bogor Agricultural University in Indonesia, who was endlessly available for advice. Thanks go to Margaret Allan, Senior Lecture in Education, James Cook University, Queensland, for her in-depth readings and advice on Vygotsky, and to Horacio Reggini. We shall long remember the excitement of arguing the future with him by the fjords of Norway and on the pampas of his own country. John Tiffin also remembers a fascinating event in Göteborg in the company of Lennart Fahlen, who is developing CGVR with the Swedish Institute of Computer Science and the redoubtable Myron Kruger, father of 'Artificial Reality'.

We have been encouraged by the response of Reidar Roll, Secretary-General of the International Council for Distance Education, and Armando Trindade, Rector of the Open University of Portugal, to the ideas in the book and we would like to thank Jack Shallcrass and William Renwick for their readings at the initial stages.

Pilgrims need guardian angels. To the Telecom Corporation of New Zealand and Ameritech we owe a big debt of gratitude for supporting our research from its initiation and in particular Laurence Zwimpfer for his faith in our ideas. We would also like to recognise the technical support we got from the Telecom Corporation of Australia at a crucial point in the Tri-Centre Project and to Robert Dunlop-Christie for his timely support.

Coming to the 'blessedness' part of the pilgrimage, we thank Paddi Wilson for her patience with us in her untiring efforts in preparing the manuscript. We also thank John Baber for his helping hand with the technology, Barry Larsen for the time he spent in the library on our behalf to chase up bibliographical detail, and Liz Mirams for interpreting so skilfully our graphic needs.

We would like to express our thanks to Victoria University of Wellington, New Zealand, for the opportunity to pursue this research. We salute our international colleagues. Finally, we would like to acknowledge all the thoughts and ideas and insight that have come from the arguments and discussions that have taken place in class, seminars and tutorials with our students and at international conferences where academic debates went on throughout the night in distant lands.

Chapter 1

The vision

Without a vision the people perish.

(Proverbs 29:18)

NEW SCHOOLS FOR A NEW SOCIETY

We live in a period of transition between an industrial society and an information society. Schools as we know them are designed to prepare people for life in an industrial society. What kind of system is needed to prepare people for life in an information society?

Public education systems prepare people for their place in society by emulating the factories and offices of an industrial society. Everyday, around the world, young people use bikes or buses or cars or trains to travel to school, just as later in life they will travel to work. They are expected to clock in at fixed times and they learn to work at desks in classrooms that are like the offices of industry and commerce. The way time is managed, subjects are segmented for study and schools are organised as bureaucracies are intimations of life after school. When the bell goes at the end of a school day, students stream out to commute home, just as factory and office workers do an hour or so later.

In *Gridlock*, an alien team of television researchers from the planet Brain, are able to comprehend humanity in a fraction of a second, except for one phenomenon, that of transport:

> The Brainians could see the long, thin arteries along which the humans travelled. They noted that after sunrise the humans all travelled one way and at sunset they all travelled the other way. They could see that their progress was slow and congested along these arteries, that there were endless blockages, queues, bottlenecks and delays causing untold frustration and inefficiency. All this they could see quite clearly. What was not clear to them was why.

(Elton 1991: 4–6)

Many scientists believe that the chemical energy used by the transport systems in industrial societies are polluting the world's atmosphere to a point where climatic change is being triggered. One solution is for people to travel less and use telecommunications more. A trend that appears to be on the increase world-wide is teleworking. Many information workers find that with a personal computer, a modem and a fax machine they do not have to be in their office every day at fixed times. They can work from home and keep more flexible hours.

People do not go to towns and cities just to work, they also go to do their shopping, to go to the bank, to see their doctor or accountant, or to enjoy themselves at the theatre or cinema. However, all these activities are becoming more accessible by telecommunications. Much of our entertainment comes by television. Teleshopping is on the increase. Telebanking, teleinsurance, teleaccounting and telemedicine are appearing. As teleactivities increase they reinforce one another. The reasons for travelling into town diminish. The information society may see a reversal of the drift to the cities that characterised industrial societies. An information society may prove to be a telesociety with a revival of rural areas and a return to the cottage industries that existed prior to the industrial revolution. The idea of telecottages is being experimented with in such countries as the United States, Australia, Sweden and Norway (Australian Telecottage Conference 1993). An industrial society depends on the physical movement of people and goods, so the critical technological infrastructures are rail, road, sea and air transport networks. The critical technological infrastructure of an information society, however, is its telecommunications network. To prepare people for life in an information society, an educational system is needed that is based on telecommunications rather than transport.

THE CHOICE

If you want to talk to someone who is not actually with you, today you have two choices which epitomise the different ways of doing things in industrial and information societies: go and see them or telephone them. Use a transport network or the telephone network. The more people use telecommunications, the more money the telecommunications companies make and the more they invest in developing telecommunications networks. The transition from an industrial to an information society gathers momentum as telecommunications improve and more people begin to use them for communication. Singapore is an example of a society that is encouraging such a trend. Its advanced telecommunications services are inexpensive, but there are heavy taxes on the use of private motorcars. Cars are even charged when they use the highways in central city areas. This is driving the country towards being an information society by pressing the brake on the transport system and the accelerator on telecommunications. It helps people to make a choice in favour of telecommunications when they want to communicate.

It is rare to have such a choice in education outside of pilot projects. If you have a class you travel to a classroom. Education needs an alternative. Students and teachers should have the choice of meeting for instruction by using telecommunications or by transport. Teaching, however, is a more complex communication process than those for which we normally use the telephone. Sophisticated telecommunications systems are needed if there is to be a sensible choice between using transport or telecommunications to get an education. However, a new generation of telecommunications is going into place around the world and the next quarter of a century seems set to see an increase in telecommunications capability of the order of magnitude that transport experienced when it shifted from using horse-drawn vehicles to railways, trains and automobiles.

TELEVIRTUALITY

The person you telephone may be at the opposite side of the world yet their voice on the telephone can have you saying, 'You sound just as though you were here in the room with me'. 'Virtual' means in effect but not in fact, and 'tele' means at a distance. So the telephone gives the effect of a presence and since the effect is achieved with people who are at a distance from each other, it is that of a virtual telepresence, but only in terms of their voices. The new breed of telecommunications brings not just sound, but also images. Video phones are available and videoconferencing in the business world is becoming standard for meetings. These technologies are already being used experimentally for education, making it possible for teachers and students to meet, as telepresences in televirtuality. Already we begin to talk of teleschools and virtual classes as an extension of, or alternative to, conventional schools and classrooms.

BALANCING CONVENTIONAL LEARNING AND TELELEARNING

Does telelearning mean the end of the classroom as we know it? The idea of people gathering together in some special site for learning goes back well before the industrial revolution, and the classroom by itself has proved a remarkably resilient and durable place for learning. What we may see happen is the reversal of the trend towards big schools especially in the secondary and tertiary levels of education, and a return to something more like the village school and the small rural college, which catered to neighbourhood communities, where the catchment area meant it was possible to walk or bike to school rather than use motorised transport systems.

Children and adults need to learn socialising skills. Team sports, swim-ming, playing music, pottery, drama and singing are all reasons for people

coming together for learning. Embedded in such activities are the interpersonal and group communication skills people need to live with one
another. Where city schools drew large numbers of students it was possible
to cater to a wide variety of educational needs. Small schools could not
offer the same range of subjects. However, telelearning promises to make it
possible to offer a variety of courses that no conventional school could
match. In telelearning there are no physical limits to the number of courses
that can be offered; it even opens up opportunities for the development of
an international trade in teaching where an individual learner can access

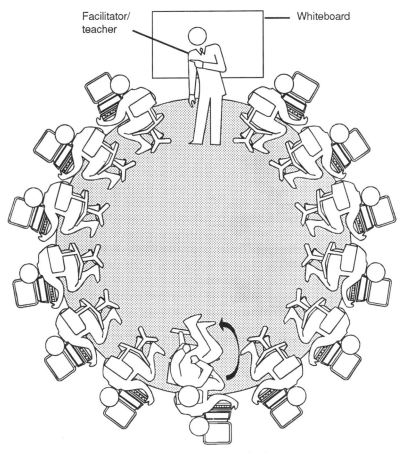

Students work independently at
their computers and then turn to
participate in group work

Figure 1.1 The experiment. In group mode everybody faced inwards towards
one another. In CAI mode everybody faced outward, linked to the computers

courses and teachers anywhere in the world in whatever subject they want to study, provided that someone, somewhere, wants to teach it.

In a research situation used by a computer company[1] to test instructional software, between ten and twenty students who ranged from mature adults to primary schoolchildren were seated in a circle in such a way that when the students all turned outwards with their backs towards one another, they faced a computer. For about 45 minutes they would work with the computer in a CAI (computer-assisted instruction) mode. At the end of that time, they would swing around 180 degrees to face one another and, for the next 45 minutes, would be involved, with the teacher, in a discussion of the subject they had studied with the computer. Swivel chairs were used to facilitate the swinging back and forth between the computer one-to-one instructional mode and the human, interpersonal, group mode. The students became fascinated with this juxtaposition of different communication modes. At times after an intense one-to-one session with the computer they would reach out and hold hands to form a human circle and declare how good it felt to be linked to humans instead of machines. They said that using both modes of instruction was better than using either one by itself. There was a point at which they became tired or irritated with the computer, and it was a pleasure to turn and join in a human discussion in which logic was less exact, interaction was less precise, meanings were more fluid and people made the kind of intuitive leaps that no computer could. They also said that after a while they became less tolerant of the silliness that sometimes developed in discussion, the subjective nature of many comments, and the undertones of personal feelings that clouded clear thinking. Then they found it a relief to return to impersonal, unambiguous interaction with a computer. What the experiments suggested was the need for a balance between computer interaction and human interaction. In the future we will need to strike a balance between telelearning and conventional classroom learning.

THE VIRTUAL CLASS TODAY

Information technology, the technology behind the information society, is the conjunction of computer and telecommunications technologies. Computers are already widely used in education and training. Computer-assisted instruction, computer-managed instruction and the use of computer simulations for training goes back to the 1960s. The use of telecommunications for teaching also has a history. Audioconferencing has been used since the 1970s and instructional television has been tried around the world since the 1950s. It is, however, the coming together of computer and telecommunications technologies that could lead to the virtual class as the primary locus of learning in society.

If 'virtual' means in effect but not in fact, how is it possible to have the effect of a class without the reality of a classroom? A classroom is a communication system that makes it possible for a group of people to come together to talk about something they want to learn, and to look at pictures and diagrams and text that help them understand. In a conventional classroom this is made possible by the walls which provide protection from outside noise and interference so that everybody inside the classroom can hear and see one another and can also see, on a whiteboard or blackboard, words, diagrams and pictures about what is being learned. The question is, can information technology provide an alternative communications system for learning that is at least as effective?

The idea of a virtual class is that everybody can talk and be heard and be identified and everybody can see the same words, diagrams and pictures, at the same time. This calls for the use of telecommunications and computers. At its simplest, it can be done using two conventional telephone lines at each site, one to link telephones and one to link computers. One line is for sound, and one is for pictures which can be generated on the video display unit (VDU) of a computer. To link more than two sites, a teleconferencing bridging system is also needed. Teleconferencing bridges can be linked to other teleconferencing bridges and theoretically there is no limit to the number of places that can be linked, or where these places are. This is one technology that makes a form of virtual class possible today, and there are pilot projects taking place in many countries which show that it can be made to work at least as effectively as a conventional class (Rajasingham 1988a; Rumble and Oliveira 1992). Such projects make it possible to think about what a virtual class could be like in the future, as telecommunications systems improve. In time it will be possible to use the public switched telecommunications system to transmit high-quality digital sound and high-definition video images. Audiographic conferencing systems are being upgraded to include videoconferencing. Not only is it possible for everybody in a virtual class to talk to one another, they can also see one another. We can expect, through the 1990s, a rapid development of teleconferencing technology and attempts by the teaching world to adapt it for educational purposes.

THE VIRTUAL CLASS TOMORROW

The telephone can provide televirtual voices. Teleconferencing can provide the effect of a meeting without people actually meeting and is already being adapted for instruction and called a 'virtual class'. However, a new technology is emerging in the 1990s called 'virtual reality' (VR). It seeks to create the effect of actually being inside a simulated reality. We are beginning to conceptualise it as a new medium and come to some appreciation of its possibilities. These are extraordinary. We appear to be facing in communication the kind of quantum change that Eric Drexler (1990) predicts for manufacturing with nanotechnology. Applications of virtual reality are being developed in such fields as architecture, medicine and arcade games. However, its origins were in the development of flight simulators for training (Rheingold 1991: 203). It is time to see how it could be applied to education and the development of virtual classes in the fullest sense as wrap-around environments for learning where students as telepresences can see, hear, touch and perhaps one day even smell and taste.

VR technology is a computer technology and can be linked to telecommunications systems. Dr Nobuyoshi Terashima, the president of Advanced Telecommunication Research (ATR) Communication Systems Laboratories, near Kyoto, Japan, leads a team which is developing virtual teleconferencing systems. This is how it works. One person sits in front of a screen and puts on a pair of glasses and a glove. This makes it possible for them to interact in a virtual room with another person who is sitting in front of a screen in another place who has the same equipment. They are linked by telecommunications. They see each other apparently sitting around a table in a conference room. They are actually looking at computer graphic images of each other, but the image is three-dimensional and their faces move as they speak. It is a bit disconcerting to look under the table and discover they have no lower body! Since people do not normally look under the table when they are in a meeting to see if the other people are altogether there, the designers felt there was no need to create a software version of people's nether halves. At the moment it is possible for three people to meet in this way and see one another in three dimensions and have a discussion. They can also use their gloved hand to manipulate virtual objects within the virtual room or to change the virtual scenario. There is no technical reason why this virtual teleconferencing system should not be used for a virtual class. It can be done now. However, today's VR technology is where radio technology was a hundred years ago. It is at the very beginnings of its development and adoption for popular commercial applications. What will be possible with virtual reality fifty years from now? What form could a virtual class take? What potential capabilities could it have? Is a virtual class likely to be an improvement on a conventional classroom as a communication system for learning in the coming information society? Will it be the place where our children and their children learn to learn?

VR offers us the possibility of a class meeting in the Amazon Forest or on top of Mount Everest; it could allow us to expand our viewpoint to see the solar system operating like a game of marbles in front of us, or shrink it so that we can walk through an atomic structure as though it was a sculpture in a park; we could enter a fictional virtual reality in the persona of a character in a play, or a non-fictional virtual reality to accompany a surgeon in an exploration at the micro-level of the human body.

Will we use this extraordinary technology to advance the way we learn, or

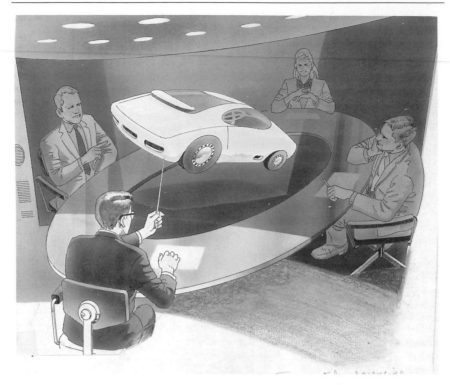

Figure 1.2 ATR system for teleconferencing with virtual reality
Source: Reproduced by courtesy of ATR Communication Systems Laboratory

will we use it to create virtual classrooms that are the virtual versions of conventional classrooms? In the 1960s, television seemed to hold great promise for education. It was described as a window on the world for the classroom;[2] a way to bring new experiences and new presentation techniques to learning. Somehow television never really worked in schools. Yet, it has become the great educator of our time. Not, however, in the way we anticipated. Not in cooperation with educational systems and intentions, but rather as a maverick alternative education, preoccupied with violence, not so much a window to the world as a mirror of what is wrong within us. In Latin America, technology is seen as a knife with two edges which can cut both ways.

THE SEARCH

President Lyndon Johnson, at the apogee of American affluence, commissioned the Rand Corporation, a prestigious think-tank with exacting standards, to examine the vast body of research into instructional methods both old and new that existed in the United States and look for what worked.

The idea was that America would increase the effectiveness of education by investing in what could be clearly shown to be the best methods of teaching. Published in 1972, however, the report found 'that research has found nothing that *consistently* and *unambiguously* makes a difference in student outcomes' (Averch *et al.* 1972: 172). There is an interesting rider to this in the summary 'there is a suggestion that substantial improvement in educational outcomes can only be obtained through a vastly different form of education' (Averch *et al.* 1972: 178). A decade later, in 1983, as America slid into recession and brooded over a loss of international competitiveness that seemed to have links with its educational system, the National Commission on Excellence in Education (NCOEIE) delivered its report, *A Nation at Risk*. This was one of many reports expressing deep concern with declining educational standards, but it caught the public's imagination with the phrase: 'If an unfriendly foreign power had attempted to impose on America the mediocre educational performance that exists today, we might well have viewed it as an act of war' (NCOEIE 1983: 5). It was apparent that the existing educational system not only lacked the potential for improvement, but it was also in serious decline. In 1992 Dwight Allen stated that the American educational system is diseased (Allen 1992). Chester Finn argued that American education is to education what the Soviet economy was to economy (Finn 1991). Stanley Progrow said that the future of education could not be the same as its past (Progrow 1983) and Philip Altbach wrote of 'The Great Education Crisis' (Altbach 1985). Yet, when Barbara Presseisen analysed eight major reports on the American educational system which tried to address the problem, it was apparent that none of them proposed any serious innovation. Although there was some advocacy of the need to introduce new information technology, essentially all the reports assumed a continuation of the conventional classroom model of teaching (Presseisen 1985). One felt in reading them that the problem was seen as a decline of educational standards from some past golden age to which the United States needed to return, for a rejuvenation of the old system rather than the birth of a new system. The cry from the movement for excellence in education in the United States is 'back to basics'.

The United States is not the world, but is there any country that is not deeply perturbed about its educational system and does not feel some resonance with the problem that the Americans, as is their way, bare to the world? As long ago as 1968, Philip Coombs wrote the classic *The World Educational Crisis* on the basis of a meeting of educators from around the globe who reflected a universal concern that educational systems were failing, that they were dinosaurs. In 1985 Coombs revisited the issue and found only that the crisis had deepened (Coombs 1985). The inadequacy of existing systems for learning is manifest in every society. The need for a better way of educating people is patent. The search for a new system of education is on.

The term 'educational system' conjures up for most of us the idea of a national or state organisation that administers and standardises what goes on in schools and colleges. Schools themselves have subsystems for administration, for play and social activities, for leisure and games and physical training. The critical subsystems of schools are the classrooms. They are where the learning and teaching, the core process of education, take place. The classroom is to the school what the coal face is to a coal mine. It is the very heart of the process, for which the rest of the system was set up. It is for this reason that this book focuses on the future form of the class and the classroom. Of course learning and teaching are not confined to the classroom, but the fact is that the classroom is the place dedicated to the kind of communication called education and this seems to be so in every nation.

A classroom is a room where classes are held. A class is a group of people joined for some course of instruction. A meeting of such a group is also called a 'class'. It is in this latter sense that we use the term 'virtual class', signifying that two or more people can come together as telepresences for instruction. We avoid the term 'virtual classroom' because it suggests that the place a virtual class is held is an electronic simulation of a conventional classroom. Roxanne Hiltz, who coined the term, used it to refer to the use of computer-mediated communications 'to create an electronic analogue of the communications forms that usually occur in a classroom including discussion as well as lectures and tests' (Hiltz 1986: 95). We use the term 'virtual learning space' (VLS) to encompass any kind of distributed virtual reality that can be used for learning. Virtual learning institute (VLI) is used to describe entities that are responsible for organising, developing, managing and administering learning in virtual environments, much as schools, colleges and universities do in conventional classrooms. Where the parallels are close enough, the terms 'virtual school', 'virtual college' and 'virtual university' are also used, but we wish to avoid the idea that the application of computer and communication technologies to education will mean a virtual version of educational systems as we know them now.

In his book on scientific revolutions, Kuhn uses the term 'paradigm' to describe a generic system of thought in which the key ideas and the ways they interrelate are accepted as axiomatic (Kuhn 1962). Kuhn applies the concept of paradigm to 'normal' science, this being the accepted scientific explanation of the world in a particular period of time. He then goes on to note how scientific discoveries lead to the development of new scientific paradigms, but how the shift from the old paradigm to the new paradigm is one of angry argument and debate between the practitioners of the old paradigm and advocates of the new. The first teams of women Rugby players had much in common with the first advocates of the new scientific paradigm known as 'chaos theory'. It was not done for women to play a man's game or for scientists to study disorder, rather than order, in the universe.

The term 'paradigm' can also be used to describe 'normal' education (Heinrich 1970). People understand education as an established set of procedures that takes place in schools and classrooms. This is a world view which will not be changed easily. In a sense, a paradigm is a supraview of an established system, recognising not just its functionality, but also the faith in that functionality. This book is an attempt to describe a new educational paradigm. When everyone believed the Sun went around the Earth it was positively dangerous to argue the case for the Earth spinning on its axis in a path around the Sun. The Inquisition dealt with such heresies. In Kuhnian terms, if this book does not make a lot of educationists angry, it is not advocating a genuinely new paradigm.

How will we find the new educational paradigm? The Rand Corporation report, referred to above, judged research into the effectiveness of innovations in education by the standards of quantitative research (Averch et al. 1972). This is the dominant research paradigm in the social sciences. It seeks to establish relationships among phenomena by careful, objective measurement, the use of established statistical procedures, and by accounting for all the variables that could be involved. To show that an innovation in education could be an improvement on existing practices using the quantitative approach, it is necessary to conduct comparative tests that take into consideration all the possible combinations of factors that could affect the outcome. One approach to the study of the virtual class would, therefore, be to select randomly groups of students and assign them to conventional classes and to virtual classes and carefully measure the results of equivalent instruction in the two modes.

Logical as the quantitative approach may seem, there is a distinct possibility that it is inhibiting the search for a new paradigm in education. Noam Chomsky argues that 'the behavioural sciences have commonly insisted upon certain arbitrary methodological restrictions that make it virtually impossible for scientific knowledge of a non trivial character to be attained' (Chomsky 1972: ix). Quantitative research measures what exists, not what could exist. By making comparative studies between conventional instruction and innovative instruction it can preclude further development of an innovation by damning it in terms of what it is, as distinct from what it could be. Qualitative research which allows for a more subjective and intuitive approach to the study and description of the complexity which characterises human phenomena has become common in recent years in the education departments of universities. However, educational planning units persist in seeking proof of improvement from the results of quantitative research before committing to any change. This creates a problem when information technology is involved. Because the technology changes so rapidly, the proof may no longer be relevant when it arrives. Imagine if the first aeroplane flights had been subject to quantitative evaluation that compared them to railways in terms of speed, reliability and load and that the results had been key to the development of aviation. It would have seemed logical at the time to arrange a test with flights taking off from a landing strip next to one station and following the railway tracks to a landing strip at the next station. Given that trains were reliable, could carry hundreds of passengers and attain speeds well over 100 miles an hour when aeroplanes first appeared, such a test could have discredited aviation.[3]

The example reflects another problem in using quantitative research to assess innovation. The aeroplane follows the railway tracks. If the race had been held over a river or mountain the aeroplane would have appeared in a different light. Comparisons of what happens when variables are changed in instruction are done within the existing paradigm. Innovations in education tend to be evaluated in terms of whether they work in the classroom. Yet what we are seeking is a new paradigm of education with new standards and outcomes, something that may have no resemblance to classrooms as we know them. A new paradigm cannot be evaluated in terms of the old paradigm from which it shifts (Kuhn 1962). It is like asking the Inquisition to judge Galileo's new theory.

Quantitative research in the United States in the 1960s compared conventional classroom teaching with teaching by television and found 'no significant difference' (Chu and Schramm 1968). Classroom teaching uses techniques that have developed over four thousand years. Television was not designed for use in a classroom and few people had any serious idea how to use it for teaching other than to imitate conventional classroom procedures. Little account was taken of the likelihood that black and white TV would become colour, or that videocassettes would become available, or that definition would improve. None of this research contributed to the development of television for instructional purposes.

Philip Jackson, the president of the American Educational Research Association, in 1990, reflecting widespread concern with the ineffectiveness of current practice, called for 'marrow bone' thinking[4] and new approaches in educational research (Jackson 1990). Action research, which seeks to advance knowledge through attempting to solve real world problems, although hardly new, may be an answer. It seems appropriate to a search for a new paradigm for instruction, because it allows researchers to create new systems to achieve set goals and to pursue paths towards their goals that are dynamic. The approach allows for changes in direction and objectives and for real world conditions where mistakes can occur and the researchers themselves have to be taken into account. This is different from the tendency in quantitative research to create laboratory conditions that exclude factors which could contaminate the study. Instead of trying to compare aeroplanes with trains in terms of a railway system, action research recognises that aeroplanes have advantages which can only come to fruition in an airline system and that to find out if aviation works it is necessary to set up a system for aviation. As Michael Moore points out in arguing the case for researching distance education at the systems level, the first attempts to set up aviation systems were made by people who bought a plane, rented a field, put up a sign and waited for customers. Those who persisted and survived and were ultimately successful in developing the aviation industry did so because they realised their mistakes, worked out what was needed and had another attempt (Moore 1993: 10). Of course that did not mean that the system then worked as they wanted. It usually meant that they were presented with another generation of problems to be resolved. This iterative pattern is the hallmark of action research. It involves the evaluation of each phase of development, a consequent reassessment of goals and a new plan by which to proceed.

Development of a complex system that is radically different means that the people involved must have a long-term vision which sustains them. The people who built railways and aviation had such vision. The people who develop virtual learning environments will need one. Another research method which helps is 'futures scenarios'. The researcher visualises a system at some determined point in the future and, by extrapolating from past trends, seeks to show that it could function and is a viable possibility for the future. Action research and futures scenarios have a logical link. Futures scenarios research creates a vision that action research can be used to realise.

THE VISION

Shirley zips into her skin-tight school uniform which on the outside looks something like a ski suit. The lining of the suit in fact contains cabling that makes the suit a communication system and there are pressure pads where the suit touches skin that give a sense of touch. Next, she sits astride something that is a bit like a motorbike except that it has no wheels and is attached firmly to the floor. Her feet fit on to something similar to a brake and accelerator and her gloved hands hold on to handlebars. She shouts, 'I'm off to school dad.' Her father, who is taking time out from his teleworking, begins to remind her that the family are going teleshopping in the virtual city later in the day, but it is too late, his daughter has already donned her school helmet. She is no longer in the real world of her real home, she is in the virtual world of her virtual school.

The moment the helmet closes over her head, Shirley finds herself looking at an information map of her school and her own academic activities. There is her individual school diary of daily activities and appointments, class timetable and academic calendar. She can for any particular class see what will happen, at what time, for how long, or when a particular assignment is due. Her overall progress in terms of her chosen career path is charted. Of course she can reschedule. This involves a session with computer-assisted counselling (CAC) which just might refer the case to a human counsellor especially if a change of classes is involved. Much of her instruction is asynchronous and computer based and presents no practical problems to creating an individual timetable. The CAC concern is with how changes affect her long-term career goals.

As she turns her head there are the notices about the society meetings and extra-curricular activities she is involved with. If she asked about any of the thousands of events and activities going on in her areas of interest, notices about them would be brought to her attention. A couple of notices have signs winking on and off to show someone wants to get in touch with her. Before responding to them, however, she looks up to check the time (the clock is always there whenever she looks up) and notices that she has fifteen minutes before her class in geo studies begins. She looks at the info map of school functions. Library, registration, counselling, health services, research laboratory, computer room and classroom are all clearly marked. To go to any one of them all she has to do is to reach forward and 'touch' them and she will be there. She could go straight to the virtual class. Maybe some other students are already there. The pre-class chats are fun with people from so many cultures. She often wonders how many students there really are in the virtual school and how many countries that represents. Today, however, she is leading her group's presentation on glacial retreat as evidence of global warming and she is not sure of her grasp of the concept involved. Putting timetable on automatic, which means that when a class begins she will automatically find herself in the class, she hits the library function and asks for the Franz Josef glacier. Then she selects the terraforming and flight overview options. As the simulation forms around her she gets the familiar feeling of butterflies in the stomach as she finds herself hovering a thousand feet above the Franz Josef glacier. She reaches for the reassuring touch of the handlebars and, kicking the accelerator with her right foot, leans forward on the handlebars and zooms down to the front of the glacier. As she reaches the position she wants, she decelerates with the left foot until she is hovering just in front of the glacier. She touches the function key that gives her the 'simulations capability index' and selects 'glacier movement' at a century per second starting at 2000 BC. The term 'glacial' to her means something that moves so slowly it hardly seems to move at all, so she is startled by the size and speed of the glacier's advances and retreats at this rate and quickly slows the simulation down to study it more carefully. Suddenly the glacier disappears and is replaced by three-dimensional images of her teachers and classmates sitting in a sun-dappled glade while deer graze among them in the Arcadian forest they have designed for their virtual learning space. The virtual class is starting.

Just how serious is a scenario like this? Everything that has been described is technically feasible within the next ten years. A child born in the 1990s could be educated in this way. A datasuit of any real sophistication with force-feedback that gives a sense of touch presupposes some rather rapid developments in this area. There is a basic assumption that computer performance and memory will continue the present trends towards greater memory, faster processing and miniaturisation and that broadband telecommunications technology will become widely available. Looking at individualised speech recognition systems that exist today it is difficult not to imagine that they will become the basic way of communicating with personal computers in the near future. The wheelless motorcycle device is simply one of many designs for an interface system that allows a person to feel secure and comfortable in adjusting to the physical discrepancy between what bodies do in the real world and what minds do in reacting to virtual worlds. If the equipment and the software were mass produced for a global population of school goers they would surely be cheaper than the buses, roads, schools, books and so on which constitute the infrastructure of conventional classroom education.

The student attends her virtual school from her home. She could as easily attend from a local community centre or conventional school. The scenario indulged in a high-tech version of the interface equipment needed for a virtual school. A simpler system could be little more than a pair of spectacles and gloves. With cellular telecommunications it would be possible to join a virtual school anywhere in the world. This is the essence of the vision. The educational system for an information society will be distance-independent. And if that is truly the case then it could also be independent of a particular country. Education could become an international as well as, or perhaps even instead of, a national service. The student may not have to attend class with people who come together simply because they live in the same area. Instead it will be possible to share class activities with people who share the same interest in a subject even though they may live at the opposite ends of the world.

Besides liberating education from limitations of space, many time restrictions could also disappear. An instructional ideal is for people to learn at their own pace. The concept of a virtual learning environment brings this closer. Asynchronous instructional activities such as reading, doing exercises and individual assignments and accessing knowledge bases need not be dependent on institutions being open at fixed times. When there is no need for teachers and students to go to a physical location for education, the need to conduct education in lock-step and in fixed time slots is reduced. Students and teachers can keep flexible hours and calendars. Every student can have their own schedule, and a virtual school could be open every hour of every day. The students and their teachers could be spread around the world.

The scenario suggested that a virtual school could have large numbers of students. There are no physical restrictions such as the size and number of classrooms or the distance of a student's home from school to create limits to the number of students who can be part of a network that enables them to find the instruction they want. Nobody knows how many million people are linked today by Internet, a network of scholars and academics which is already being used for virtual classroom instruction. It links people in communities with mutual interests, lets them enter the catalogues of great libraries in many countries and write books together even though the authors are in different places. The people who use it, like the hypothetical student, are only aware of the part that they are involved with. Although they can explore its multitude of possibilities, its size is so great and it changes so much, so quickly, that no individual could know it as a whole in the way in which they could be aware of a conventional school. An advantage of an educational system as an international network is the variety of courses that could be accessed and the opportunities to link with like-minded learners around the world.

This is a vision of the kind of educational system that could become possible in an information society, a virtual network of learners, teachers, knowledge and examples of the problems the learners want to solve. The whole emphasis in instruction tilts towards the learner who is encouraged by the process to become a selective, sophisticated, lifelong customer for educational services that bring learning to the learner at the learner's convenience.

This vision is premised on the basis of the development of the information technologies that permit virtual reality. Writing of this technology Barry Sherman and Phil Judkins note:

at their outset, most technologies can be considered neutral. It is we, the people, who determine how, where and for what they are used. And as the world grows more sophisticated, and its parts increasingly interrelated, so these decisions get more difficult and more important. Virtual Reality is the most recent of links in this long chain, and like these other fundamental changes – radio and television included – it will offer us visions of hell as well as the more widely promised glimpses of heaven.

(Sherman and Judkins 1992: 13–14)

In arguing the case for a new paradigm of instruction based on virtual learning environments, there is a tendency to focus on the positive possibilities. There is, however, another side to the vision. In their research the authors had to deal with problems caused by differences in time and culture which are inherent in interacting between countries. Some of the problems they met were predictable, such as the way some teachers felt threatened by the technology and the fact that students wanted real social contact with one another. Other difficulties were less expected. There were intransigent problems in the technology itself and unexpected behaviour patterns such as the exaggerated communication on E-mail known as 'flaming'. These are some of the concerns in the telelearning pilot projects that are taking place around the world. What will be the social, economic, political and psychological consequences if the virtual class becomes the dominant mode of instruction?

With growing momentum, the copper cables of the telephone system are being replaced by cables of glass fibres. They are criss-crossing the oceans and going into place on the main trunk lines. Glass is beginning to replace copper on branch lines and inner-city loops. Heavy users of information such as universities, hospitals, airports and large businesses are acquiring their own fibre optic networks. Some time in the next century fibre optics will reach out to individual homes. Major developments are taking place in satellite and cellular telecommunications. The infrastructure of the information society is going into place now. In Singapore and Japan intelligent cities are actually being constructed. As Bernard Woods points out, 'the new systems will come about rapidly, driven by their potential profitability, by the new markets they create and by the new solutions they offer in the social sector' (Woods 1993: 133). Woods argues that we are living in a dual reality; what is possible now and what will be possible in the near future as information technology infrastructures being planned now come on line (Woods 1993: 133–4).

In civil engineering, planning horizons may be twenty years ahead as people think of the amount of water and waste disposal that will be needed to match birth rates, and the kinds of dams, roads, seaports and airports that will be needed to match economic plans and forecasts. A similar planning horizon is needed for education. It must go beyond trying to match schools and teachers to birth rates as if there were no other way. It must begin to look at how educational systems can be matched to the needs of the societies of the future and at the alternatives that the technologies that are transforming every other aspect of life could provide for learning. It must go yet further and consider that radically to change the ways in

which we learn is in its turn radically to change society. By thinking ahead in this way and describing future scenarios that are possible with new information technologies, it is possible to create a debate about foreseeable advantages and dangers and to influence the shape the future actually does take in education.

Chapter 2

Education is communication

. . . it is clear that communication either affects conduct or is without any discernible and probable effect at all.

(Shannon and Weaver 1949: 5)

Education, like religion or journalism, is the practice of a kind of communication. This chapter examines education in order to establish the fundamental communication functions for it to take place. We can then look at how the classroom facilitates such communication functions and how we could use information technology to improve on the classroom.

We make the assumption that all of us in the long run need some assistance to acquire complex sets of skills that are external to us. The term 'education' is used in an extended sense to include training, apprenticeship and bringing up children. It is also taken to include learning without direct supervision, through mediated instruction as in the case of distance education or teach-yourself materials. Having said this, however, the primary place where education takes place is seen to be the classroom.

Classroom communication is an emergent field of study concerned with intrapersonal, interpersonal, group and cultural communication in classroom settings. It studies verbal (Wilkinson 1982; Sutton 1981; Malamah-Thomas 1987) and non-verbal (Hansford 1988: 112–42) communication in the classroom. There is also a concern for the communication difficulties that learners experience such as communication apprehension, lack of listening skills and issues of self-perception (Hansford 1988: 39–53). But as Hansford notes, 'Given the immense amount of time most persons spend in classrooms . . . there is a paucity of research regarding the impact of such physical settings on the teacher–learning process' (Hansford 1988: 115).

Where the physical qualities of the classroom have been the focus of research it has been in terms of the psycho-social environment they provide. This is like saying that where the physical qualities of motorcars have been the focus of research it has been in terms of the mood the interior decoration sets for the driver. Cars are the mechanical component of people/machine transport systems dedicated to terrestrial travel. Class-rooms are the mechanical component of a people/machine communica-tions system dedicated to education and training. The classroom, like the car, does not function without people and, although people can travel and learn without them, they do so more effectively with them. Although we are fascinated with the way the car functions to do its job, we seem to have forgotten about the way classrooms function. They have been around so long that we take what they do for granted. There is no body of study of the classroom as a communication system for learning.

Given the potential of information technology, can a communication system for learning be designed that is more effective than a classroom? When we begin to look at the classroom as a communication machine and try to discover the fundamentals of educational communication so that we can build a better machine with information technology, then the tradi-tional research methodologies and theories of communication and educa-tion are limiting. They describe and explain what exists, rather than what could be. What does become relevant, however, are the methods and theoretical structures that lie behind information technology itself. Some way is needed to bring together the ideas of information technology with the ideas of communication and education. At the moment the profes-sionals in these three fields are like the wise but blind men who tried to understand what an elephant was from touching its different parts.

As industrial societies become information societies, conventional com-munication systems are becoming information systems. Where communi-cation was based on paper transactions and face-to-face meetings in rooms, there is now increased use of information technology. From depending on transport systems to get people and paper to the places where business is done, society is depending more on telecommunications to move informa-tion to where it is needed. Of course information technology has been used for some time to facilitate conventional communication. Television has supplanted the theatre in the lives of many people. The telephone supple-ments travelling to talk to people. But the change that is taking place is more than this. It is a change in the way communications are systematised.

Take the example of banking, a conventional communication system which changed little for many hundreds of years. People travelled to banks to pay in and withdraw money that existed mainly as information on paper notes or cheques. Transactions were primarily face to face or by post. Banks were among the first users of computers, but it was as a backroom aid for storing and organising data. Today computers are linked to tele-communications systems in banking so that bank cards can be presented for services and the cost directly debited from a person's account. Auto-matic tellers replace human tellers. Credit cards can be used around the world. Banking is becoming an information system. The same process is happening in business and commerce and wherever there is an organised

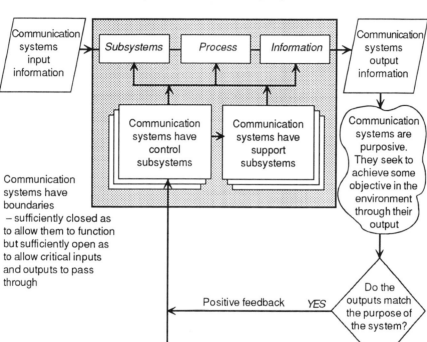

Communication systems have environments
and are part of communication suprasystems

Communication systems input information

Subsystems — Process — Information

Communication systems output information

Communication systems have control subsystems

Communication systems have support subsystems

Communication systems are purposive. They seek to achieve some objective in the environment through their output

Communication systems have boundaries
– sufficiently closed as to allow them to function but sufficiently open as to allow critical inputs and outputs to pass through

Positive feedback   YES

Do the outputs match the purpose of the system?

Negative feedback   NO

Figure 2.1 How a communication system functions as a system. Any communication system can be analysed in these terms

communications system. Since education is a communication system, it
will, in its turn, be transformed. It has to be, if it is to prepare people for a
society where information systems are the norm.

What usually happens as people first consider applying information
technology to an area of conventional communication is that a systems
analysis is applied. This means thinking of how communication in a
particular situation acts as a system in order to see how it can be improved
by using information technology. In conventional or traditional communication people seldom give much thought to the way they communicate. It
is something that is habitual and copied from existing examples. Although
the questions asked in a systems analysis are usually simple and obvious,
like, 'What is the objective of this communication process?', they make the

people involved re-think the nature of what they do. This is the purpose of this chapter – to look at education as a communication system so that later we can see how information technology might improve its effectiveness. In order to do this, we begin by examining the nature of education.

WHAT IS EDUCATION?

Is it what you are born with or the way you are brought up that counts most in life? The question divides the study of education. Of course both a person's genetic endowment and their environment contribute to the way they develop, but the question as to where responsibility really resides for what a person becomes is a legal and political issue of our time. Is a violent, unsociable, unemployable person the consequence of a genetic predisposition, or a lack of parental guidance, or what they see on television, or a failure of classroom teachers?

Even if the genetic factor proves to be the most important, the concrete way in which we have to prepare people for their part in society is by creating an effective educational communication system for those who need it.

One advocate of the environmentalist approach in education whose work has provoked interest in recent years is Lev Vygotsky. His concept of a Zone of Proximal Development (ZPD) provides a basis for looking at education as communication.

The zone of proximal development

Vygotsky defines the ZPD as 'The distance between the actual developmental level as determined by individual problem solving and the level of potential development as determined through problem solving under adult guidance or in collaboration with more capable peers' (Vygotsky 1978: 86).

Stated simply, the ZPD is the difference between what a person can do by themselves and what they could do with help from people more experienced than themselves.[1] An educational system exists to provide that help. The ZPD makes it possible to think about education without having to do so in terms of schools and classrooms. It provides an answer to the question 'What is the purpose of education?' by saying that it is to provide assistance to the learner that enables them to achieve levels of development that they would not be able to achieve by themselves.

Vygotsky was seeking a theory of education as a fundamental human activity (Moll 1990), and Tharp and Gallimore believe that the ZPD can be used as a basis for conceptualising a new educational paradigm (Tharp and Gallimore 1988: 20). However, as Barbara Rogoff cautions, we are looking at the 'refraction of Vygotsky's ideas . . . through a foreign lens – through differences in time and place, language and intellectual climate' (1990: 14). In appropriating the concept of the ZPD we transform it to some extent.

The ZPD implies that any educational system involves people who have roles as teachers and as learners and a communication process between them that allows the teachers to help the learners to solve problems that they would not be able to solve by themselves.[2] In addition, 'problem solving under guidance . . . or in collaboration with' means practice and feedback, and a two-way interactive communication process between teachers and learners that is dynamic. What Vygotsky did not have in mind in the pre-computer era he lived in is the possibility that the helping hand for the learner need not be human. Nor could he have realised that developments in telecommunications as well as computers would mean that the teacher, human or otherwise, could be anywhere and only present with the learner in a virtual sense.

Vygotsky had in mind the development of children. Today, education is seen as a lifelong process rather than merely as a preparation for adult life. The ZPD does allow for this and most neo-Vygotskians accept the broader application. Another post-Vygotskian development that may be important in a new educational paradigm is the notion of teaching as a team activity and learning as a group activity. This is a theme that is being explored by Michael Cole and his associates in the Fifth Dimension Project at the Laboratory of Comparative Human Cognition in San Diego. At different youth centres, children explore as groups a computer maze of educational games. They are represented by icons and have an existence in a world with its own rules which they have to learn in order to cope with different levels of problems. This extends Vygotsky's ideas beyond the classroom mindset of learner–teacher interaction. It addresses the 'social embeddedness' of learning and is an attempt to use a simple computer-based virtual reality for exploring new educational paradigms (Nicolopoulou and Cole 1993).

Bloom (1956) and later Gagne (1965) developed taxonomies of different kinds and levels of skills in the course of which 'problem solving' in education acquired specific meaning. Gagne in particular saw problem solving as a major aim of the educational process, and placed it at the highest level of the intellectual skills which he saw as being the main concern of schools (Gagne and Briggs 1974: 35–52). Neo-Vygotskian thinking accepts that Vygotsky's use of 'problem solving' in the concept of the ZPD can be broadly defined. According to Tharp and Gallimore, 'for any domain of skill a ZPD can be created' (Tharp and Gallimore 1988: 30–1).

Problem solving in the Vygotskian perspective is culturally based. A particular culture expects problems to be resolved according to the ways that culture has devised for solving its problems. As Rogoff puts it: 'Interactions in the zone of proximal development are the crucible of development and of culture' (Rogoff 1990: 16). Although some initiative and ingenuity can be shown by someone in solving a problem, essentially they are expected to draw on a culturally sanctioned repertoire of solutions. Education is a process of enculturation, of learning how to deal with the world and solving the myriads of problems it presents, according to the ways of a particular culture.

Education is not just an interaction between people in the roles of learner and teacher. It is also an interaction between problems and the knowledge in a culture of how to deal with them. 'Problem solving' can be seen as having two sides, like a coin: 'the problem' and 'the knowledge that can be applied to the problem'. Such areas as health, social relationships, dress, shelter and spatial relationships present problems to all peoples. Their existence has provoked cultures to develop ways of dealing with them which, over time, have accreted to form bodies of knowledge. Culture is a society's way of dealing with the world and education is the process whereby the accumulated accepted knowledge of a culture is passed on.

The four critical factors of education

In his ZPD, Vygotsky specifies three factors in the educational process:

- someone in the role of learner;
- someone in the role of teacher; and
- something that constitutes a problem which the learner is trying to solve with the help of the teacher.

By implication there is a fourth factor – the knowledge needed to solve the problem.

We believe that it is the interaction of these four factors – learner, teacher, knowledge and problem in a particular context – that constitute the fundamental communication process that is education. All these factors need to be present for education to take place, but the factors only exist in relation to one another and only for the period of time it takes a learner to master an ability to solve a class of problems. When a person 'knows' how to solve a 'problem' they do not need a 'teacher' and they are no longer a 'learner'. There is no ZPD. In this view of education, 'knowledge' only exists in relation to a class or domain of 'problems', and the role of teacher only exists in relation to someone who assumes the role of learner with regard to a class or domain of problems. The four factors can take many forms and can exist at different levels of complexity.

Example 1

There is a problem on the blackboard which a group of learners are trying to solve. They have a textbook that contains the knowledge they need to solve the problem and there is a teacher to help them if they have difficulty.

In this case the four factors have a separate embodiment. Of course, if the textbook has nothing to do with the problem and the teacher is not qualified to teach the subject and the learner does not want to know how to deal with the kind of problem that is written down, then there is no relationship between the factors and there is no educational process.

The problem does not have to be on the blackboard. It could be in the teacher's head. The teacher could give the problem to the learners in the form of a verbal question. It then also resides in the heads of the learners. The knowledge of how to solve this kind of problem is in the teacher's head as well as in the textbook. The teacher can transfer this knowledge to the learners by an explanation. The learners now have a problem, and the knowledge as to how to solve it, but they cannot see how the two fit together. The teacher uses the blackboard to relate the knowledge to the problem. There are smiles and nods from the learners as the relationship clicks into place. The teacher provides a few more examples of problems to ensure that the learners really have understood, but the ZPD is evaporating. With respect to this kind of problem, the learner is no longer a learner and the teacher no longer has a role because the new practitioners know how to deal with this class of problem.

Example 2

A group of students are learning how to work together as a team in order to record a video programme in a television studio. To do this they are guided by a professional studio team who, in this case, act as a team of teachers. Each student takes on a studio role as talent, camera person, floor-manager, technical director and so on. They act as a team to produce a short video sequence.

Although each student in turn has to master a skill such as presenting to a camera or manipulating a camera, they also have to learn to work as a team. This is learning to solve a problem as a group. The team of teachers, although they are helping individual students at one level, are at another working with one another to make the activities come together. The problem is how to use the studio and the equipment in it to record a video programme. The knowledge is in a book the students have studied before doing the exercise and in the professional studio team. Although the students theoretically know what to do to begin with, they have great difficulty with the problem. As a group they manifest a ZPD and need assistance from the team of professionals. However, as they rotate through the different tasks a change takes place. By the time they have all per-formed in each of the roles, the teachers are no longer helping them. Something akin to learning to ride a bike has taken place at a team level. Although there is more to learn, the basic ability to coordinate different actions has been developed. The students know how to deal with the problem of recording a video in the studio.

Example 3

In 1964, Ethiopia decided to switch from driving on the left to driving on the right-hand side of the road. The direction of the flow of traffic is something that affects everyone in a country. Pedestrians as well as drivers have to learn to follow the rule together. People learn as individuals how to follow the highway code of a country, but in this case a whole country had to re-learn a rule of the road together and to do that overnight. It was not the kind of change that could be introduced gradually. The problem was how to drive on the opposite side of the road and how to adapt to the new direction of traffic. The learners were a nation of people most of whom were illiterate. The teachers were a miscellaneous group of foreign advisers and Ethiopians at the Imperial Highways Division of the government of Haile Selassie who had the detailed knowledge that was needed to deal with the problem. For weeks before the changeover they conducted a national educational campaign using radio and posters, and sending advisers to every market place, every school, everywhere that people met. In this way the knowledge that resided in a government department was transferred to a nation. Despite forecasts of the biggest road accident in history, the change took place without a single fatality. What had been a problem (the nation did not know how to drive on the right-hand side of the road) became knowledge (the nation did know how to drive on the right-hand side of the road), and the country in this respect was no longer in the role of learner and had no more need of teachers. The National ZPD had disappeared.

These examples are intended to show that education can take place at many levels. Whatever the level, however, for the four factors of learning to interact, there has to be a communication process.

WHAT IS COMMUNICATION?

There are three fundamental communication functions – to transmit information over space, to store information over time and to process information so that it is regenerated. It is through these three functions that the interaction between the four factors of learning takes place.

Transmission

What most people have in mind when they talk about communication is moving information across space. To get a message from one place to another requires energy. Speech is carried on sound-waves, people see

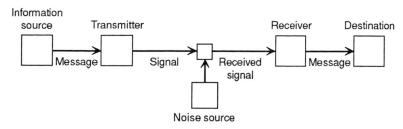

Figure 2.2 Shannon's model of a communication system
Source: Shannon and Weaver 1949

because of light-waves and the telephone system uses electrical energy. Communication that exists as energy is subject to the physical laws that govern energy. The first person to recognise this was Claude Shannon. As with Vygotsky in education, he provides a point of departure for studying communications that most people can accept.

Claude Shannon argued that the primary concern of communication is to reproduce a message sent from one place to another place as faithfully as possible (Shannon and Weaver 1949). Shannon illustrated the path for transmitting information over space with a diagram which has been reproduced in articles and books around the world. Because of its simplicity and obviousness, it has dominated the way people think about communication so that they see it as a linear action with a beginning and an end, a source and a destination.

Shannon created his model while he was working in the research laboratories of the Bell Telephone Company. He had in mind a telecommunications system. A telecommunications system has inputs of information at one place and outputs of information at another place. It transmits information from one place to another place as quickly and as accurately as possible. In Shannon's day, telephones often had some kind of background noise that made it difficult to hear clearly, especially on long-distance calls. Shannon gave a specific meaning to the term 'noise' as that which was added to a message that impeded perfect transmission. Although telecommunications has vastly improved and physical noise has been reduced, it has not been eliminated. Audio noise is a serious technical problem in using the public telephone system for education.[3] There are other kinds of noise which come from the fact that humans are never the same in the way they understand things and never find themselves in exactly the same circumstances twice. Noise is semantic when the destination of a message does not understand what the sender intended, syntactic when the grammar of a message is incorrect and pragmatic when the purpose of a message is not clear.

Shannon's diagram describes the most basic unit in transmission over distance, the half duplex dyad (Figure 2.3). Shannon went on to analyse

Node A   Node B

Figure 2.3 A half duplex dyad; a one-way link between two nodes which can be thought of as source and destination

Node A   Node B

Figure 2.4 Full duplex dyad

mathematically the function of communication at this most fundamental level and he did so with a logic that has remained mathematically unassailable. Warren Weaver, in reading Shannon's original publication describing his mathematical theory of communication, believed that it represented a general theory of communication, and wrote a foreword to a subsequent publication of the theory which presented it in this way. As a result it has been perceived, criticised and partially accepted as a general theory of communication. This has tended to prescribe the study of communications. What was a key to a room in a mansion was mistakenly seen as the key to the whole edifice. Communications studies have used Shannon's model to see the macro in terms of the micro. Perhaps the most enduring image we carry of the educational process is that of a teacher explaining something to a student. How deceptively easy it is to transpose this to Shannon's model, with the teacher as source and the student as destination and any difficulty in learning as due to noise (Hansford 1988: 9, Figure 1.5).

Shannon was analysing the minimal communication function over distance. Turn his half duplex dyadic link into full duplex (a two-way communication link) or see it as part of a bigger network, and the message source becomes a destination as well. Communication starts to become a complex process.

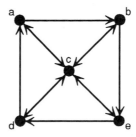

Figure 2.5 Star and ring network with five nodes in network *abcde*. The dyad *ab* represents Shannon's model with *a* as source and *b* as destination. In the wider context of the whole network *a* could also be destination for a message from *d* and either source or destination for communications with *c*

Imagine that the network *abcde* is a school telephone network. The node *c* is a switchboard that links the school network into the local loop of the public switched telephone network. The local loop of a telephone network will have a switch that links it to the trunk network, and the trunk network is linked by a switching system to the international network. In this way networks are linked to networks. But this is simply to look at the inter-connectibility of telephone networks which are only one of the communication network systems that people use. They also use networks of roads and railways and sea-lines and airways which allow them to travel to meet and talk with other people.

The ramifications are endless. The receptionist who operates the switch-board at *a* meets for lunch with his network of friends and, although he is not supposed to, he discusses the messages that passed through *c*. One of his friends hears something about a student who is the daughter of a neighbour. She decides to go and see her . . . and so it could continue. The potential for complexity as networks interlink is extraordinary, and raises the possibility that communication at the macro-level could be better understood in terms of complexity theory (Waldrop 1992) than Shannon's theory. Seen in this light, the view of a teacher and student as source and destination for the transmission of knowledge is simplistic. Teachers and learners are nodes in classroom networks, which are linked to school networks, which are linked to school district networks, which are linked to regional educational networks, which are linked to national educational networks. Every one of the learners and teachers are nodes in other networks, such as family networks, religious networks and political

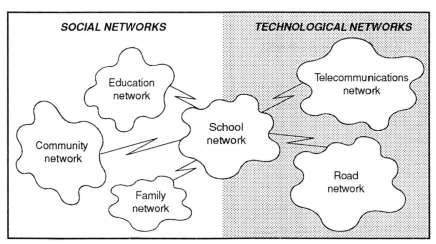

Figure 2.6 The interconnectibility of networks. Social networks link with one another and the school via the technological network. People can walk to talk or use the telephone

networks. The network activity in a classroom is in fact linked to network activities in a complex chain of networks in which the flow of information does not necessarily form stable patterns. No two lessons are ever the same and classroom communication can be highly volatile.

Storage

The second function of communication is to store information over time. Part of the classic picture of a teacher lecturing students is of the students diligently making notes. Information carried on sound-waves becomes ink marks on a piece of paper. Information as energy becomes information as matter. The way to preserve information is in some way to record it on some relatively non-volatile matter.

One of the reasons students take notes is that they have become only too conscious of the limitations of the human brain as an information storage system. They get tested and examined at regular intervals, and this demonstrates to most of them that their memory seems to be limited as to how much it can remember, how long it can remember and how accurately it can remember. This is a common-sense understanding of learning and memory which everybody who has gone through a traditional educational system shares. It is deeply embedded in societies where educational systems evaluate the extent to which memory in an individual is unstable and decays with time, and reward those who have special ability to remember or the determination to study something over and over until it is finally remembered. Herman Ebbinghaus gave scientific credence to this concept of memory and learning (1964). He undertook a series of experiments on himself which established a long line of laboratory research into the capability and limitations of memory. It has also served as something of a model for diligent students. He learned strings of nonsense words and then tested recall over different periods of time and showed how, with time, memory loss stabilised. He also tested what happened when he re-learned the string after different periods of time and showed that memory savings improved with each iteration.

For hundreds of years, around the world, first-year tertiary students have sat in lectures and tried to write down everything the lecturer says. They do not know what they are expected to remember or what they will be tested on, so they play safe and try to remember everything. In this, as in the Ebbinghaus experiments, there is an echo of the uncritical eidetic memory patterns of childhood. Eidetic memory is what is often called 'photographic memory'. Steven Rose writes that 'Many, if not all, young children apparently do normally see and remember eidetically, but this capacity is lost to most as they grow up' (Rose 1992: 103–4). He then speculates on the significance of the dramatic change in the nature of remembering that takes place with the approach of puberty when people shift away from eidetic memory:

Consciously or unconsciously, we [then] select salient information that we need to commit to memory from the blooming, buzzing confusion of the environment around us. To help in this selection, we possess quite elaborate blocking or filtering devices to prevent new information from cluttering up our memories. At birth, we may guess all types of input may seem to be of about equal relevance; within only the widest possible classification rules everything must be registered and ordered so as to enable each individual to build up his or her own criteria of significance. At this time eidetic memory, which does not prejudge the importance of inputs, is vital because it gives us the greatest possible range over which inputs can be analysed. But as we grow up we learn to select from the key features of our environment.

(Rose 1992: 104–5)

And so, as first-year students become second-year students, they begin to take notes that relate more to the meaning behind the words than the words themselves. They are the students' own comment on, and construction of, the field of knowledge the lecture addresses.

Western education is critical of rote learning. It seems childish and in line with eidetic memory to remember things indiscriminately. A contemporary view of memory in education is of a more mature process of selective memory that allows us to construct our own versions of knowledge. This in itself, however, is inadequate. There is a collective memory of knowledge that exists independently of us. Oral cultures have used rote learning to pass on collective tribal memory. Artificial memory which is also used for collective memory is as old as history. In the classroom, besides the memories of the people present, there are textbooks, workbooks, video-cassettes, audiocassettes and compact discs which contain the problems and knowledge needed for learning. Computer-based memory grows exponentially. We are looking at a growing role for artificial as distinct from biological memory. Steven Rose explains the significance:

Where there is no artificial memory, each individual animal lives in its own unique and personal set of memories which begin with its birth and end with its death and can represent only its own experience . . . artificial memory presents the same picture, set of words, video image to many hundreds, thousands or millions of us, resetting, training and hence limiting our own individual memories, creating instead a mass consensus about what is to be remembered and how it is to be remembered.

Thus whilst for each of us the experience of collective memory is an individual biological and psychological one, its existence serves purposes which transcend the individual, welding together human societies by imposing shared understandings, interpretations, ideologies.

(Rose 1992: 326–7)

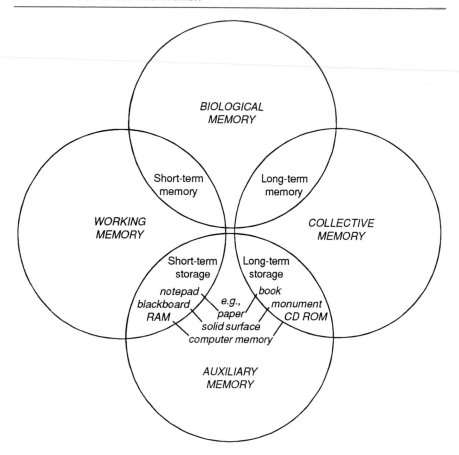

Figure 2.7 Kinds of communication storage

Processing

The computer, the brain and a sundial are all systems that process information. What constitutes process in communication is when the change at a node in a network results in new information. This happens when transmitted information intermeshes with stored information. The result is the generation of information that is in some way different from the incoming and stored information from which it is derived. The newly generated information can then be stored and/or transmitted.

Intuitive models of the way we think suggest a similarity with the workings of a sundial in the interaction between memory and perception, between the influx of new information transmitted through the senses and the information we have from past experience. The result is the generation of new information. Von Weizsacker expresses it as 'information is that which generates information' (Von Weizsacker 1980: 26).

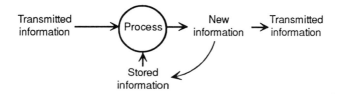

Figure 2.8 Communication processing takes place when transmitted information intermeshes with stored information. The outcome is new information that can be transmitted and/or stored

Figure 2.9 A sundial is a simple communication-processing system. The hours are inscribed upon a dial. This is a programmed memory. The sunlight strikes the stylus and casts a shadow. In this way the intersection of incoming information with stored information creates new information. The sundial tells the time

In humans, the output of new information has some degree of originality. A person's memory is based on a unique set of experiences and a unique cerebral capability. The information an individual receives, even if it is a mass-media message, is unique because of the time and place in which it arrives and the kind and amount of noise that accompanies it. The intersection of the unique information with the unique memory results in a unique output of information. Even if it is years later, even if it is tangential, even if it is only in a tone of voice, a gesture or eye movement, at a particular point in time, at a particular point in space and in a particular

Figure 2.10 A person's brain is a complex communications-processing device. Years of experience are inscribed in memory. Reflected light is focused on the fovea at the back of the eye. This incites neural activity that matches what the old man sees with what he remembers. He thinks

context, there is always some degree of originality in the ensuing information. We are part of an endless flow of information. We attend to some parts of the flow and as a result subtly shift the direction of that flow, so that downstream, in time, things change.

Computers process information and can generate original information. The whole field of science is rapidly advancing in its understanding of the universe because of the information generated by supercomputers. A computer's capability to intermesh information is programmed into it by humans, just as the dial and positioning of sundials are the results of human ingenuity. But are not humans programmed in their turn? What is education and training if not a form of programming? Education can be thought of as humans programming humans, but will that be the case in the future? Already children use machines to help them learn arithmetical skills. Are they not, therefore, already being programmed by machines?

Figure 2.11 A computer is a communications-processing device, though it is usually referred to as an 'information-processing device'. Information is transmitted to the computer by someone using the keyboard. This interacts with information stored in the computer's memory to process information. When words are keyboarded in to interact with a stored applications programme such as a word processor, the information processing is called word processing

We have described communication processing in minimalistic terms as a process that people have in common with things like sundials and computers. This is like using Shannon's model of transmission processes to explain an operatic performance by Dame Kiri Te Kanawa. It does not explain adequately the complexity of conscious thinking in a human being and the capacity that is called intelligence.

Conventional education systems are based on human transmission systems, human memories and above all, on human processing – the thinking in education. That we can use technology for transmission or as an auxiliary memory in a future educational system is something most people would probably accept. They are also likely to be comfortable with the use of low-level processing systems for instruction such as computer-assisted instruction (CAI). What, however, is controversial is the idea that a future educational system could include a technological version of the high-level complex communication processing that people engage in when they think.

Whether we already have created, or ever can create, artificial intelligence is one of the academic debates of our time. On the one side we have a group of people who, like Marvin Minsky (1986), argue that the artificial intelligences of the future will regard us as pets, if we are lucky. On the other side we have John Searle (1992), Roger Penrose (1989) and Gerald Edelman (1992) who argue that machines can never possess intelligence. The debate is without a clear foundation because intelligence is an elusive attribute of the human brain which, like consciousness, mind and memory, defies definition and is essentially understood through personal experience. Whether artificial intelligence ever does rival or surpass human intelligence, it continues to develop in a direction which seems intelligent.

The fractal dimension in communications

Communication, in its fullest sense, embraces the three functions of storage, processing and transmission. It is possible to see a sequence of communication events, rather like the links in a chain in which information is stored, transmitted, processed, stored and so on. When we write, we link thought to paper, processing to storage. When we read, we link light to thought, transmission to processing. When we take a photo, we link light to film, transmission to storage. When we project a movie, we link film back to light, storage to transmission. Information is shifted between the different links in the chain by transducers. These are devices such as microphones, cameras, television sets, video players which allow information to be transferred from one kind of function to another. Even a fountain pen, or a light playing on the page of a book, are transducers, as are eyes, ears, noses, mouths, hands and skin. A library is designed to

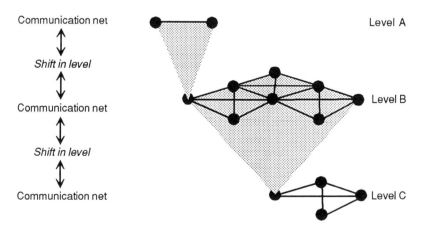

Figure 2.12 The fractal dimension in communications. Nodes *a* and *b* are, on closer examination, networks themselves at a different level

store information. A telecommunications company is designed to transmit information. A computer is designed to process information. Some communications systems, however, may be concerned with all three functions of communication. A television station is one example, a school is another.

The concept of a network embraces the complexity of communication as a whole. The term can be used for human as well as technological communications systems.

Diagrams of communication networks consist of lines that represent communication channels and points where the lines intersect, which are referred to as 'nodes'. Lines between nodes are called 'links' and the basic unit of a network is the dyad. This is the link between two nodes which Shannon's model describes, without which there can be no network. We used the idea of a network to explain the transmission of information between nodes. We looked at processing as something that happened at a node where incoming information interacted with stored information. The inference here is that information is stored at a node. Nodes, then, can have a storage function, a processing function and a transmission function. It is also useful to remember that nodes are not necessarily static. People are transmitting, storing and processing nodes in social networks and they move around. A laptop computer can be used as a portable transmission, storage and processing node in a network such as Internet.

What gives a communications system an internal cohesiveness is the way it functions as a network. However, no communications system exists in isolation. Communications systems have communications suprasystems and subsystems. Networks can be seen as part of supranetworks and as possessing subnetworks.

When communication is looked at in this way it seems to have something in the nature of a fractal dimension. Fractal geometry was conceptualised by Benoit Mandelbrot (1983) as a method of describing structures such as clouds and trees that do not have a regular formation. If a structure is described at different levels or scales and the same fundamental elements keep appearing, it is said to have a fractal dimension. Fractal geometry seeks algorithms that describe fractal dimensions (Jürgens *et al.* 1990: 60–5). An example which is widely used is that of a coastline. It is an irregular shape which at any scale is an intersection of land and water in headlands and inlets. There appears to be a fractal dimension in communication in the way that a node in a communications network can prove, on closer examination, to be a communications network itself. Conversely, a communications network can at another scale be seen as a node in another communications network.

To understand this let us attempt a thought experiment. You are a node in a network, you have a relationship with a significant other, so the network is a dyad. Bring in a third person. You have a triadic network. Now think of being part of a group of friends, an N–adic social network.

What we are doing here is increasing the size of a network. The network remains at a level where all the nodes are individual people. Now let's begin to shift levels and observe what appears to be a fractal dimension.

Imagine the social network you are part of meeting in a classroom. At one level a classroom can be seen as housing a network of people each of whom is a node. At another level, the classroom itself can be seen as a node in a network of classroom nodes that constitutes a school. Any large building can be seen as a communication network in which the rooms are nodes and the passages and stairs and elevators are links.

Shift levels again to consider a road with buildings along it. The buildings are now nodes in the street network. A network which consists of a single link with nodes along it is called a bus network, an interesting reflection on the way houses can be linked by transport along the road, as well as by postal services or telecommunications. Zoom out now to some point in the sky where you can look down on the roads and the railways and the way they intersect in towns and villages which now become the nodes. At night, from an aeroplane, it is sometimes possible to look down at the patterns of light made by cities and roads and it looks like an illuminated diagram of a network. Shift scale now to the perspective of a satellite where whole cities can be perceived as nodes. At these levels maps are good ways of looking at the networks formed by roads and motorways, air lanes and sea lanes. A research project in Japan known as the Triple-T (Tourism, Transport and Telecommunications) sees the development of networks across the Pacific which permit the free flow of people, goods and information. This project attaches great significance to the development of giant nodes where different kinds of networks intersect. Places such as Singapore, Shanghai, Hong Kong and Tokyo/Yokohama are seen as conjunctions of seaports, airports and teleports where different kinds of communication channels intersect to form supercommunication nodes known as Triple-T hubs (JANCPEC 1992).

Reverse the process. From a hemispheric view of networks zoom into your own country and its communication networks with its city nodes. Zoom into your town or city communication network. Keep going on this fractal zoom. First you see the neighbourhood you live in as a node, then as you get close, it becomes a network. Now you see your house as a node, then you are back into it and it is a network of rooms. Move into a room, there is a network of people. Don't stop. Imagine you can enter the brain of one of the people who is a node in the social network and see the billions of synaptic links between the neurons that make a brain a network with between ten and a hundred billion nodes.[4]

The study of communications implicitly recognises the existence of communication networks at different levels. Intrapersonal, interpersonal, group, organisational, mass and global communications are seen as the social levels within which people communicate (Williams 1992). The

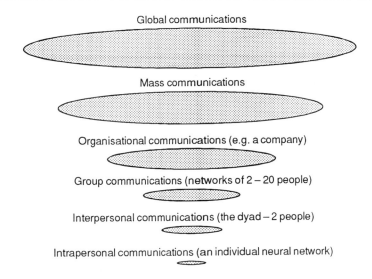

Figure 2.13 The levels in communications studies

nature of communication is different at each level and people can be seen as shifting levels to satisfy different communication needs.

Education systems are communication systems and therefore they are networks which can exist at different fractal levels. The networks have transmission, storage and processing functions and interrelate learner, teacher, problem and knowledge nodes so that learning can take place. We need to look at this in more detail before seeing how it applies to classroom education and how it could provide a basis for designing a network for a virtual class in the future.

WHAT KIND OF COMMUNICATION SYSTEM IS NEEDED FOR EDUCATION?

What are the critical components and functions of a communications system for education? From the previous analysis of the nature of education and communication we can state:

> Systems for organised learning are complex communications systems concerned with the transmission, storage and processing of information. Their purpose is to assist learners so that from being unable to deal with problems they become proficient problem solvers. This depends on communications networks that intermesh four related factors: learning, teaching, knowledge and problem. There appears to be a fractal dimension in that the network that intermeshes the four

related factors can prove to be a node in a network at a higher level. Similarly, a processing node in a network can, at a lower level, prove to be a network. The existence of different levels in a communications system for learning allows learners to shift levels in the process of learning.

To apply this to the conventional classroom and to designing a new educational system for the future we need to revisit the basic communication functions, looking at them now in terms of how they relate to educational systems.

Transmission systems for education

Learning in any entity depends upon stimuli from the environment. Of course, people can learn on occasion without direct external stimuli. We are all familiar with the ruminative kind of self-reflective thinking which produces insights from which we can be said to learn. However, such thinking depends in the first place upon stimuli previously received. Implicit in the reason for education is that there is some body of knowledge or skills external to the learner which has to be communicated to the learner.

We can think of the five senses as five channels, each with a fixed channel capacity through which information in the form of energy can reach the central nervous system of a human. It is through these channels that learning takes place. Thomas Aquinas said: 'man's knowledge starts from the senses' (Aquinas 1975: 5). Education is something transduced into people through their senses.

Proximal stimuli is energy that physically impinges on the receptor nerves of the body. A distinction is drawn with distal stimuli, which refer to the origins of stimuli that are not adjacent to the body. Somebody shouting is providing distal stimuli, while the impact of the sound-waves on the receptor nerves of the ear provides proximal stimuli. A human being is only aware of the world outside his or her body through proximal stimuli. It is this which makes virtual reality possible. The senses can be tricked into believing that an artificial world is a real world.

Of the five channels available for learning, education has been heavily dependent on those of sight and sound. This is because most classroom instruction is in spoken or written words and numbers. Yet coping with real world problems means dealing with information through all the senses. Not surprisingly, training, with its orientation towards concrete practical skills, has always had a strong concern with touch, taste and smell, especially in such fields as viniculture, cooking and sports. Advocates of multimedia systems in education, like their predecessors in the audiovisual movement of the 1960s, argue that education needs to be less abstracted into words and should make greater use of images and sounds which portray the world as it is. In contrast, Neil Postman believes that the decline of literacy which he sees in the United States heralds a new barbarism. Because people do not learn to read they lack the ability to think about things in the abstract and instead know the world more directly, as animals do (Postman 1985). These are extreme positions. There are occasions when a picture evokes a thousand words, others when a word is worth a million pictures and still others when to learn we need to smell, touch and taste. Learning can involve all the senses of the learner and a transmission system for learning needs to provide for this. Classrooms do.

When we need to see a picture to learn, then we need to see it clearly. The same is true of listening when we are learning music, or of taste when we are learning cooking, or of touch if we are trying to discriminate surfaces, or smell if we are defining perfumes. Learning like this needs high-fidelity information. That means transmitting large quantities of information in real time and to do that requires a lot of bandwidth. For the moment let us accept that the amount of bandwidth is a measure of the amount of information that can be transmitted at a given time by a channel. In the world of telecommunications bandwidth costs money. The irony of the current situation is that the classroom is a broadband environment and can be used to transmit as much information as the senses can absorb. Yet we mainly use it for learning with words which require little bandwidth.

Multichannel learning means learning through more than one sense at a time and usually refers to learning by sight and sound. There is a popular notion that multiplying the stimuli on different senses multiplies the impact of instruction. There is no evidence that this is the case. It seems more likely that the information input that we are conscious of is distinctly limited (Best 1992). It is self-evident that when we consciously focus on one sensory input, it is at the expense of the others. If, for example, you were now to give some thought to what the inside of your mouth feels like, whether you are thirsty or hungry, or what the big toe on your right foot is feeling, then you will realise that you have given them very little attention for some time unless you have been learning to climb or to make ice cream. And having really got into touch with your big toe and tongue, try reading this at the same time. In learning, people need to be able to switch between sensory modalities and adjust bandwidth.

There is nothing intrinsically different in the way information is transmitted for instruction as distinct from other purposes. However, there is a distinction in the pattern of interaction that takes place between the learner and the teacher. Education and training are concerned with achieving a permanent change in the processing capability of the learner and with verifying that this change has taken place. Despite the serious faces of television newscasters and the time and effort that goes into preparing the news, nobody cares whether anyone remembers it the following day, or whether they do anything about it. What distinguishes the instructional process from communication that informs, entertains, manages or persuades, is that some, if not most, of what is learned is supposed to stick. The learner needs to be able to remember things so that they are able to do things that they could not do before they started the instruction, and they need to be able to do them effectively, especially if they are learning to be a doctor or a pilot. This requires a process of verifying that learners have acquired knowledge and can apply it to a class of problems, and this in turn means that the instructional process must allow for some kind of practice in problem solving. The learner then needs to receive feedback as to whether or not they have learned to solve the kind of problem they are studying. They may also need some kind of help that either corrects or improves what they are doing so that they gradually become skilled. All of this implies a two-way broadband multimedia link between teacher and learner in which both can initiate communication and both can receive feedback from each other.

A learning network that is simply a full duplex dyad would be a tutor with one student where the tutor was a master of a subject. This is the traditional situation where the teacher is the source of knowledge. An example is a musician with a gifted student.

It is possible to think of cases like the above where unique knowledge may be resident in the teacher. However, in most fields of education the body of knowledge exists independently of the teacher. It has a separate existence in some kind of storage system such as a book. Text does not need a lot of bandwidth for delivery at reading speed. However, knowledge is sometimes contained in media such as 35-mm film that do need a lot of bandwidth. Soon we will also have libraries of high-definition video and virtual reality software.

The problems which are the *raison d'être* for an educational system, because an individual cannot learn to solve them without help, may exist as real world phenomena that can be touched, smelt and tasted as well as seen and heard. As such, therefore, they too have an existence independent of the teacher, the learner or the body of knowledge concerned with how to deal with them. The illnesses and accidents and decay to which people are prone is the problem domain of medical knowledge. In this domain a sick person is a problem to be treated by a doctor with the relevant medical knowledge. Doctors learn in teaching hospitals with real people. Ships and the sea constitute a problem domain which is addressed by the art of navigation. Sailors learn their craft at sea. Fundamental to education is practice in problem solving. If the problem is a real-world one, this may not be feasible or practical or even safe. In this case the problem can be simulated or abstracted, though this may carry the danger that when the learner really does have to face real-world problems, they cannot transfer the skills they learned. A training hospital or a flight simulator provide problems for instruction. Transmission systems for education need to be able to link problems and knowledge with teaching and learning however these factors are manifested. In the best of all worlds the links will be broadband and allow for information in all five sensory modalities.

So we come to a statement about the transmission needs of a communication system for learning that is beyond any existing telecommunications capability, but within the capacity of a classroom.

> To be capable of a broad spectrum of instruction, education needs a transmission system that is full duplex (two way), synchronous and asynchronous with sufficient bandwidth, and the kind of transducers that will allow for the transmission of high-fidelity information in all sensory modalities. Such a network would link learning, teaching, knowledge and problem entities. It should also be possible to dynamically adjust bandwidth and switch modalities.

Storage systems for education

Learning in any entity depends upon an ability to store the capability acquired so that it can be accessed when needed. Any teaching entity must also have some stored knowledge of a class of problems and how to deal with them. Knowledge and examples of problems in classroom education are also stored in texts. Increasingly, knowledge is stored in computer-accessible formats such as CD-ROM or databases that are accessible by telecommunications. There is a trend towards the development of banks of test items and case studies – in other words, the storage in various forms of practice problems. Education increasingly means a symbiosis of biological and artificial memories. Instead of acquiring all the knowledge needed to solve a problem, the learner acquires basic principles and concepts so that they can access and use detailed stored knowledge. For this to be possible it must be easy to find and access knowledge in artificial memory systems.

In educational systems there is an elaborate hierarchical process whereby the content of what is taught is critiqued before it becomes incorporated into a body of knowledge that is regarded as appropriate to education. Universities have a research and teaching function whereby academics write books and articles about their research discoveries that are scrutinised by their peers. Knowledge is then transmitted to students who move out into professional areas and in some cases become teachers themselves. In this way there is a slow trickle-down of new knowledge and information into the educational system. Associated with this is a process of refining the new knowledge and integrating it into the corpus of established knowledge.

Today most knowledge is stored as written text. Ever since the days of the great library at Alexandria, the bodies of knowledge contained in libraries have been seen as the raw material of the educational process. It is not just the totality of the text in the library that represents this accepted body of wisdom. Books that are regarded as sources of knowledge cite other books. There is a textual network where books that are part of the hierarchy of knowledge link with one another by quoting and referring to one another. It is this interlinking network which holds together what is regarded as accepted knowledge.

New knowledge can be added to the pantheon of accepted knowledge as long as it can be linked to the accepted ideas and tenets of existent knowledge in the same field. In other words, it conforms to Kuhn's normal or accepted paradigm. What, however, happens to divergent perspectives? What about the danger that a highly structured self-reinforcing system like this fossilises knowledge?

Training has proved more responsive than education to the changing instructional environment. The results of training are specific, observable and measurable, and there has been growing concern with the importance of introducing new skills into a workforce as quickly as possible. People find themselves unemployed because they lack new skills and increasingly are prepared to pay for training that gives them marketable skills. Instruction that is associated with marketable skills is becoming expensive. A new genre of training sees high-powered specialists in the latest information technology systems arriving, like the snake-oil salesmen of an earlier age, in the smartest hotel in town, charging top people top prices for the privilege of being trained in the latest high-tech trend. The downside of the rapid introduction of new knowledge is the danger that it is unsound, unproven knowledge.

The characteristics of storage subsystems for learning systems can be described as follows:

> To be capable of a broad spectrum of instruction, education needs a symbiotic relationship between human and artificial memory that allows for rapid, on-demand access to information in any sensory modality about the knowledge and problems which are the subject of study. New knowledge and new cases of problems need to be incorporated into education rapidly, but in a manner that indicates the degree of confidence that can be attributed to their validity and reliability.

Processing systems in education

The critical process in education lies in changing learners so that they acquire the ability to deal with a class of problems. This happens when the four factors – learning, teaching, knowledge and problem – intermesh. The result is that the learner can deal with a problem that they could not cope with before.

For learning to take place there must be a communications network in which there are nodes that can function as learners and teachers, and as sources of knowledge and problems. These are critical functions. Take away learners and the system has no purpose. Take away the teaching function and there is no ZPD, no assurance that the skill is acquired, no help if there is a mistake. Without the problems there is nothing for the learners to attempt to solve and practise on. Without the knowledge that relates to this class of problem, the only way the problems can be solved is through the intuitive discovery of the knowledge.

There appears to be a fractal dimension in the processing function of communications networks. If the analysis of learning systems as communication systems is valid it should be possible to see how processing nodes in learning networks are themselves networks. We examine this in the next chapter.

> The process system in education needs to intermesh information from learning, teaching, knowledge and problem entities. These entities are embedded in the nodes of networks which appear to have a fractal dimension. The nodes in a network where learning is taking place can be networks themselves at another level. The intermeshing of information is dynamic. The ability to shift fractal levels may be critical.

Control systems in education

So far we have looked at communication systems for education in terms of their basic instructional purpose. In all complex, purposive systems, however, there is also a control subsystem. It is a management function in any system that has any kind of intelligence to take notice of feedback and then to adjust what the system is doing to ensure that the output of the system matches the requirements of the environment it is serving. When this is the case, the feedback is positive and good management ensures that things carry on as they are as the system's objectives are achieved. However, if the feedback is negative and there is a discrepancy between what the system is doing and what the environment it is serving wants, then the message to management is to change direction. This is the cybernetic process that is critical to any purposeful system. The term 'cybernetic' comes from the Greek *cyber,* meaning helmsman, which gives us an image of a boat as a system with a helmsman as the controller constantly adjusting the rudder so that the boat is always headed towards its destination. Without the constant

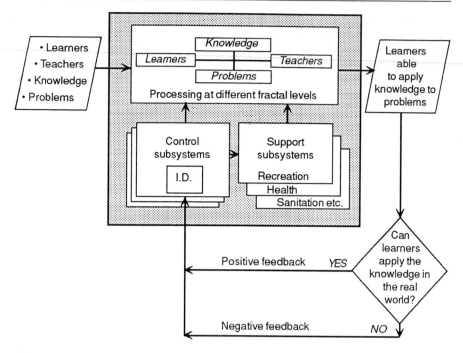

Figure 2.14 The education system as a communications system

adjustment of the rudder the boat would begin to deviate from its intended route.

Control in a system matches what is going on in the world outside the system with what is going on in the system itself and puts into place changes that guide the direction the system is taking. In this we can recognise the management function of school principals and the need for school administration systems. The function of control is also present in a classroom lesson. Teachers manage lessons, taking notice of feedback from learners and adjusting the course of the lesson accordingly. The control function is within the learner too. There comes a point when in trying to learn how to do something learners realise that they cannot manage and need some help. So they switch from studying as an individual to studying with a teacher, from one fractal level to another, in order to learn.

In education, control includes the function of design. Traditional teaching is in part an intuitive communication process and in part teachers doing unto students what was done unto them when they were students. Increasingly, however, education involves designing instruction. The idea of a design exists in a school's brochure, a teacher's lesson plan and the way learners are assisted to plan what and where they study in terms of a career path. However, there is a more rigorous approach.

Instructional design (ID) as a serious discipline developed in the second part of this century. It studies design issues from the micro-level of individual instructional events and individualised instruction to the macro-issues of designing national educational systems or the total training programme of an army or a commercial company. The approach was initially applied to training, where it has been able to demonstrate that, given clearly stated objectives as to what is expected of learners under specific conditions, it can develop effective instruction.

The ID approach has not been so readily and widely adopted in education. This appears to be changing with the growing emphasis on rationalisation and accountability. Instructional design provides a methodology for describing educational objectives in measurable terms that can be priced. This appeals to parents and politicians where government control and spending is under question. Instructional design takes a systems approach and so provides a vehicle for introducing information technology to institutions.

There is yet another subsystem of any complex communications system that involves human beings which needs to be taken into consideration. Whether it is a bank, a television station or a school, there is likely to be a canteen, a first aid station, a parking system, security services, toilets and so on. These are support systems that deal with basic needs and so allow people to get on with the main purpose of the system. Even if the teachers were machines they would still need some kind of maintenance.

We need to add to the list of criteria for a communication system for education:

> To be capable of a broad spectrum of instruction educational systems also need support and control subsystems. The latter needs to include an instructional design capability.

Chapter 3

In a class of its own

What is it?
He whose eyes are not open enters it
He whose eyes are (wide) open comes out of it.
(Riddle from a tablet excavated at Ur. It dates back to *c*. 2000 BC. The
answer is a classroom – Kramer 1963: 236.)

Archaeologists believe that ruins found in the ancient Sumerian city of Mari
in the valley of the Euphrates are those of the oldest known classroom
(Kramer 1963). Inscriptions that described school life found in other parts
of Sumer of a comparable age read like pages out of *Tom Brown's Schooldays*.[1]
Classrooms have probably been around for at least 4000 years (Kramer
1959, 1963; Gadd 1956). Whether in schools or churches or temples or
battleships, the classroom has proved a remarkably durable system for
communication. This chapter looks at the reasons why. It also looks at
ways people are educated outside the classroom, in the home and the
workplace.

THE ERAS OF EDUCATION

In *The Coming of Post-industrial Society*, Daniel Bell (1973) used the case of the
United States to classify the development of societies in three phases. He
described America when most people were employed on the land as a pre-
industrial society. When the main field of employment became manufacturing he held that America became an industrial society. In the 1960s, when
the dominant form of employment became the service industries, he
argued that America became a post-industrial society. In this text, we use
the terms 'pre-industrial' and 'industrial society', in conformity with Bell,
but prefer the term 'information society' for what comes after the industrial
society. The idea of the information society has moved into popular usage.
It implies a society based on an infrastructure of information technology
where the main form of employment is as an information worker.

Almost everyone in an industrial society does time in the classrooms of
its schools. The industrial society is linked to classrooms in the same way as

it is linked to factories. So strong is the association that organisations such as the World Bank have invested billions of dollars building classrooms in the belief that the factories will follow,[2] that educational systems lead to industrial societies, and that this is progress.

Classrooms may have existed in pre-industrial societies for thousands of years but they were for the children of the elite. They were the places where the privileged learned to play their part in society. The battle of Waterloo, it was said, was won on the playing fields of Eton, a British school for the upper classes. This supposes that the battle was won by the officers. How did the ordinary soldiers acquire the knowledge they needed for battle? In a pre-industrial society, how did people who did not go to school find help for their ZPDs so that they acted as good citizens and had the skills to make a living? Education is a ubiquitous activity that can take place anywhere, anytime when someone wants to learn how to solve some kind of problem. We focus on the classroom because it was specially designed for the communication of education, but the home and workplace have also been important locations of learning.

THE HOME AS A COMMUNICATION SYSTEM FOR EDUCATION

The term 'family' comes from the Latin *familia*, which means household. The home is the family's support system for shelter and storage. It is also their communication system, providing a walled-off place that allows the family to communicate among themselves, giving them some privacy and separation from the flow of communication and noise in the world about them. Home is where couples assert their independence, mate, have children, play with them, protect them, feed them and educate them.

The family at home constitutes the primary educational system for most people in the first years of their lives. The members of the family constitute the teachers, learners and source of knowledge. Along with the home environment they also provide the problems children have to learn to deal with.

A baby cries and as a result is picked up by a parent. As Barbara Rogoff points out, it has acquired a pair of legs that work (1990). The baby has learned to solve a transport problem by itself. Halliday argues that from the moment a child makes its first sounds it is using them to control its environment (1978). Babies are born with a network of ten to one hundred billion nodes, each capable of between two thousand and two hundred thousand synaptic links. If day-old chickens can learn problem solving by themselves with a similar but much smaller network (Rose 1992), then we can surely accept that babies too begin life with a capability for self-learning. New babies also seem to have a capability for turning anyone who is close to them into a teacher. Vygotsky's concept of a ZPD applies to them (Rogoff 1990), and they have the ability to shift fractal levels in order to learn. They move with ease between their own neural network – the most complex network known – to that of the simplest network, the dyad, as they get the attention of a parent or a sibling. A child is also part of the group network formed by a family. This is another fractal level in which a child learns in the home. However, children do not spend all their time at home. They visit other families, go to shops and clinics and for walks. In so doing they shift to another fractal level in which they can learn – that of the community in which the family live – a network in which the family can be seen as a node. Communities in their turn can be seen as part of the wider network of a culture or nation in which is resident the knowledge of how people are expected to deal with the problems they encounter in their roles as part of society. In industrial societies mass-media communication networks, especially television, have taken over much of the family communication including some of the educational role. Children learn to deal with problems because of the knowledge, examples and teaching they get from the media.

Communication in the traditional home educational system is broadband, interactive, face to face and multimedia. And it works. On the curriculum for the first three years is learning to become house trained, walk, run, hold things, put on clothes, wash, eat, behave in a culturally acceptable manner and, starting from scratch, learning to speak a language. This is true across cultures and, in contrast to much classroom education, the success rate is high. Yet the home is not a dedicated educational system, the teachers are not professionals and the knowledge is scattered through the memories of the network of family and friends rather than organised in texts and curricula. A very complex instructional process seems in action to be unplanned and spontaneous. Is the instructional design for early education in the DNA of humans as Piaget and the geneticists argue? One possibility is that it lies in the early childhood instructional network itself.

Any person can be seen in the context of their family/community network as having a dual role as learner and teacher, as having a problem with something or knowing how to deal with it. When there are other children, the amount of time parents can give to one child is limited and some of the teacher role may be passed on to older children. Children teach one another. A young mother may seek advice from *her* mother and so revert to the role of learner. In the extended family, grandparents, uncles and aunts and even family friends may also be involved as occasional teachers. Children can be seen as having many teachers and a new baby as the central node in a complex web of instruction. Knowledge is endlessly trickling through from the older members to the younger, from the past to the present. In the process it is filtered, adapted, adopted and sequenced. Herein is an organic design process. As Barbara Rogoff writes: 'From birth (and probably before) children's development occurs in a biologically given social matrix characteristic of our species' (1990: 37). In the future, in

Figure 3.1 Fractal levels in a family educational network

information societies, this social matrix may be largely replaced by networks of information technology.

In many societies television is the surrogate child-minder for several hours a day. What will happen to child education when the next generation of computers opens the home door to the superhighways of information? The home is now seen as the next great market for personal computers. By the time it is as ubiquitous as the video in the homes of countries with advanced economies, the PC will be multimedia and linked to networks that carry video and sound as well as text. In all probability it will be possible to talk to them and they will carry virtual reality. It is the development of this kind of computer and communication capability that will impel the technology into the home.

It is in the first years of life that the home and family have been critical in providing an educational system for teaching basic survival skills. When children are 5 or 6 years old they go to school, or begin work. The emphasis in education has then shifted from the home to the classroom or the workplace. Home and family have continued as an educational system for many years, but in a reduced role. If, however, it is the home that becomes the primary locus for the technology that provides access to the virtual class, then we could see the home continuing to be, physically, the place where people do most of their learning. If trends towards learning becoming a lifelong activity, rather than a rite of passage, continue, then we could see home learning as something that once again involved all the generations in a family, but not so much in a social matrix as in shared access to the technologies of instruction.

THE WORKPLACE AS AN EDUCATIONAL SYSTEM

The workplace can be anything from a factory to a mine, a farm to a battlefield, an office to a shop. Its primary function is work, not education. As in the home, there is extraneous noise, and instruction has to adapt to the conditions that exist.

On the first day in a new job most people are conscious of a ZPD. They need someone to help teach them what to do. The guidance they get may consist of little more than a few words of explanation and correction in the first few days, or it may take the form of an internship that lasts for years. The workplace is a place for learning by doing. A person learns to be a seaman in a ship, to be a nurse in a hospital and to be a farmer on a farm. In industrial societies there has been a growing trend for part of learning to work to be taught in classrooms. Naval cadets go to colleges, trainee nurses go to class, as does anyone who wants to occupy a professional position in farming. In other words, learning how to do a job of any complexity is now likely to involve a mix of theoretical and practical instruction taking place in classroom and workplace. There is also a growing use of simulations

Figure 3.2 The new apprentice. A tradition in the nineteeth century in coastal areas in Britain was for boys to be apprenticed to the master of a coastal craft or fishing boat. The picture shows a young apprentice saying goodbye to his parents who might not see him for years. The family network link is about to be severed and a new network of the workplace formed. He will live on the boat and be the responsibility of its master, who not only has an agreement with the parents, but also a legal responsibility to look after and educate the boy. An able seaman and two other boy seamen look at the newcomer speculatively. They too will act as teachers

because on-the-job training can be dangerous. It is in the development of simulations for training that virtual reality first proved itself.

The oldest educational system associated with the workplace, that of apprenticeship, had a traditional communication network which resembled that of the family educational system:

> I was first put to work when I was fourteen in the Blackburn Aeroplane factory outside Leeds. It was 1916 and they were making bombers. I had to learn to use a file and these two men tried to show me how, but I didn't like the way they did it and I bent the file across one of them. I had to leave then and my parents paid for me to be indentured to Braithwaites. They were a big plumbing company in the North of England and I was with them as an apprentice until 1922. That's how long it took to learn to be a plumber. Of course there was no books to

learn from in those days and no one wanted to teach you. They didn't like giving knowledge away. The fewer knew how to do plumbing the better your situation was. They were supposed to teach the apprentices but they didn't want to because we were seen as a threat. So we had to learn by watching. When I got my own business I didn't mind teaching the apprentices but I was a master plumber then and it was up to me when we had a big job on to make sure they all knew what to do . . . men as well as boys. By then apprentices were going to night school regularly and learning from books, but my lads always came top in their classes and I always reckoned it was because of what I taught them that was handed down.

This description of the workplace as an educational system given to the authors by a 92-year-old plumber gives some feel for the fractal levels of communication that were involved. A new apprentice had a close link with someone who was established as a qualified worker in the field. They worked together and that was how the apprentice learned. The qualified worker may have been a 'master' in the profession or craft, or responsible to a master. The situation could be that of knight and squire, housekeeper and servants, or an apothecary with a live-in apprentice.

As in the family situation there is a fractal dimension. Apprentices are given a job to do. The job is the problem, and they try to apply the knowledge of what they have been told about this class of problem or what they have learned from watching others in similar circumstances. Apprentices are their own teacher as they try to work things out for themselves. If they cannot manage to do the job they are in the situation envisaged by Vygotsky with the ZPD. They need the guidance of an older apprentice or a craftsperson, and the fractal level shifts to that of the dyad or that of a team of workers. At yet another level it is possible to think of a large company with a body of apprentices (learners) and qualified workers (teachers) and of the company existing to address a class of problems using a body of professional knowledge. It is possible to see an apprentice as part of an extended network of learner/teachers extending back to a craft, guild or professional association as the source of knowledge. Lave and Wenger place apprentice learning activities as 'peripheral participation' in a 'community of practice'. They see a cyclical pattern in which, over a period of time, newcomers become old-timers (Lave and Wenger 1991: 98, 116–17).

The idea of the master in some craft was traditionally of someone who was part of, and responsible to, a guild or professional association of fellow craftspeople who maintained the standards of their skills. In the medieval guilds knowledge of how to deal with a particular problem domain was often kept secret from people not part of the profession or craft. Access to knowledge was guarded and only became available, step by step, through

Figure 3.3 Fractal levels in apprentice training

long apprenticeship. With the advent of publishing, the knowledge of guilds and crafts became widely disseminated. Trainees could access knowledge directly from technical texts. This meant they had to be literate. It brought classrooms into training and a separation of practical knowledge from its practice. The popularity of 'do-it-yourself' books in the second part of the twentieth century further contributed to the demystification and democratisation of trade and craft skills.

As with education in the home, traditional on-the-job training seemed a random process conducted intuitively by people who did not have training in instruction and were sometimes unwilling to act as teachers. Practice and experience created an instructional design of what could and could not be expected of a trainee at different stages in their development. Over time this became embodied in the standards, curricula and examinations of trade and professional associations.

Again, as with education in the home, education in the workplace is changing. At the beginning of the nineteenth century, following principles outlined by Fredrick Taylor, the nature of work, especially in manufacturing, was carefully analysed and described (Taylor 1947). These time and motion studies made it possible to segment the different tasks that were involved in producing some manufactured item. In this way workers could concentrate on the jobs they were best able to do. It also meant that less time needed to be dedicated to training a worker. The separation of knowledge from function which Taylorism brought about promoted the development of the factory system and automation. If a job can be broken down into a set of simple procedures that can be done automatically, then why not develop a machine to do it instead of a human? The change from an industrial society to an information society does not mean that primary and secondary industry is in decline. What is in decline is employment in these sectors. Production continues to grow, while the number of people needed to effect this continues to diminish. It is in information work that there is, in the information society, a growing demand for workers. The workstation of an information worker is a desktop computer or computer terminal in an office. The convergence of computer and communications technologies at the desktop provides not only a place where work is done but also a place where information workers can access training as and when needed.

A glance around the offices of large information technology corporations in Japan and North America shows desktop computing being pushed to one side as people work with portable computers that allow them to take their work home. This is the hallmark of a mind worker, a person whose work is not bounded by conventional office space or times. For this person education that is associated with work takes place anytime, anywhere. As the amount of teleworking continues to increase, the home becomes a workplace and a place where people learn to work.

THE CLASSROOM AS A COMMUNICATION SYSTEM FOR EDUCATION

Unlike the home or the workplace, the classroom is dedicated to teaching/ learning. Most people in an industrial society will associate it with schools, which are normally clusters of classrooms with an associated infrastructure for administration, management and support. However, classrooms can also exist in the buildings of large companies and in churches or temples. Any large military establishment will have its classrooms. For the Romans it was a room in a wealthy house or at the side of a street. The classroom at Mari was an integral part of the city itself. In Ethiopia, priests use parts of the church to teach. In India, students have gathered under trees for learning for thousands of years. Then there are science laboratories, gymnasia and classroom workshops for teaching metalwork, woodwork and domestic science. The places dedicated to instruction take many forms, but for most people in most countries a classroom is a rectangular room with rectangular desks and a rectangular blackboard. This formula for facilitating learning has spread around the world. This is what we mean when we talk of the conventional classroom. It is a remarkably successful and resilient communication system for instruction. If we are to improve on it we need to understand how it has survived and multiplied.

The purpose of classrooms

Classrooms emulate the places where people live and work, especially the work world of offices. They are designed to teach people how to deal with problems as they are represented in abstract by language and mathematics. Classrooms developed in early civilisations to teach reading, writing and arithmetic. The growth of cities depended on systems for recording and storing information in language and numbers, and a cadre of clerks was needed. However, as the ancient Greeks realised, the ability to abstract reality in language and number also made it possible to manipulate and control the world, create scenarios of what could be and search for explanations of why things were. The tools of the mind in the form of written language and mathematics have in urban civilisations been the real source of power and control rather than the tools that are used to deal directly with the world. The classroom is first a learning system for acquiring the basic skills of literacy and numeracy, but it then has the potential to give access to the storehouses of written knowledge which are the sources of power. It is hardly surprising that classroom learning should be associated with the ruling elites of pre-industrial civilisations, or that in the development of democracy in industrial societies there should be a demand for classroom education as a right for all citizens that is as basic as universal suffrage.

The industrial revolution created a need for an army of tallymen, clerks and shopkeepers. An industrial society had to have a literate and numerate workforce. The desks in nineteenth-century European classrooms were modelled on the rows of desks occupied by the clerks who were needed to keep track of business transactions. The demand for universal education in industrial societies was supported by those who invested in industry as well as those who worked in it. Newly industrialising countries see a simple and direct link between education and advancement. People in such countries hunger for their children to go to school and learn in class-rooms. They believe it will open a door to a better life. Since the 1960s attention has been drawn to the idea that classroom education leads to a better standard of living and that the more time people spend in classrooms the more likely they are to be able to earn a high income (Becker 1964; Denison 1962; Schultz 1961).

The coming of an information society in turn is seen as depending upon a workforce educated in the skills and literacies of information technology. It is hardly surprising that the information industries are supporting reform in education. There is a growing argument for a better-educated population as a solution to unemployment as industrial societies restructure to become information societies. There is also a growing tension between those who see education as a preparation for work and those who see education as development of the whole person.

How does the classroom function as a communication system?

Like the home and work educational situations, the classroom permits broadband, fully meshed, fully interactive communication that can be multimedia and address all the sensory channels. Classroom education does not, however, normally involve people in tasting or smelling or even touching in the way that family or work education can. It is essentially concerned with sight and sound. The walls keep external sounds out and internal sounds in. Ideally, windows allow in light that does not carry distracting information and is sufficiently diffuse to make reading easy. In old classrooms, thick walls, wooden floors, high ceilings and a minimum of reflective surfaces create a quiet environment where people can hear one another easily. Windows are usually high and difficult to see out of. They throw light down so that it is not reflected as glare, and late and early sun does not create problems. In the classrooms of Mari there are no windows; in fact, there is no ceiling. The light comes from above, though there would have been some kind of partial roofing of laths or branches to give some shade. Mari was in a desert, so rain was not a problem. The mud and stone surfaces would have made it quiet. In contrast, modern classrooms have big, low windows which let in sound and sights as well as light. All surfaces, from the vinyl floors to the low, glossy ceilings and smooth walls and whiteboards are reflective. They give classrooms the sound qualities of a bathroom and encourage people to be noisy. On a sunny afternoon it may be difficult to read from the blackboard, let alone use video or projected media, and students complain about the sun in their eyes. School architects now reproduce the form of classrooms without thinking of their function.

Such concerns may sound like trivia. They are not, and the lack of attention to the communication aspects of modern classrooms explains some of the problems encountered in them. Educators focus on methodology and style, and lose sight of communication factors. You cannot tell if a television programme is well produced if the television aerial does not work. It is no good worrying about how a lesson is taught if students cannot see the writing and pictures they are supposed to look at or hear what is being said. A team of instructional designers at the Federal University of Pernambuco in Recife, Brazil, laboured for months over the way learning deteriorated as classes proceeded in a newly designed course.[3] The course used new technologies and methodologies, but students continued to do badly whatever methodological variable was adjusted. Then someone remarked that the classroom got so stuffy in the afternoon they could hardly keep awake. All that was needed was improvement in the ventilation. When this was done learning improved dramatically, and to everyone's relief it was possible to say that the expensive new instructional system was a success. The students needed oxygen.

The problem described above came from the fact that the classroom was becoming, in terms of the flow of air, a closed system. In systems theory a closed system is one that does not have exchanges of inputs and outputs with its environment. A closed system is contrasted with an open system. If the classroom had no walls there would have been ample ventilation but also another set of problems from external sounds and the weather. Systems need a balance in the extent to which they are closed or open. The flow of information is critical to classrooms. In this respect, classrooms tend to be closed systems when they are in use and open at the beginning and end of a lesson. Classrooms are bounded systems which, paradoxically, isolate learners from the problems of the real world in order to study the problems of the real world.

Communication channels within a classroom, by contrast, are unbounded. The images and sounds in a class are broadcast. Everybody needs to be able to see what is on the blackboard and hear what is being said. When teachers are discussing something with a class they try to impose a star network on a potentially fully meshed network. In a star network communication radiates from a central node (teacher) to the other nodes (learners), who are expected to communicate with one another through the central node. In a fully meshed network, all nodes can communicate directly with one another. However, if a class of students does this there is chaos. When a

Figure 3.4 Patterns of communication in classrooms, 1: a star network with teacher as central node

Figure 3.5 Patterns of communication in classrooms, 2: the observed dyad. Teacher questions a student while the rest of the class listens

Figure 3.6 Patterns of communication in classrooms, 3: fully meshed network. All the students are talking. Students go to class to socialise as well as to learn. For some, socialising is the main reason for attending a class and this can make them disruptive, because they may not give priority to the established objective of learning and their own objective is not acknowledged or sufficiently catered for. A classroom serves as an introduction agency for people of a similar age, interest or socio-economic status and an arena where they can perform for one another as well as for a teacher. This could be one reason for the success of the classroom

teacher and a learner initiate a dyadic exchange in a classroom they are both conscious that the rest of the students are listening. The teacher takes this into account, hoping that the interaction with one student has a vicarious effect on the others. To the extent that a student's question or answer is representative of the thoughts of other students on the issue, this is an efficient method.

The things that everyone associates with a classroom are desks and a blackboard. These two subsystems are critical in the sense that without them there would be no classroom. One is a subsystem for writing and reading as an individual activity (a set of desks or tables and chairs) and the other a subsystem for reading, writing and drawing as a communal activity (blackboards or whiteboards).

The blackboard/whiteboard system is the heart of the classroom process. The desks or tables are for activities which are adjunct to blackboard-centred activities. Desk-based activities may also link with extra-classroom activities. A student can take a book home but not the blackboard. Blackboards and whiteboards can also be contrasted to paper-based storage media such as textbooks and exercise books. Blackboards

Figure 3.7 Triadic relationship between learner, teacher and problem solving. T and L are teacher and learner in a triadic relation with, in the case of tying a shoelace, a real-world problem-solving situation RWPS which occurs when knowledge K is applied to a real-world problem RWP. In the case of Pythagoras's theorem, symbolic knowledge SK is applied to a symbolic problem SP which is derived from a class of real-world problems RWP which can be resolved through symbolic problem solving SPS

are the short-term memory systems of a class, holding a topic against the ephemeral flow of words. This contrasts to the permanent words in a textbook or the students' attempts to make words permanent in exercise books.

The essence of the educational process is a teacher helping a learner apply knowledge to a problem. There is in this a point in time and space when the teacher–learner relationship focuses on the interception of knowledge and problem; for example, when a parent helps a child to tie a shoelace. The unlaced shoe is the problem, the knowledge of how to tie it is in the parent and the focus of the interaction between the child and parent is the shoe as it is laced. In classroom education it is the blackboard or whiteboard which provides this focal point. Knowledge and problems exist in a classroom in symbolic form and the blackboard/whiteboard is a medium for expressing them as such. Of course, the blackboard/white-board can also be adapted for projected images from film, slides or over-head projection to show problems or knowledge, and small, controllable realia, such as plants or pets, can be introduced to classrooms. Essentially, however, the classroom is a place for learning about the world at second hand through words, numbers, pictures and diagrams of various kinds, and the blackboard/whiteboard is the device where this is shown.

Think of a teacher writing Pythagoras's theorem on a blackboard and asking students to copy it down. This is using the blackboard for know-ledge. The teacher could as easily have got the students to turn to a page in their textbook that contains the same knowledge. Next, the teacher writes down a problem on the blackboard and tells the students to apply the theorem to the problem. Again, there is no special need for the blackboard or, indeed, for this to be a classroom activity. The students could be given

Figure 3.8 Patterns of communication in classrooms, 4: the blackboard/teacher/ learner triad

the assignment as a handout to take home, and if they can solve the problem there is no ZPD and no need for the teacher or the classroom.

Imagine, however, that there is a ZPD, that although the students have some knowledge of the theorem, the results of an assignment show they have not mastered it. Now, the teacher uses the blackboard to explain how the theorem can be used to solve the problem, getting the students to explain how they went about it, confirming where they are right and correcting where they are wrong. The juxtaposition of the theorem and the problem on the blackboard allow them to be related to the problem solving. This weaving together of the weft of learner and teacher with the warp of knowledge and problem is something that no text or handout can do. It is the essence of education, something we can recognise in the competence of good teachers, but something that defies analysis because it is dynamic and intuitive and does not work on demand, even with the most gifted teachers. Of course, the process could have been done at the dyadic level with the teacher spending time with each student and using a page in their exercise books instead of the blackboard, and it may be, if a teacher can find the time and opportunity, that they will do this. What validates the classroom is the economy of scale that comes from the group interaction made possible by the blackboard, and there is the tantalising possibility that, when the interaction is done skilfully, there can be a synergy which may make this at least as effective as dyadic interaction between learner and teacher. It also means that there are several fractal levels of communication in a classroom.

THE FRACTAL LEVELS IN THE CLASSROOM

Level 1: the learner

If we were able to look inside the head of a learner working by themselves we would find a neural network of extraordinary complexity. We understand little of how it works but, from our own experience of what it is like to be a learner, we are conscious of the way we struggle with problems as we try to work them out. At times we act as our own teachers. A conversation may take place in our heads that is like an echo of a teacher–learner discussion of a problem. Vygotsky (1962) calls it 'inner speech'. Sometimes it works. We see how knowledge and problems fit together. The meshing of information from the four critical factors appears to take place in the networks of the mind.

Level 2: the dyad

An individual learner is trying to solve a problem by themselves, but cannot manage. Perhaps they reach out for a book and open it. The fractal level has shifted: they are now in a dyadic link with another node that contains knowledge. On the other hand, they may turn to a fellow student or call on a teacher and ask for help. Again they are opening up a dyadic network, but this time linking with a teaching node who could also be a source of knowledge.

Level 3: the class

This is a communication network in which the nodes are textbooks, exercise books, blackboards, students and teacher. The knowledge nodes are likely to be the teacher and the textbooks, and the problem nodes the blackboard and exercise books, but the teacher and textbooks could also be sources of problems and knowledge that could be written on the blackboard and in exercise books. Analysis of classroom discourse and interaction shows that there are common intermeshing structures. Sinclair and Coulthard have shown a widespread pattern they call IRF (initiate, response and follow-up), in which teachers initiate questions, there are responses from learners and then a follow-up from the teacher (Sinclair and Coulthard 1975).

Interaction within a class as a whole may not last for the whole of the lesson. A teacher may set an exercise which has students working by themselves or in small groups. In other words, a classroom provides an environment in which learners can shift between fractal levels. If a learner has difficulty in acquiring knowledge of how to solve a problem at one fractal level, then they have an opportunity to learn at another fractal level.

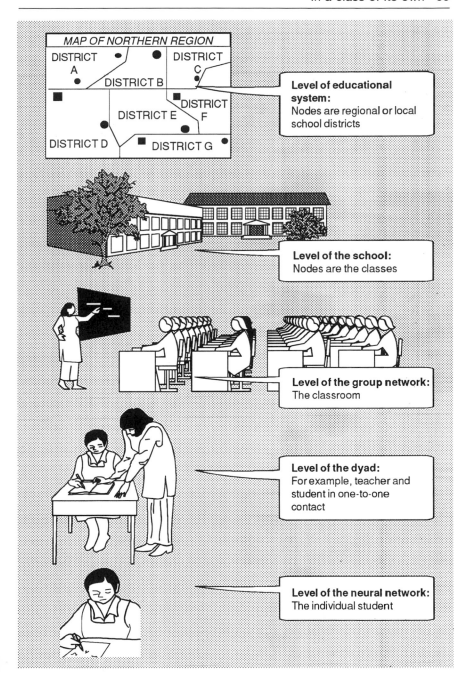

Figure 3.9 Fractal levels in conventional classroom education

It is particularly the shift from someone trying to work inside themselves in an intrapersonal communication network and finding it inadequate to an interpersonal communication network seeking to learn outside themselves that is described in Vygotsky's concept of the ZPD.

Level 4: the school, college, university

A class can be seen as a processing node in the network of an educational institution, the school library as a knowledge node and problems as examinations.

Scale changes in every way. Where a cycle of learning at the level of an individual learner may last a few minutes, and at the level of a class 40 or 50 minutes, schools work in the order of terms and school years. This reflects the size and degree of the problems the learners are trying to master. At the end of an academic year the learners take exams or complete grades that show the extent to which the learners, teachers, knowledge and problems have intermeshed at a macro-level.

The school itself could be considered as a processing node in some larger regional or national educational system. At this level, however, the purpose of the system begins to change and to be more concerned with the implementation of policy, administration and support.

CLASSROOMS IN TERTIARY EDUCATION

Knowledge in living cultures is dynamic and growing. This means that some knowledge is new and unstable and not fully validated. As new ideas and techniques are applied to a problem domain and create a new layer of knowledge, the new knowledge creates a new generation of problems calling forth yet another generation of knowledge. Yesterday's solutions to the problems of distance are today's pollution problems. Every attempt to explain the nature of the universe has led to a new set of questions.

Primary and secondary education are about understanding and applying established knowledge. Tertiary education is where students question the knowledge of their time and culture instead of taking it for granted. This is the idea of universities, and of degrees being earned not just by acquiring knowledge and being able to apply it, but also by being in contact with the potentially new knowledge that comes from research.

There is not a great deal of argument as far as a primary student is concerned as to the outcome of an arithmetical problem or the words that groups of letters make when they are trying to read. At this level, instructional objectives are behavioural in the sense that it is possible to describe a precise relationship between problem and knowledge (given conditions X, the learner will be able to do Y to the standard of Z). This can be extended to on-the-job training where an automatic response is required in the

Figure 3.10 Lecture theatre. Note the length of the blackboard, projector system and production and tiered seating. The emphasis is on clarity of exposition

application of knowledge to a problem. (Drivers should stop when traffic lights are red.) However, medical students do not learn that there are always automatic answers to the problems they will address. They learn to critique the problem/knowledge axis in their profession.

The critical approach to knowledge in universities has lead to variations of the classroom for lectures, seminars and tutorials.

The word 'lecture' has its roots in the Latin *legere*, to read. One version of the origins of the lecture is that in the ancient monasteries from which the European university tradition is derived, before the invention of printing it was the duty of the lecturer to read a text aloud so that students could copy it down. Students swear the tradition continues, but so does another one. Some of the early universities were communities of scholars who invited and paid for eminent scholars to spend time with them, occupying a 'chair' and discoursing on their theories. They would read to a critical audience from papers they had written. The learner, teacher, knowledge and problem were there, but the knowledge was called into question and the learned person had to defend their position. This was the tradition of Abelard, Luther and Melancthon (Cubberly 1948) and it continues. Universities still invite distinguished academics to give papers, and large lecture theatres are designed for this. They are a theatrical form of the conventional classroom. Seats are tiered and organised as an auditorium and there is a podium for the lecturer. The blackboard/whiteboard is there, but it is bigger than in a

Figure 3.11 Seminar room. Note the way the blackboards are distributed for easy access by everyone. The arrangement of chairs and tables allows everyone to face each other. The seminar allows for presentations but is primarily for group discussion

classroom because the lecturer may need it to develop an extended argument. Unlike the classroom there will also be a lectern, and unlike a theatre there will be facilities for the audience to make notes. A lecturer focuses on the exposition of knowledge and needs good presentation facilities and so there will usually be projection systems.

CONTROL IN THE CLASSROOM

In the conventional classroom the teacher has the function of control and may also have some responsibility for the design and planning of instruction as well as for its implementation. Teachers follow models of teaching which are acceptable to parents, their profession and the culture they are teaching in. As in the home or workplace, the design of instruction is something that has evolved, almost in a Darwinian sense, through trial and error over many years by generations of teachers sensitive in various degrees to what works and the subtle checks and balances that come from the way classroom education networks into societies.

Industrial societies in developing national compulsory education systems have undertaken educational reforms which involved designing school curricula, instituting national examination systems, setting texts and

Figure 3.12 Office used for tutorial. Students discuss their studies or an assignment in a small group or as a dyad with the tutor (teacher). Note the tutor's 'library', providing easy access to stored knowledge

teaching materials and standardising procedures. This, along with a control infrastructure of ministries, departments, school boards, committees and principals, has meant that design, planning, management and administrative functions in education have become officially embodied in a bureaucracy separated from the teaching function. Such reforms changed what was taught, but it is doubtful if they have had any effect on the communication process in the class.

CLASSROOMS AS THE INTEGRATORS OF EDUCATION

In this chapter we have looked at the factors within the classroom that explain why it has been around so long. And they are many. It is a room and rooms are our primary systems for communication. It facilitates all the functions specified in Chapter 2 as critical to a communication system for education. The subsystems make it possible to intermesh learners, teachers, knowledge and problems at a variety of fractal levels. It is a broadband, multisensory, multimedia communication system. It is possible to have a symbiotic relation between human memory and artificial memories and to turn quickly to knowledge that is in written form. Finally, there are support and control systems and designs that are based on experience.

What may also explain its survival is the way the classroom is integrated with the education systems of the home and the workplace. It works not just because it is an effective communication system for instruction, but because it is a keystone in society. And if that is the case, we need to be careful how we replace it.

Chapter 4

The writing on the wall

We don't need no education.
(Pink Floyd, 'Another Brick in the Wall – Part 2',
from the CBS album, *The Wall*, 1979)

Learning processes are lagging appallingly behind and are leaving both individuals and societies unprepared to meet the challenge posed by global issues. This failure of learning means that human preparedness remains underdeveloped on a global scale. Learning is in this sense far more than just another global problem: its failure represents, in a fundamental way, the issue of issues.
(Botkin *et al.* 1979: 9)

There is only one problem and that is education, all other problems are dependent on this one.
(President Domingo Faustino Sarmiento, founder of
Argentina's national education system)

THERE'S TROUBLE AT SCHOOL

School does not work as it used to. World-wide, societies face the dilemma that their education systems are designed to meet the needs of agricultural and industrial societies, not the coming information society. Moreover, the gap between the needs of evolving information societies and the response of their education systems appears to be widening. Educational systems are preparing people for the past, for the ideas and attitudes and values of a way of life that is fading away and for work in areas of shrinking labour requirements. Schools seem unable to respond to the new needs of the societies which support them.

History shows that in the past human learning has been largely successful. Throughout its cultural evolution humanity has adapted to its environment – successfully if often unconsciously – shaping its surroundings in ways that ensured survival of the species and that gradually increased the wellbeing of larger and larger numbers of its

Figure 4.1 The end of an era. A school from the industrial revolution stands derelict. Weeds grow in the playground and the windows are broken

kind. Some societies thrived by developing their human learning potential, compensating for inhospitable climate, poor geographic location, or
lack of natural resources. Others, even some with great wealth and
power, were too slow to learn; unresponsive to impending changes,
they disappeared. But on balance, human learning processes viewed at
an aggregate global level have been adequate to meet the challenges as
they presented themselves. Serious doubt must be raised as to whether
conventional human learning processes are still adequate today.

(Botkin *et al.* 1979: 9)

It is no longer sufficient for people to become literate and numerate. The
growth of the knowledge industry has brought a demand for new skills and
new literacies (Drucker 1986; Coombs 1985). Education systems are failing
to provide the quantity and quality of workers which countries will require
for sustained economic growth in the twenty-first century. They are also

failing to address that part of the education of an individual that is needed to prepare them as citizens of an information society.

Why is education out of step with society's needs? Does the problem lie in the way education is administered, the methods of instruction and the content of curricula? These are the issues that advanced industrial societies focus on as they attempt to find a solution. Our concern is with the extent to which the problem lies with the classroom as a communication system for learning. Our argument is that the classroom is a technology that emulates the way people live and work in an industrial society. It does not relate to the way people will live and work in an information society. Some countries are sufficiently into a transition to an information society for the discrepancy to be obvious.

THE SIZE OF THE PROBLEM

Around the world the demand grows for more education. Poor countries seek universal primary education. Countries that have managed to provide primary education for everyone seek universal secondary education. Those that have universal secondary education want to raise the school-leaving age and extend tertiary education. Rich nations fret about the proportion of school-leavers who go on to tertiary education, seeing this as reflecting their future economic muscle. In 1992, the President of Argentina declared on television that 'The future of Argentina no longer depends on its soil, its climate and its minerals. It depends upon the capability of its people, and that depends upon how they are educated.' Carlos Menem is far from being the only politician to express such sentiments. Education is fast becoming the key issue of our time.

The western educational tradition which has so profoundly affected so much of the world has its origins in ancient Greece and in particular the educational systems of the city states of Sparta and Athens. The idea that the first twenty years of life constitute a period of preparation for adulthood dates back at least this far. It is as though these years constituted a supra-ZPD in which young people, whether at home or in class or at work, need the assistance of mature citizens to develop so that they can cope with the problems of life in the ways of their society. This deeply ingrained idea is changing. Education is coming to be regarded as a lifelong activity. That people will spend a proportion of their whole life in education is one of the characteristics of an information society. The move to lifelong education has been around for some time. The increase in the number of tertiary students in most countries is in part because more school-leavers are going on to further education, but it also results from the growing number of adults returning to the educational system.

There is also a growing demand in industrial societies for educational opportunities for early childhood education. The second half of the twentieth century has seen women in industrial countries taking control of their child-bearing role and becoming waged labour. Women in industrial societies have fewer children and those they do have they put into crèches and kindergartens while they continue with a career or go to class themselves.

Research at Otago University in New Zealand provides weight to the argument that the first three years of a child's life are the most critical to its future development.[1] It may even be that a rich variety of learning experiences in this period is more important than three years in a university later on. If this is the case, then we may see an upgrading of the quality of pre-school instruction and erosion of the entrenched idea that education only begins with formal school. Seymour Papert (1980) has shown how early a child can begin to learn the logic skills needed for integrating with information technology.

There has also been an increase in the second half of this century in the use of classroom teaching as an adjunct to on-the-job training. The edges between training and education are blurring. Community colleges form a bridge between university education and technical training. Industry becomes increasingly involved with universities.

Expansion in the demand for education takes place in developed countries as more people seek education and as they spend more years in education. In the newly industrialising countries of Asia, young and rapidly growing populations are striving for rapid expansion of their education systems and see this as the key to economic growth (UNESCO 1983). Another wave of expansion comes as women around the world demand equal access to education. Then there are estimates that the world population could double in the next fifty years and the only humane way to stop it doubling again and again is through education.

Can this world-wide demand for more education be matched by an expansion of existing classroom-based educational systems? The last decade of this century sees even the rich nations drawing back from the growing costs of classroom education (Lacayo 1993), while the poorer nations find themselves in a losing battle, unable to expand what classroom education they do have to match the rate of growth of their populations (UNESCO 1993).

Part of the reason for the failure of classroom-based educational systems to expand to match the demand is that they are wasteful of resources of space and time.

PROBLEMS OF SPACE

Classrooms are normally clustered together in schools and colleges. With urbanisation these have grown in size. This brings advantages of scale. Besides being able to separate administrative functions from teaching, it is also possible to cater to a wide variety of student needs, offer a broad variety of curricula, and have sporting and social activities. Schools and colleges also provide support systems such as libraries, playgrounds, health centres, canteens and sometimes dormitories. All this means a substantial investment in school grounds and buildings and their maintenance.

Of course, schools and universities existed long before the industrial society, but they were for the rich and they were often residential, so that they were utilised around the clock. The extraordinary thing about the modern state-supported school, college or university in many countries is how little teaching facilities are used. Children usually go to school for about 7 hours a day, 5 days a week, 40 weeks a year – a total of 1,400 hours. This means that the facilities may not be used for 7,300 hours a year. In some universities, classrooms may be unused as much as 90 per cent of the time.

Classroom education could, therefore, in some countries be expanded by using existing facilities more efficiently. Schools in Brazil and in many countries in Asia run in shifts. In both North and South America it is common to find college classrooms in use from early morning to late at night throughout the year. Adult education has developed by making use of existing facilities in the evenings and at weekends or in vacation periods.

The larger the catchment area of a school, the further students have to travel. The second part of this century has seen a growth in the number of students who, along with their teachers, commute to school by bus, train or car. Transport systems cost money, but they are frequently subsidised. If the environmental costs of motorised transport could be calculated we would probably find that motorists pay only a fraction of what it actually costs to use the roads when they drive their children to and from school. School buses or the cost of using public transport may also be subsidised. Many teachers and students in developed countries go to work by car and car parks have become a standard part of schools. Part of any city's commuter traffic is caused by its educational institutions. Classroom education is a transport-based activity, but the costs in terms of pollution, health, stress, policing and maintaining the transport infrastructure are hidden and not related to school costs.

The classroom mimics the transactional systems of urban society. A shop is a place that brings together shoppers and shopkeepers during shopping hours for the purpose of buying and selling goods. A bank is where bankers and their customers come together in banking hours for transactions that involve money and credit. In the same way, a classroom brings teachers and students together during school hours for a transaction called 'instruction'. All such transactions, which are the very *raison d'être* of towns and cities, are fundamentally inefficient. They involve an additional cost for the transport needed to bring the players together and for the upkeep of institutions for the periods of time when they are not committed to the transactions. These kinds of transactions are tied to time and place. Either by law or custom, times and locations become established for the transactions in a transport-based society. People do not get the service they want when they want it and where they want it. They have to go to markets on market day in the hours when the market is open, to business centres on business days in business hours and to schools on schooldays in school hours.

The development of efficient, fast, transport systems has led to the growth of transport-based transaction systems and the great cities of the world. But this growth has proved self-defeating by creating urban traffic congestion along with urban growth. Travelling to make transactions has become one of the problems of our time, and education is part of it.

Akiru Morita developed the Walkman so that no matter where people are, even if they are moving about, they can listen to radio or cassettes (Morita *et al.* 1987). This is the opposite to transport-based services. It provides a service when and where the customer wants it. This is the promise of information technology in an information society. As other services follow the telephone and television and we get telebanking and teleshopping, it seems difficult to imagine that there will not be teleteaching.

PROBLEMS OF STORAGE

The great library at Alexandria existed from 323 BCE to circa CE 400. It may have held up to 700,000 texts in the form of papyrus rolls (Edwards 1968: 5–9; Harris 1984: 37–42). It probably acquired the library of Aristotle and the Pergamum collection. The custodians of the library scoured the world for writings. Ships visiting the harbour of Alexandria were searched for books. Here in one place was the accumulated written knowledge of the ancient civilisations of the Mediterranean and the Near East. To it were drawn the best minds of the day and those seeking answers to the great problems of geography, mathematics, science and philosophy. From all over the known world teachers and students travelled to Alexandria, because that was where knowledge was. From the earliest times, the higher the level of learning, the more it involved travel.

In the home, at work or at a primary-school level, knowledge is mainly resident in teachers and passed on orally. Location is not critical for learning. It is in the later years of secondary school, in colleges, and above all, in universities that libraries become important and anchor an institution. It is not just the size and comprehensiveness of libraries that attract scholars and students. It is also the quality and completeness of individual collections of texts within them. The great universities of the world have, or are associated with, the great libraries of the world. They are fixed in their sites. People who want to go to them must travel as they did in ancient times to Alexandria. Students and academics are still among the great travellers of the world and this still means that access to the great storehouses of knowledge is for those who can afford to travel.

Knowledge powers the development of information societies and this is leading to exponential growth in the creation of knowledge. Universities are closely linked to this and grow with their libraries, but the cost of keeping collections up to date is exploding. The numbers of texts and journals in a field for which there is a demand keep growing, as do the costs of paper as a medium of storage and the costs of storage space. It has been obvious for some time that as long as knowledge is primarily on paper, storage systems face a problem of exponential growth. Library systems have to adopt new electronic storage systems. As they do, location ceases to be a serious issue.

PROBLEMS OF TIME

The transport-based classroom model of instruction means that besides organising a place for learning and the means to get there, it is necessary to organise when teachers and learners meet and how they use their time. Typically, classroom instruction provides set chunks of instruction at set times on set days at set rates for set periods to set groups of students. This emulates the way people work and conduct business in industrial societies. But how efficient is it compared with providing the instruction the individual learner wants, when the learner wants, at the pace the learner wants, for the length of time and with the frequency that suits the learner? Romiszowski suggests a scale of frequency bands in which individualisation takes place, ranging from the level of a course, to units in a course, down to individual learning steps (1976, 1981). He makes the point that it is only in the recent history of mankind that the major part of instruction has ceased to be individualised (or small group) and has become large-group centred. He points to the growing development of individualised instructional programmes, especially with the development of computer-based learning systems (Romiszowski 1986: 19, 20).

We need to recognise, however, that many people prefer to make some compromises in their use of time in order to learn in a group. What would seem to be important is to have the option to do so.

If membership of a class is based on the fact that people are of the same age, or live in the same locality, then ability in a particular subject could vary a great deal. In a class like this, the pace of instruction may be too slow or too fast for the majority of students. If, however, membership of a class is based on ability in a particular subject, most members would be clustered around the mean with relatively few at the extremes for whom the pace of the class could be too slow or too fast. People may be assigned to conventional classrooms because of their capability or common interest in a subject, but in transport-based schools they are also there because they live in the locality the school serves and are in a certain age group. The argument in favour of mixed ability classrooms sees social advantage in people of the same age who live in the same community learning together. This provides an argument for retaining some aspect of the conventional classroom. Rheingold points out that virtual communities are drawn together because of intellectual affinity as distinct from the accident of living in the same locality (1993). Telelearning offers the possibility of classes of common interest and compatible range of competence which is attractive for cognitive learning while conventional classrooms offer the possibility of developing social skills and community ties and values.

Today, classroom teaching is tied by a whole set of time-related restrictions derived from administrative and bureaucratic procedures that have nothing to do with learning. How many students around the world sit in silence with their arms folded, or their hands on their heads, waiting for the bell to go because they finished some task early and became noisy? How many teachers are just completing an instructional sequence that looks as though it's going to bring everything and everyone together when the bell goes and the students react like Pavlovian puppies? Tertiary institutions, secondary schools and even some primary schools divide the teaching day into a set of time periods. These make it possible to allocate class time to subjects and teachers and students and seek the holy grail of a timetable that allows everyone to fit their class periods together in a way that suits them. The timetable, however, has nothing to do with learning. The length of classroom periods is not based on pedagogical research. They are traditional time slots to be filled. There is no fractional situation, no flexibility, no fuzzy edges to classroom teaching times. What we do know of periodicity in instruction suggests that concentration spans are considerably shorter than classroom periods.[2]

The quality as well as the quantity of different times affects learning. Teachers know that a class at 9 a.m. when students are fresh is worth far more than one at 3 p.m. when most students are tired. The authors find this noticeable in teleseminars across date lines which juxtapose students who are starting an instructional day with students who are finishing one. However, there are always some students on a different internal clock from others.

There are distortions in the use of time for learning that come with examinations. Weeks are lost because teachers are involved in marking, students in revision and what is taught after an examination is not valued because it will not be tested.

There seems to be no instructional justification for the length and times of the school day or for that matter the school week or the school term. Arguments can be made as to why education should be temporally organised in the way it is, but they have little to do with learning. Sickness and ill health and all the problems to which people are heir mean that learners fall behind and have to catch up within the framework of the administrative system. How many students find themselves repeating a year because of some minor issue which saw them lose credits for a course?

It is especially the mature students arriving in tertiary education in increasing numbers who have difficulty fitting into the lock-step time structures of classroom systems. Many have family responsibilities and jobs which constrain the time available for learning. They have certain days, hours and times of the year when they could learn and are frustrated when these do not match with the terms and times of educational institutions. They know their pace of learning and how much or little of a course they want to do and how much they would like it spread out or concentrated. Societies that are moving from an industrial to an information base are finding that transactions must be where and when the customer wants them. Banks have to provide round-the-clock, hole-in-the-wall services, supermarkets and gas stations stay open all hours, television never stops. When will teaching learn?

PROBLEMS OF TEACHER-TO-LEARNER RATIOS

Classroom teaching has a high teacher-to-learner ratio compared to home education or on-the-job training where there may even be more teachers than learners. The higher the teacher–learner ratio, the lower the cost of instruction, but the less opportunity there is for dyadic interaction between teacher and learner. This leads to the argument in favour of reducing the sizes of classes.

There are no established quantitative criteria for how much teacher–learner interaction is optimal at particular ages or for particular subjects. Interactive dyadic communication between teacher and learner varies and can be asynchronous as well as synchronous. Listening to a child read is a detailed and intensive, synchronous, cybernetic process. Contrast this to the asynchronous feedback that takes place with a doctoral student who may spend a year drafting a thesis before submitting it to a supervisor who then has to find the best part of a week to assess it. A teacher can tell a story to a couple of hundred primary students in a school assembly and a professor can give a lecture to several hundred students in a large lecture theatre, but they cannot mark assignments with such numbers on a regular basis. In one of our courses we introduced an E-mail system that allowed graduate students to get unlimited feedback on assignments. When an assignment was marked and graded, students were given the opportunity of using feedback to re-work the assignment for a higher grade. They could continue to do this until they felt satisfied that they could not do any better in solving the particular problem the assignment addressed. The use of E-mail meant that assignments could be marked and returned in hours. With motivated, mature people, interaction was intense. What, with some twenty students having a single shot at an assignment, would normally have been some four or five hours' marking became something that took the best part of a week. Not only did students keep on re-submitting by E-mail, but they also were moved to come in for frequent face-to-face discussions. One student submitted an assignment eight times until we could find no fault with it and she got a 100 per cent mark.

The system worked. This was neither criterion- nor norm-referenced assessment. It was enabling assessment that made it possible for students to reach their maximum potential in a skill. Yet it created such time pressures on the teachers that the innovation had to be dropped. There was no way that the level of marking could be sustained with existing staff. The experience prompts the question: 'What would happen to teacher/ learner ratios if learners were able to seek the amount of individual tuition they needed, as distinct from that made available to them?'

There was an interesting corollary to the story. The first assignment assessed in this way was to write an effective c.v. The student who got the perfect mark gained an excellent position when she graduated. Her boss later confided that what clinched the job for her was that she had written the most perfect c.v. he had ever seen.

FAILURE TO ADAPT

Philip Coombs saw the principal problem of education globally as its inability to adapt to change (Coombs 1985). How long does it take for new knowledge to seep through the system to schools and their students? How long between the recognition that society needs to know something and its introduction in the classrooms? How long before schools and colleges and universities acknowledge that their customers, the students, are asking for up-to-date services, and respond?

The problems in ZPDs come in different sizes; from needing help to tie a shoelace to learning to be a citizen of a society. If zippers replace shoelaces, then adjusting the instructional process is simple and straight-forward. But what happens when societies change? And societies are changing. What needs to be done to an educational system to make it fit an information society when we hardly know what an information society is?

In the adoption of new communication practices for learners, schools have proved reluctant to adopt what was becoming standard practice in the community for which they were preparing students. There was a time when some schools forbade the use of fountain pens. 'Proper pens' that were dipped in inkwells had to be used so that students would learn copper-plate handwriting. Ball-point pens in their turn were frowned upon when they appeared. The generation that first got their hands on Apple IIEs returned home crestfallen when they handed in printouts of their assignments and had to write them out again 'properly' because they had to learn to write quickly with a ball-point to pass exams. Even today, most students learn to handwrite, even in countries where computers are the norm in the workplace.

On the other hand, national educational systems in developed countries are prone to fadism in the adoption of new communications technologies for teaching. There is often a storeroom in a school that is full of the skeletons of old video equipment, epidiascopes and audio equipment. By the early 1980s, teachers and parents were in a panic that they would be left behind if their charges did not know how to program the new personal computers (the idea of using them for word processing came in the second half of the 1980s). In New Zealand, there were xenophobic fears that Australia was overtaking them in the introduction of computers to schools. Australia regarded the possibility that Britain would get ahead of them in this field on a par with losing to them at Rugby. Thatcherite Britain had to be more educationally computerised than the United States. America, for its part, saw its future at stake in its trade battles with Japan if it did not have enough computers in its schools. No one really knew what to do with the computers or why they were getting them, but parents were conscious of growing unemployment and believed that computing was a growth area. There was (and still is) a gut feeling at the community level that education has to take the computer on board. Parents set up cake stalls, raised money, bought computers for schools, and said in effect to the educators, 'There you are, get on with teaching our kids to use them'.

Educators who actually visited Japan in the 1980s were surprised at how little computers were used in schools. As a Japanese teacher explained to one of the authors, it was one thing to sell computers to the world, it was quite another to use them in their own schools. They would use computers in schools when they were sufficiently developed for educational purposes. In the 1990s, computers are being widely adopted in the Japanese educational system. One may well wonder how many millions of dollars in the form of early varieties of the PC now gather dust in the rooms where schools keep the fossils of their fads.

In the mid-1960s all graduate students at Wisconsin University's Department of Geography were expected to do a course in computer science. Richard Hartshorne, the distinguished American geographer, is remembered for what he said to a geography student who could not see why he had to study computers: 'If you don't learn how to use a computer, you will be an illiterate in the eyes of your children when they grow up.'[3] Fifteen years before the knee-jerk response of educational systems to the advent of personal computers, the logic of the development of the computer was understood, the need for educating people in their meaning and use was recognised, good universities were teaching computer science and pilot programmes in computer-based education were in existence. Yet, educational systems were caught napping. There was no long-term planning. Vision in education is always of the past.

Learning to use a word processor and to E-mail and access databases is the shoelace-to-zippers level of adaptation in education. At this level, training institutions and colleges almost manage to keep pace with the rapid changes in the technology of the workplace. However, at the macro-level, at the level of preparing people for an information society, things move more glacially. It is here that there is a wide gulf between what is taught, and what will be needed in the society that is emerging. Children starting in school today will leave the educational system sometime in the next millennium. Can we imagine that the skills of handwriting that they are labouring over will have any value other than as a folk craft? Will the skill of keyboarding even be of value? By then it will be possible to talk to the technology. Some disabled people already can. Personal computers are becoming personal assistants (PAs) for the disabled so that they can interface with them by speech. Not only is it possible for someone to do the conventional PC functions such as word processing, spread sheeting and diary, by speaking to a computer, they can also control the electrical environment by telling the computer to switch on the television, record on video, adjust the air conditioning or start the oven.

Dictating or talking clearly is not an easy skill to acquire. There is good reason for this. The most fundamental skill taught in classrooms is reading and writing, not talking and writing. Listen in to the classrooms of the world as children are taught not to speak; hear the vast chorus of teachers shouting, 'Be quiet!', 'Stop talking!', 'The next person to open their mouth will be . . .'. Teachers are not to blame. Educational systems evaluate and reward the ability of students to express their thoughts in writing, not to articulate them in spoken words. The child who does well is the one who can write. Good talkers are troublemakers. The nature of a classroom as a communication system means that providing positive feedback to talkers tends towards chaos. For the first three years or four years of their life children are encouraged to speak. Thereafter, if they go to school, they are taught not to speak unless spoken to.

Let us suppose that the all-talking and-listening personal computer has arrived on the educational scene like the Apple IIE did in 1980. Imagine it as something the size of a paperback that fits into a pocket and serves as new-age phone and computer combined. There is no need for a keyboard, but there is a video display unit with definition equal to that of a printed page. This PC does as you tell it, writes as you tell it, and is a textbook and exercise book whenever you want it to be. Now let us further imagine that just as in the 1980s there was a world-wide shortage of people who could keyboard, so in the first decade of the second millennium there is a demand for people who can speak clearly to computers. How will educational systems cope? Will they be taken unaware yet again, or will they have recognised the growing need for oral skills? Learning to write by speaking is a skill of similar magnitude to learning to write with a pen. The whole process of teaching has to be reconceptualised. Teachers have to be trained and the trainers of teachers have to be trained and texts written and curricula developed. And how on earth do teachers cope in a classroom when everyone is talking to their computer?

Two hundred years ago in Europe, universities were falling into disrepute as places where the idle rich passed their years learning to drink (Rudy 1984: 77–99). What was taught had little value to anyone who did not seek a life as a clergyman because it explained the world in the terms of theology. The great debates of the Reformation and Renaissance were exhausted. What resurrected universities was science. For fifty years universities went through a time of trauma as they adopted scientific criteria for what constituted accepted knowledge. Then, however, they became the knowledge engines that drove the development of industrial technology and the source of curriculum development for free, universal, national education systems. This was the macro-level adjustment that took place as industrial societies re-invented education. What will be the equivalent educational change as industrial societies transform to information societies? Botkin *et al.*, in their report to the Club of Rome, said:

> Traditionally, societies and individuals have adopted a pattern of continuous maintenance learning interrupted by short periods of innovation stimulated largely by the shock of external events. Maintenance learning is the acquisition of fixed outlooks, methods and rules for dealing with known or recurring situations. It enhances our problem solving ability for problems that are given. It is the type of learning designed to maintain an existing system or an established way of life. Maintenance learning is, and will continue to be, indispensable to the functioning and stability of every society. But for long-term survival, particularly in times of turbulence, change or discontinuity, another type of learning is even more essential. It is the type of learning that can bring change, renewal, restructuring and problem reformulation.
>
> (1979: 10)

Science constitutes an approach as well as a subject concerned with the nature of physical reality. What may constitute the critical focus of education in the development of the information society is the study of communication and information. Already this is probably the most rapidly growing area of study in universities as people try to get to grips with the implications of information technology. But it needs to be more than just a subject. It needs to be an approach concerned with information and communication in the educational process itself.

The failure of the classroom educational system rapidly to devolve new knowledge imperils the democratic process. People do not understand what is taking place around them because the educational system cannot keep pace with new knowledge. Consequently, people are without an informed voice in changes that, through government and taxes, they may be responsible for. *Time* magazine made a case that around the world the democratic process is failing (*Time*, 20 April 1992). The industrial revolution was not accomplished in Europe without the continent being put to the torch in the revolutions that swept through it in 1848. It was after this that education became an issue. Benjamin Franklin warned: 'The best guarantee of a democratic system is an educated population.' We are losing this guarantee because people are educated for the past, not for the future. Will it take angry, bloody-minded mobs of alienated, unwanted, uneducated and unemployable people venting their fury to bring about educational reform at the macro-level? History has not ended. It may be oscillating.

REMOVING THE FENCES

We think within fences of the mind that were erected in the past for purposes we can no longer remember. In the 'free' educational systems of industrial societies, which are in fact paid for by taxes, generation after generation of bureaucrats, operating at every level of the system, created layer after layer of rules and regulations and procedures which now provide endless obstacles to students getting the learning they want. It is possible that in the future education will again become commercial. A basic precept of good management in business is that the seller should remove obstacles to customers buying their products or services. What if this precept were to be applied to education and obstacles to learning removed? What if marketing analyses were conducted of what students want? What if the learners become customers in an information society?

Education needs to become more accessible than it is. It should be possible whenever an individual wants to learn something, no matter where that individual is, for them to be able to access instruction that suits their needs. The search for the virtual class is the removal of impediments to attaining this goal. It is the idea of developing a telecommunications-based model of education as an alternative to the present transport-based model that makes it possible to re-envisage education as something that is free of restrictions of time and space.

Education needs to be less expensive than it is. Unless education becomes less expensive it will not expand to deal with the world crisis in education. The conventional classroom system is incremental in costs. For every extra thirty or so students there needs to be an extra classroom and teacher and support facilities. There is no reduction of costs as numbers increase. A system is needed that reduces unit costs with numbers.

Education needs to be up-to-date and relevant. It needs to be linked to

Table 4.1 Salient characteristics of education in pre-industrial, industrial and information societies

	Pre-industrial	Industrial	Information
Language	Latin and Greek	National languages	English
Learners	The young of the elite	The young people	Everyone
Age of learners	6 to 20 years	6 to 16 years	Any age
Payment	Parents	Through taxes	User pays
Providers	Church	State	Corporations
Where available	Sites of knowledge	Towns and cities	Anywhere
When available	Arranged times	Set times	Anytime
Economic system	Traditionalism	Taylorism	Neo-liberalism
Source of curriculum	Teacher	State	Learner needs

knowledge networks, so that what is taught is related to research, and the demand for skills can be forecast.

Education needs to be tailored to fit the needs of individuals. In business, the customer is always right and if the customer wants a certain size, colour and texture in a product then something is done to make this possible. This means not only providing education where the learner wants and when the learner wants, but also, at the learner's pace, in units that are of a duration and frequency that suit the learner.

The learner-centred, market-driven model of education does have dangers. One of the greatest hurdles to accessing learning is examinations. Do we then remove these too? Most students would probably agree that it would be nice not to be examined, or at least, to let them examine themselves and be their own judge of what they have learned. In a skill that sees development in terms of self-satisfaction, this is fine. A golfer can determine whether some training has improved their swing. But who would be happy to know that the pilot of the aeroplane they were flying in was self-assessed? There is no real gain without some pain in learning and the awarding of qualifications recognises this.

Mature, self-directed, motivated learners who link education with work find the commercial model of education attractive. But what happens to the immature, directionless, unmotivated learner in compulsory education? They tend to be found where classroom education is linked with home education. We see how the idea of the virtual class could be applied to the autonomous learner, but how will it serve the dependent learner?

The classroom by itself, as it is, is an inadequate communication system for all an information society's education needs. But it would be a mistake totally to replace what happens in it with a virtual class. The purpose and function of the conventional classroom needs to change, and much of what is now done in the conventional classroom could be better done in a virtual class. The classroom, although it may change, will be around for a long time to come and needs to coexist in parallel and harmony with the virtual class.

Chapter 5

Roads to the virtual class

> Errors benefit us because they lead us to study what happened, to understand what went wrong and through understanding, to fix it.
>
> (Seymour Papert – Brand 1988: 127)

Two by four by six education, where learning is contained between the two covers of a book, the four walls of a classroom, for six hours a day may be in trouble but it has proved remarkably durable. There have been many attempts to solve the problems of education with communications technologies. One of the first was to use postal services. The 1940s and 1950s saw the introduction of film and radio, and the 1960s and 1970s saw the rise and fall and rise again of educational television. The 1980s were the decade of personal computers in schools. The 1990s look set to be a time for experimenting with telecommunications in education. So far, however, none of these technological initiatives has posed a serious threat to the dominant technology of education, the classroom. We need to know why. This chapter seeks to draw lessons from three major movements along the road towards a better way of learning.

In retrospect, the idea that television, correspondence or computers could, by themselves, provide grand solutions was naïve. As we have seen, the conventional classroom is a sophisticated, fully integrated, broadband, multimedia environment which is capable of most of the communication processes involved in instruction. The mono technological approaches did not have the same technological capability. However, these first attempts were espoused in their day by priests, politicians and parents as panaceas for educational problems. They had their converts and believers and their successes, but they also had their failures and they have never looked as if they would supersede the classroom. Where these technologies have been successful is in such areas as pre-schooling or providing distance education where there is no existing classroom infrastructure.

THE ROAD TO DAMASCUS: CORRESPONDENCE EDUCATION

Typical of many religions is a tradition of proselytising where adepts leave the place of worship to go out into the larger world in order to minister their religion and seek converts. The preacher is teacher, the convert is learner, the world is full of problems and the sacred word is the source of knowledge as to how to cope with them.

One evangelist, St Paul, applied the communications technology of his time to the task of religious teaching. His Epistles make him the founding saint of correspondence teaching. Scribes wrote his words on papyrus, and these were taken by messengers to the early Christian colonies around the Mediterranean. Even then the advantages and disadvantages of correspondence teaching were obvious. Papyrus was tough and flexible and could survive long, hard journeys. Clear as St Paul's message was, however, it had the problem that faces all correspondence courses. Written materials by themselves are not dynamically interactive. It is possible to build in some programmed interaction, and Paul did this with rhetorical questions and answers, but this does not allow for the learner/teacher discourse to assume its own path. As with all successful correspondence teaching, St Paul had to build in some face-to-face teaching to complement the correspondence lessons. In one of his letters in the New Testament, he said: 'these and other things I will explain when I see you'.

Correspondence education, like the classroom, may have been around a long time but its serious growth took place as societies industrialised and efficient transport networks, postal services and high-speed printing came into existence. These are the technologies that underpin modern correspondence education making it possible to mass produce instructional materials and deliver them rapidly.

Norway and Sweden were pioneers of correspondence education, as were the settler societies of Australia, New Zealand, Canada and the United States. They have all used correspondence education as a solution to problems of rugged topography and scattered populations. However, distance from educational opportunities can be measured not only in kilometres but also in terms of social or economic inequalities. It may be just as difficult for someone living in an urban area to attend classes on a campus as it is for someone living in a remote rural location. As the demand for education grew in the second half of the nineteenth century, increasingly correspondence education has been seen as the way of providing education opportunity for all those who, for whatever reason, could not attend regular school or college.

Some educators (Peters 1973) have seen correspondence education as a form of industrial mass teaching that responds to the escalating costs of labour-intensive conventional teaching; as a less expensive way to teach the less advantaged. Correspondence education has come to be regarded as second-class education tied to notions of deprivation; good enough for people on the periphery of society. To some extent, the picture of correspondence courses as second rate has been self-fulfilling. Quality has often been distinctly economy class, and drop-out rates have often been high. On the other hand, in an attempt to compensate for the lack of interactivity, some correspondence courses achieve standards in clarity of exposition, organisation of content and instructional design which would be exceptional in classrooms.

The Achilles' heel of correspondence education is the limited degree of teacher–learner interaction. Learners can work at their own pace as long as it is slow. Interaction between teacher and learner depends on the postal service and is normally in writing. Problems and the knowledge needed to deal with them are in workbooks. The intermeshing of learning, teaching, knowledge and problem takes place primarily in the space between the correspondence student and the materials in front of them. The difficulty comes with the ZPD, when the learner needs help from another person. When this shift in the fractal level of instruction takes place in a classroom a learner turns to the person sitting next to them or puts up a hand and gets a teacher's attention. In correspondence instruction the learner has to write a question, post it off and wait for the response. Shifting fractal levels to that of the group or the institution is also not easy. To deal with this, correspondence schools include block teaching units in face-to-face mode. Like St Paul, they tag on some conventional teaching.

Correspondence education institutions are conscious of the limitations of using postal services and progressively adopt methodologies and technologies that help to overcome them. Instructional design is widely adopted. Hot lines are provided for students to access a tutor on demand by telephone. There is growing use of audiovisual aids as well as written materials, and students can communicate with their instructors by audio cassette as well as by writing. Computers are increasingly being used for everything from administration to desktop publishing and teacher-assisted marking. With all this, however, the days of using conventional correspondence systems for education are numbered. Postal services grow more expensive. Fax and E-mail become ubiquitous and less expensive. Postal networks in industrial countries diminish while telecommunications expand.

The institutions using correspondence for teaching are responsive to feedback and more aware of technological changes than most conventional educational systems. Many of them are planning and preparing for the changes information technology brings, and it may be that they will provide institutional leadership in moving down the road to the education of the future. Correspondence teaching institutions are not finished. They are becoming transformed into telelearning systems.

THE ROAD TO PUEBLA: EDUCATIONAL TELEVISION (ETV)

In 1975 one of the authors set out from Mexico City to travel to Puebla with the intention of visiting the television schools (*telescuelas*) en route, in order to find out how effectively they were using educational television. The research had been commissioned by the Organisation of American States (OAS) which had invested large sums of money in the development of educational television (ETV) in Latin America. There was a belief that ETV provided a better solution than expanding conventional classroom schooling to the continent's endemic educational problems. However, the OAS was growing increasingly concerned with the lack of convincing results (Tiffin 1976, 1978, 1979).

The *telescuelas* were part of a national programme known as the Tele-secundaria whose purpose was to use television to provide secondary-school education where there was none in the poorer parts of Mexico. Any community that wanted their children to have a secondary-school education could get together, find a building and buy a television set. The Telesecundaria provided para-teachers who were responsible for running the *telescuelas*, but not for instruction. This was delivered by television programmes from the Telesecundaria studios and supported with work-books. In a country desperately short of secondary-school teachers, television was being used to provide instruction. Here was an attempt to use a transmission technology to expand education. The students in the Telesecundaria system took the same final examinations as the students in the conventional secondary-school system. What was particularly exciting was that their results were marginally better. In consequence, the Telesecundaria system was expanding rapidly.

The man who founded the Mexican Telesecundaria system, Carlos Fuentes, described the new way of teaching as opening a window to the world for the children of the poor in Mexico. This was an idealism to which all those who worked in educational television in the heady times of the 1960s and 1970s could subscribe. Around the world, countless millions of dollars were being poured into educational television in the belief that an answer had been found for the educational needs of the world.

The year 1975 was a high water mark for educational television, or 'instructional television', as it is called in the United States. Latin America was particularly interesting because of the numerous attempts to use television instead of conventional classroom teaching to expand access to education. The United States was funding an educational television experiment in El Salvador. Colombia and Venezuela had national educational television systems. Some of the most innovative uses of ETV were in Brazil. Soap operas were used for teaching basic literacy skills nation-wide. Secondary education in the poverty-ridden north-eastern states of

Maranhão and Ceará depended upon television schools which used group dynamics in conjunction with television programmes. Students watched a television lesson in a group of eight around a table. After the telelesson, the group would ensure that everybody in the group had understood the lesson and had learned the skills that were being taught. Then an inter-group competition would begin in which the different groups would probe one another to see if anybody had not fully understood the lesson. An adult was present to act as a facilitator, but, as in Mexico, had no role as a teacher. The student groups took charge of their own learning, using texts, work-books and television without the intervention of an adult. Exercises were collected and taken to the system's administrative centre in the television studio complex for marking. The results were related to behavioural objectives and the television teaching programmes modified accordingly. The students manifested a remarkable degree of maturity, sensitivity and learning autonomy.[1]

In North America, Japan and Europe educational television was introduced to well-founded conventional classroom systems to enrich the existing teaching programme by providing the kind of instructional content that would be difficult for a teacher to obtain. Although this 'enrichment' model had some success in primary schools, by 1975 it was becoming clear that it was not having any serious impact on secondary schools. It was in parts of the world where there were no teachers and no conventional classroom teaching that educational television had the opportunity to create an alternative model and, for a brief time seemed to have found a way that worked.

One of the most exciting experiments was conducted in Niger. Villages were used where there was no school and nobody could speak French. Education was solely dependent upon television as the source of instruction. The result was some ingenious adaptations of a television system as a stand-alone instructional system with minimal support. Students learned to write from a television screen by writing on it or in the sand in front of it. And learn they did, by television, to read and write in what was to them a foreign language, French. The system was never intended to do more than educate at the village level, but the students inevitably went to the capital, Niamey, and sat public examinations, where, it is rumoured, they did so well that they aroused the wrath of teachers in the conventional educational system.

From the British Council and the British Overseas Development Administration, from the Konrad Adenauer Foundation and the Eberhard Stiftung, from USAID and EDA, from UNESCO and the OAS, idealistic missionaries of a new era in education spread the good word on ETV around the world. But on the road to Puebla one of them lost his faith. The first *telescuela* he visited lay on the slopes of Mount Popocatapetl, in a television reception shadow cast by the famous mountain. The television school had no television pictures.

The para-teachers and the schoolchildren were politely amused at their visitor's concern. No, they never got the television pictures, but they did get the sound, and of course they got the workbooks and the school was doing very well. But why bother to get a television set if they could not get the pictures? Because, if they did not have a television set, they could not be part of the Telesecundaria system, and everyone wanted to be part of Telesecundaria because then they got a secondary-school education.

Two days later, having visited the rest of the *telescuelas* along the road, the researcher arrived in the beautiful old city of Puebla. His visit had been timed to coincide with the announcement of the results from the public secondary-school examinations. The para-teachers from the school that got no pictures were there. Once again the results from their school had been the best in the whole district. How could this school be doing so well when it did not get the pictures that were the whole reason for using television?

An analysis of the public examination papers was undertaken which asked: 'To answer this question, is there any critical information that a moving television image would give, that could not be got from the workbook or the sound channel of the television?' There was not a single question to which the answer was clearly 'Yes'. The reality was that if the purpose of the secondary school education was to pass the public examinations – and these were the children of the poor to whom passing the secondary national examinations was a passport to a better life – then there was no need for television. Radio and text could do the job at a fraction of the cost.

Study any public examination and see if television pictures are needed to get the knowledge to answer them. Subjects such as geography and science do call for interpretations of still images, maps and diagrams, but these can be provided and explained in books. Some degree of quasi-motion helps in teaching mathematics and there may also be some value in using moving images to explain laboratory procedures and practical work. The hard fact is, however, that established public examinations evaluate what is taught in conventional classrooms, and what is taught in them is how to deal with written problems using knowledge that exists in written words. If what was taught by educational television had been tested with images, the story of ETV might have been different. Will the virtual class in its turn introduce multi-sensory educational environments only to evaluate problem solving by writing?

This explained why the school without the television pictures had managed to do the examinations, but not the disconcerting fact that it had done better than the *telescuelas* which had the benefit of pictures. Are moving pictures a distraction if they are not critical to instruction?

Educational television inherited from the audiovisual movement an approach to instruction based on the idea that the more the learner's senses are engaged, the more they learn. Hit the learner with sound and sight, with text, with music, with pictures and cartoons and they will learn more. Associated with this was the belief that learning should be fun and that printed words are not as much fun as pictures and spoken words are not much fun without music in the background. Given this approach to learning, television was seen as the ideal super-medium for teaching. Whether pictures were actually needed was not the point. What mattered was that the message should be accompanied by lots of sound and motion. What sold detergents would surely sell education. In studios concerned with producing education television programmes, there were often two distinct groups of people who had difficulty reconciling their perspectives. On the one hand, there were educationists trying to adapt their teaching to a medium they were not trained to use. On the other hand, there were experts in television who knew nothing about instruction convinced that they could transform teaching into entertainment.

There is, in fact, no scientific basis for supposing that extraneous information improves the learning process, that adding lively music or vivid pictures to a verbal message helps people to understand the information in a way that is relevant to learning. On the contrary, the study of perception suggests that there is a limit to the information that people can consciously process (Best 1992). We appear to have the capacity to focus on one communication channel and in this way to be more sensitive to the information within it. When we look carefully at something we do not pay as much attention to what we are hearing. All of this suggests that if learning is to be an intense, concentrated activity, then we need to be parsimonious in the way we use different channels for instructional information. If some instructional content is best conveyed in written words, then let it be in written words. Adding music or showing pictures is likely to distract, unless there is a complementary relationship between the different modes or channels of communication. For example, if someone is learning to read, then hearing how a new word is pronounced while looking at it helps. A simple rule of thumb is that, where there is a complementary relationship between the information in different channels or modes, then this can contribute to learning. However, where there is no relationship between the information in one mode and that in another mode, then what is irrelevant becomes noise and distracts.

The cognitive need for full motion images in classroom instruction seems to be relatively rare. It arises mainly in training such as sports, crafts and medical skills. Even here, a question hovers as to the extent to which full motion video is necessary. In a video describing a surgical procedure, the motion in the face of the surgeon describing procedures is not critical. A single frame of the surgeon's face is enough. By the same token, any diagrams, X-rays, shots of apparatus, any picture showing conditions where there is no movement can all be transmitted as single frames. Try this on most educational television programmes and you will find that you have removed well over 90 per cent of the number of frames. What is interesting is that when frames are removed from what seem to be sequences of critical motion they can then become easier to understand. When motion in a tennis serve or a suturing procedure is removed so that they are viewed as a series of stepped images, the motion is easier to see and understand than when it is shown in normal full motion. When instruction involves images and the learner is trying to see something they could not see before, simplifying the image by removing some of the motion can help. What all this points to is the possibility that educational television saturates learners with information. And if that is the case then what will virtual reality do?

The principle of parsimony in designing instruction will become critical when we use virtual reality for education. It has far greater potential than television for providing multichannel information and inundating the senses. If it is used as indiscriminately as ETV is, then its impact could be even less.

Educational television tried to join the cognitive and affective processes together with only mixed success. It is as though teachers were to decide that, because people are happier in playgrounds than in classrooms, they should try to teach in the playground instead of in the classroom. However, the instructional process differs from the information processes whereby we are entertained or informed. Learners attempt to retain and apply what they learn and there is some attempt to test and measure whether they do. This involves focusing attention and mental struggle. Learning from television may be a fun process, but it has failed to provide the austerity of thought and critical analysis associated with serious instruction. The development of television as a medium of entertainment created progressively more passive viewing habits. When educational television was introduced to places like Ethiopia, Haiti, Ghana and the Amazon forest, educators noted the avidity with which the learners viewed the television screen. However, when they acquired commercial television, viewing habits changed. Like a drug, the first time it is used television has a powerful impact, but the more people become addicted, the less effect each fix has. Think of the endless repetition that advertisers find necessary in their commercials to get us to remember even a minimal message. How little we remember of yesterday's television viewing, let alone the great wasteland of watching in which we spend so much of our lives. A heavy television viewer spends one to two years of their lives just watching commercials. Will virtual reality prove as addictive as television? Will it engender habits of mindless, reflexive responses such as we see in people playing arcade games?

Television can actually teach false concepts when it is used to show images where recognition is critical. The use of colour television in medical instruction could lead to misdiagnosis because of the difference between television colours and real life coloration. In a teleclass in the north of

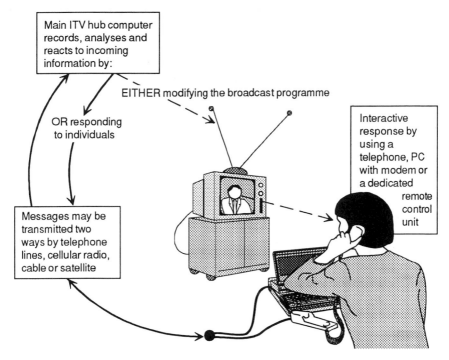

Main ITV hub computer records, analyses and reacts to incoming information by:

EITHER modifying the broadcast programme

OR responding to individuals

Interactive response by using a telephone, PC with modem or a dedicated remote control unit

Messages may be transmitted two ways by telephone lines, cellular radio, cable or satellite

Figure 5.1 Interactive television

Brazil, one of the authors watched groups of students earnestly convince one another that a triangle was composed of three curved lines, because that was the shape they had seen on a badly adjusted television receiver. In the end one girl stood alone arguing the case for straight-sided triangles. But the power of the belief of her peers proved too much. In tears she recanted, and then there was a lot of hugging and kissing as everybody became united in the knowledge that triangles had curved sides. There was no teacher to correct the situation, only a facilitator who also believed in the knowledge presented by television.

The biggest weakness of broadcast television as a medium for education was that it was a one-way medium. It provided knowledge and expounded problems and showed their relationship, and it could, at a generic level, be good at this. What it did not do was to provide the teacher–learner interaction and relate that to the knowledge–problem axis. Today, interactive television tries to do this in telelearning situations by making it possible for learners to interact with a television teacher. There are various ways of doing this, but the extent to which the viewers can respond is limited.

With a few exceptions, educational television in its first incarnation as a medium for broadcasting instruction was never able to establish that it was a more effective or a less expensive way of teaching. The various educational television projects around the world did not attract the student numbers that would have made them an economically viable alternative to conventional education and there was little benefit to show from television as an add-on to an existing system.

A problem analysis of education television systems in Latin America came to the conclusion that the effectiveness of every one of them was impeded by serious problems to the point where any future development could only come about as a result of massive changes which would involve huge capital investment (Tiffin 1976). Given the lack of political conviction as to the effectiveness of educational television, this was not forthcoming. The late 1970s saw the digging of what Latin Americans called the 'cemeteries of educational television' (Tiffin 1980: 257–61).

Broadcast educational television systems have not all disappeared. There have been successes. The children's television workshop, one of the few educational television projects based upon solid research into the relationship between the television medium and the instructional process, came up with a format in *Sesame Street* that has proved popular and successful around the world. It catered to the reality of children's attention spans. Not that *Sesame Street* competed with conventional classrooms. It targeted the pre-schooler and took the role of an electronic nanny. There was no contradiction between the school's timetable and the television timetable, no rivalry between the television teacher and the classroom teacher, no argument as to what should be in the curriculum and no examining or testing system.

With the development of videocassette recording, broadcast educational television became more a delivery system than an instructional medium. In Europe, North America and Japan educational television has moved into the publishing business. Blockbuster series such as the *Ascent of Man*, *Cosmos* and *Civilisation* were produced with a major authority who also wrote a book to go with the series. Besides being of general interest, both the text and the video of the series could be used for education. Teachers were able to record the programmes off air, or acquire the videocassettes. The Annenberg Foundation in America began the collection of a library on significant issues by famous authorities which would create a critical mass of knowledge in video format. Although television acquired an *alter ego* in video, it continued to lack the dynamic interactive function which is at the heart of education.

Broadcast television is the medium *par excellence* for the grand event; for creating the global village with its fêtes and fairs and sports events and its preachers and politicians. The whole world watches the Olympics, and Tosca is simulcast globally as it is performed in Rome in the three historic locations where the story takes place at the actual time of day in which the three acts of the opera are set. If we are to look at education as a global activity, then cultural and sporting events can be shared through the use of international transmissions that act almost like the traditional assembly that creates a sense of the school or college as a whole. Television, with its sense of occasion and ability to capture the interest of great masses of people could serve a major role in developing collegiality in the virtual colleges of the future.

When the best of the educational and television worlds come together, as sometimes happens in educational documentaries, we realise that television is a powerful medium for lecturing to large groups of people. In this capacity digital high-definition television (HDTV) could mark a more mature approach because it will be possible at last to take the pictures seriously. When pictures are needed in instruction in such fields as architecture, medicine, biology, art and photography, then the pictures must be of high resolution. This is something that has not been possible with television so far because its images have been of such low quality that they have needed a presenter to explain to the viewers what they were looking at. The tradition of scientific film making, where directors such as Benedito Duarte have sought to use their cameras to seek clarity and objectivity in the visual depiction of phenomena has eluded television, where, by contrast, directors have resorted to the tricks of television to give an impression of veracity.[2] Virtual reality will initially be a low-definition medium which resorts to artifice to trick the senses into accepting it as reality. And that represents one set of problems if it is used for instruction that prepares people for real-world problems. But what about the time when it has advanced to the stage where it can immerse an individual in a virtual world of high fidelity that purports to simulate real reality? Virtual reality is digital. This means that it can be subtly manipulated and adjusted.

THE ROAD THROUGH SILICON VALLEY: COMPUTERS APPLIED TO LEARNING

Television is attractive to those who see teaching as explanation. It is the technology of the lecture. It has the potential for presenting education at the national, pan-national and global levels. These are the macro-fractal levels where learners are masses, problems are things that societies face and knowledge is a conjunction of common sense, pseudo-science and the sweet voice of reason in the presenter.

By contrast, computers are attractive to those who see learning as interaction. It is the technology of the practice mode in education. It operates at the fractal level of the dyad where the computer is the learner's ever-patient, untiring teacher, source of knowledge and problems – what Gabriel Saloman calls an 'intellectual partnership' (Saloman 1990:

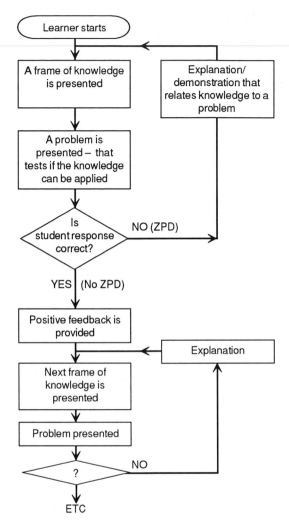

Figure 5.2 Basic CAI model

26). Education on television uses a broad brush. Computers applied to learning use a fine pen.

Computer-assisted instruction (CAI) was first based upon the principles of programmed instruction. This places the four factors of instruction – learning, teaching, knowledge and problems – in close proximity. It does this by breaking down instruction into easily assimilated units which are placed in a sequence that the learner can move through in easy steps. A unit of knowledge is presented which is then followed by a problem in the form of a test. If the learner gets the test item correct, they move to the next bit of knowledge and the next test. In other words, knowledge is followed by a problem, and as long as the learner can solve the problem by themselves there is no ZPD. However, if the learner gets the test item wrong then there is a ZPD. Teaching is needed. This is provided by a remedial loop that explains the relationship between the knowledge and problem, or breaks the knowledge and problem down into even smaller units. Such programmes seek to explain through simplification.

This was the pattern of early CAI programs and it underlies many of the more sophisticated programs that are now developed. For low-level skills it works. However, where the overall learning task has some degree of complexity, the model is not so successful. The linear sequencing, which makes this approach easy to program does not make it easy to synthesise what is being learned. Learners are stuck at the dyadic level, and this may be an impediment when the subject is complex. Shifting fractal levels helps learners to see problem–knowledge relationships from different perspectives and so more holistically.

Like the use of television for education, the application of computers to instruction grows more sophisticated with the technology. Computers can be used for discovery learning. This presents the problem first and allows the learner to get the knowledge they need to solve it from a database. A variation on this is to present the learner with a problem for the resolution of which they have to use computer functions. Game playing allows learners to work with computers as a group, in competition with one another as individuals or as a team. This is popular in military and manage-ment training, as are computer simulations. These present a model of a real-world situation and allow the learner to manipulate the variables involved. The learner can try to deal with problems that might emerge in the simulated environment using knowledge that the programs make acces-sible. It was in the application of computer technology to simulation that virtual reality technology had its roots.

All these applications of computers to learning belong to what Blagovest Sendov calls the 'first wave'. This is using computers as an adjunct to the existing classroom – as a way of automating routine instructional functions and making learning more lively. The computer does instructional tasks under the control of the teacher (Sendov 1986: 16).

Also belonging to this first stage is computer-managed instruction (CMI). This is a macro-level version of CAI. There are three databases. One contains information about the learners, one contains assignments and test items (problems) and the third contains content and resources (know-ledge). The computer acts as a counselling-type teacher interacting with learners to advise them on the overall pattern of their problem–knowledge activities.

Knowledge and problem are related together in an instructional hierarchy that determines the sequence in which learning takes place. As with CAI,

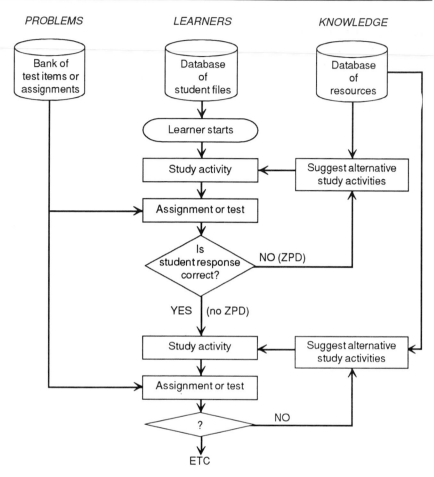

PROBLEMS   LEARNERS   KNOWLEDGE

Figure 5.3 Basic CMI model

the learner absorbs some knowledge, although this time it may be that the learner is told to read some text or do some conventional learning activity with a teacher. Then there is an assignment or test to see if the learner can solve the problem that the knowledge addresses. If they can, there is no ZPD and they proceed to the next unit of knowledge. If there is a ZPD, then an alternative study programme is prescribed. Whether a student can solve a problem or not, the results of their tests and assignments are placed in their file so that their progress through a learning sequence is monitored. This makes it possible to build a profile on an individual student that can be used to advise them on study paths. It can also be related to counselling programmes in such areas as career guidance. When the progress of large numbers of students through a course of study is compared to course objectives, the information can be used to improve instruction.

Like CAI, CMI has taken different forms, but an obvious question is, Why not link the two together so that the two fractal levels are available to learners? This is done in training, especially military training. But in schools first-wave computing in education is like computing in banks. Automatic tellers deal with individual banking transactions. This is the CAI level. Then there is the backroom use of computers to keep track of people's accounts and monitor the flow of money into and out of the banking system. This is the CMI level. In between, there are people who deal with the human aspects of banking and help to relate the overall picture of people's accounts to their individual concerns. This is equivalent to the teachers in education. At the moment, when you walk into a bank, it doesn't look all that different from the way it looked in the past. Neither does the conventional classroom.

But banking is changing. Automatic tellers are linked to a bank's main-frame activities, as are each individual transaction that takes place with a plastic card. Studies are taking place as to how artificial intelligence can be applied to some of the functions of tellers. In the same way, education is moving into Sendov's 'second wave'. He characterises this as 'the mass presence of the computer in the social environment'. Sometime soon, students will have their own computer. It will be as basic a piece of equipment for a learner as pen, ink, paper and text have been in the past. Sendov says, 'the basic problem now is not how to introduce computers in education, but how to build education in the presence of the computer' (Sendov 1986: 16).

The technology of correspondence changed slowly, the technology of television changed in stages, the technology of the computer is evolving rapidly and dynamically. Form and function do not stay stable so that educators can adapt it. When students get their hands on their own computing devices in the future, it may no longer be a device they interface with by reading and 'typing'. The new generation of personal computer is multimedia. It combines sound and image with text and graphic capability and can draw on multimedia databases on compact discs and via telecommunications. Soon we will be talking to it.

As the case of television showed, increasing media capability does not in itself lead to better ways of learning. Perhaps more important is the work that has been done in the application of artificial intelligence research to the development of expert systems for education and intelligent computer-assisted instruction. This suggests that student computing devices could become vehicles for courses that are managed and taught by computers.

Computers could take over the functions of correspondence education and educational television, and what makes this possible is that they can also be jacked in to what is beginning to be called 'cyberspace'.

Chapter 6

Telelearning in cyberspace

Henceforth, it is the map that precedes the territory.

(Baudrillard 1983: 2)

TRACKS TO SUPERHIGHWAYS

The 1990s is the decade of telecommunications. Strictly speaking, 'tele-communications' means communicating at a distance with or without wires. Until recently the term conjured up images of the plain old telephone system (POTS) and its attendant telegraph system, the inter-connecting network of cables and wires supplemented by satellite and microwave links that span the world. This network is changing from narrowband to broadband, from analogue to digital and from dumb to intelligent. The transition in telecommunications is to the information revolution, what the change from horse and sail to steam-driven transport was to the industrial revolution. In this chapter we look at the attempts being made to apply telecommunications to instruction while the changes are taking place. It is unlikely that the technologies being used for tele-learning in the 1990s will be around in the next millennium any more than the current generation of personal computers. The current applications of telecommunications to instruction are like the first attempts at educational television in the days before tape-recording and colour television. They are makeshift and succeed because of the enthusiasm of brave innovators. But do they represent yet another step along the road towards the virtual class or the point at which the journey stops and the foundations are laid? First we need to overview the transformations in telecommunications and the emerging forms that telelearning is taking.

One change is that copper is giving way to glass as the medium of wired telecommunications. The 'twisted pair' of copper wires that links a tele-phone to the telecommunications network typically has a bandwidth of 5,000 hertz. Bandwidth can be thought of as a measurement of information capacity of a telecommunications channel. Since the human voice normally uses a bandwidth of 10,000 hertz, it has to be compressed for transmission by telephone. NTSC television, the US standard, uses 6,000,000 hertz, so until recently it was assumed that it was not possible to transmit television by telephone if the results were to be worth watching. By contrast, a strand of fibre-optic wire has a bandwidth in the region of 2,000,000,000 hertz. It is this giant leap in capacity that leads to ideas of superhighways of information that can handle the full range of the human voice, high-fidelity sound (200,000 hertz) and high-definition television (24,000,000 hertz). It is this capacity which will make possible the transmission of high-definition, multi-sensory virtual reality.

Fibre-optic cables are going into place around the world for long-distance telecommunications but it is not proving easy to bring fibre optics to the home. An interim technology is developing that brings 'fibre to the kerb' with coaxial cable providing the final link to homes. Coaxial is what is used for cable TV. It has a bandwidth of about 10,000,000 hertz, which is an improvement on the 'twisted pair' but does not match fibre-optic. However, developments in compression techniques are making it possible to use coaxial cable and even the 'twisted pair' to transmit information more efficiently than had previously been imagined. The plain old telephone system can even be used for videoconferencing.[1]

Another of the changes in telecommunications is that information will be transmitted in digital rather than analogue form. It means that information is represented in binary, as it is in computers. When telecommunications and computers use the same language it becomes possible to integrate their functions so that telecommunications networks can acquire computer 'intelligence'. Digital transmission also makes it possible to transmit video, voice and data at the same time. In this way, it becomes possible to think of telecommunications delivering many kinds of services simultaneously. People at home could talk on the telephone and at the same time receive a fax and have a video downloaded. This is the idea behind ISDN (Integrated Services Digital Network), an international set of standards intended to implement this new stage in telecommunications. It means that information can be piped into a house for many purposes, rather in the manner in which electricity is used to pipe in power.

The use of satellites for telecommunications is also changing. Today's telecommunications satellites are called GEOs, because they are in geostationary orbit 22,350 miles above the Equator. It is only at that height and only above the Equator that a satellite will orbit at a speed that will keep it in the same position relative to a place on the Earth. In other words, it appears stationary in the sky to an Earth station. The distance between GEOs and Earth stations attenuates signals and have required large dish-type antennas to send and receive signals. However, as satellites become more efficient and powerful there is a corresponding decrease in the size of dishes, which then become more widely distributed and more economic to use.

There are a variety of ways of receiving and transmitting from an Earth station to a satellite. A teleport is a large Earth station that acts as a hub from which messages can be sent and received via microwave or fibre-optic cable to other terrestrial centres. A teleport could serve a whole educational system, internationally as well as nationally. VSAT (very small aperture terminal) networks may function as a star network with a central controlling hub Earth station which could be a teleport and a lot of small stations with small 'dishes' that link with one another through the central hub. However, VSAT networks may also be fully meshed. This means all the Earth stations can communicate with one another directly by satellite. In either case, this is a means whereby schools and colleges and training institutions could be linked with one another by satellite independently of the conventional telecommunications system. Even smaller dishes are used in direct broadcast satellite (DBS) systems. These dishes are only used to receive television broadcasts. They are used by individual schools or homes. Any response to the broadcasts is normally by cable or telephone. Finally, there are mobile terminals which use suitcase-sized devices that can link a portable computer transmit/receive terminal to a satellite.

All of these systems provide ways of bypassing conventional terrestrial telecommunications systems with existing geostationary satellite technology (Gabriel 1994; Singh 1994). However, it is the next generation of communications satellites that is likely to seriously challenge Earth-based telecommunications. Called 'Low Earth Orbiting Satellites' (LEOs), they will begin to operate in the latter part of the 1990s. Satellites will follow each other in orbits in such a way that, no matter where a user is, there will be a satellite in line of vision. Because the LEO satellites are much lower than the GEOs, a user can link to them directly with a mobile phone, which in turn can be linked to a portable PC.[2]

The promise of future generations of satellite technology is that it will be possible to make links from anywhere to anywhere else by phone or computer. If we think of people one day using the kind of datasuit described in Chapter 1 to link from anywhere to anywhere else as a full-bodied telepresence, then 'Beam me up, Scottie' could take on a whole new meaning.

The application of new developments in telecommunications to instruction is called 'telelearning'. There are two basic modes, synchronous and asynchronous.

Synchronous communications are when the transmitter and receiver operate in the same timeframe – as, for example, in educational television. Asynchronous communication is when the transmitter and receiver of a message are not acting in the same timeframe – as, for example, in correspondence courses. Communication in a conventional classroom switches easily between synchronous and asynchronous modes as teacher and learners move from discussion of a topic (synchronous) to an exercise that the teacher writes on the whiteboard as an assignment to do at home.

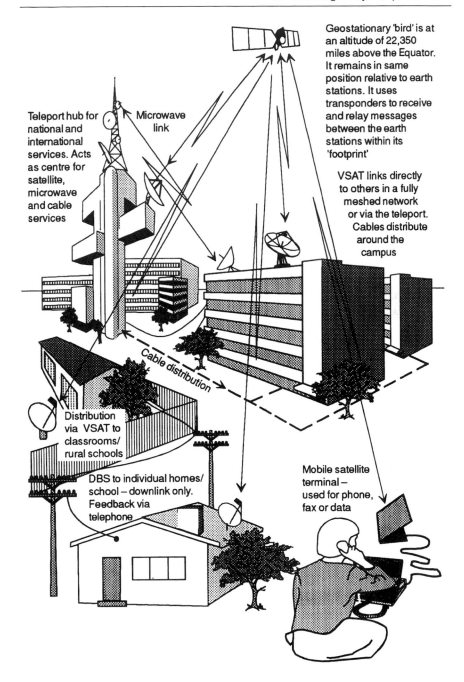

Geostationary 'bird' is at
an altitude of 22,350
miles above the Equator.
It remains in same
position relative to earth
stations. It uses
transponders to receive
and relay messages
between the earth
stations within its
'footprint'

VSAT links directly
to others in a fully
meshed network
or via the teleport.
Cables distribute
around the
campus

Teleport hub for
national and
international
services. Acts
as centre for
satellite,
microwave
and cable
services

Microwave
link

Cable distribution

Distribution
via VSAT to
classrooms/
rural schools

DBS to individual homes/
school – downlink only.
Feedback via
telephone

Mobile satellite
terminal –
used for phone,
fax or data

Figure 6.1 GEO networks

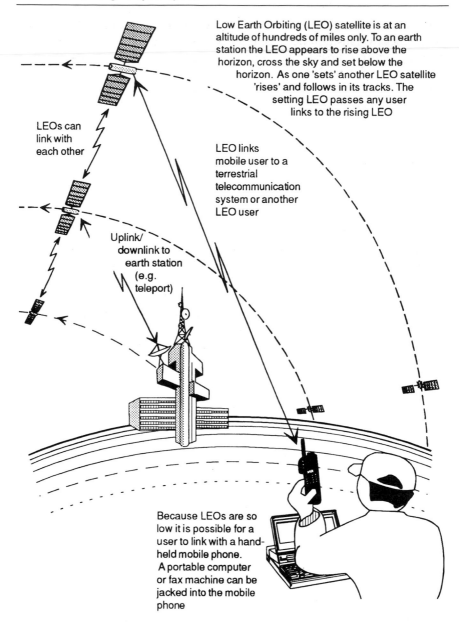

Low Earth Orbiting (LEO) satellite is at an altitude of hundreds of miles only. To an earth station the LEO appears to rise above the horizon, cross the sky and set below the horizon. As one 'sets' another LEO satellite 'rises' and follows in its tracks. The setting LEO passes any user links to the rising LEO

LEOs can link with each other

LEO links mobile user to a terrestrial telecommunication system or another LEO user

Uplink/ downlink to earth station (e.g. teleport)

Because LEOs are so low it is possible for a user to link with a hand-held mobile phone. A portable computer or fax machine can be jacked into the mobile phone

Figure 6.2 LEO networks

Telecommunications can also switch between the two modes, but it is not yet a smooth transition because it means using different technologies. Fax, E-mail, bulletin boards and computer conferencing are asynchronous technologies for telelearning. Teleconferencing is the synchronous transmission system that brings teachers and learners together in realtime as electronic telepresences. It is this which makes possible the idea of a virtual class.

SYNCHRONOUS TELECONFERENCING

Synchronous teleconferencing today takes three forms: audioconferencing, audiographic conferencing and videoconferencing. In the second half of the 1990s distributed multimedia conferencing systems will develop. In Chapter 7 we look at how, in future, it will be possible to teleconference using computer-generated virtual reality. The argument of this book is that this is the direction in which teleconferencing will move and that it is at this level that it will profoundly change education. In this chapter, we look at the use of existing teleconferencing techniques for instruction.

Each form of teleconferencing is an attempt to use telecommunications to reproduce the kinds of synchronous communication that take place in classrooms. Ideally, therefore, although the people in a teleconference are in different places, the following communications should be possible:

- Everybody should be able to hear and talk to one another.
- Everybody should be able to see the person who is talking.
- Everybody should be able to see what is on a whiteboard and be able to draw and write on it so that everyone else can see.
- Everybody should be able to see any audiovisual materials used such as video or slides or multimedia presentations.
- Everybody should be able to handle and interact with any object, machine or equipment that relates to the class.
- Everybody should be able to take away a copy or record of what was studied in the class.

All these functions are possible in a conventional classroom at the cost of travelling to the classroom at fixed times. Note, however, that there are some restrictions, such as the number of people who can be in a particular classroom, and the objects that can be introduced. Students can study twigs in classrooms but not trees. Although audiocassette recording and laptop computers are now appearing in lecture theatres, records of what transpires in class are seldom more than paper-based notes and handouts. These kinds of restrictions suggest ways in which teleconferencing could actually improve on the classroom. However, although today's teleconferencing technology solves the transport problem it cannot provide all the communications facilities of a classroom. Moreover, there is added cost for each additional facility it does provide.

Audioconferencing

The most basic way of using telecommunications to hold a virtual class is audioconferencing. The intention is that teachers and learners in two or more sites can all talk to and hear one another. This is not a computer-mediated form of communication. It uses existing analogue telephone technology.

The telephone system was designed to link two telephones for two people to talk. To link more than two sites requires a 'bridge'. Conference calls, which bridge several telephones, are standard telelcommunications services, and inexpensive bridges can be installed at teleconferencing sites that link five or six telephones. Such bridges can be linked to one another to provide a mosaic of connections that is user-controlled and theoretically unlimited. Bridges that link large numbers of telephones together from a central hub are expensive and, because all calls radiate from the centre where the bridge is, transmission costs can be high, especially if the other nodes are widely distributed and involve trunk calls.

Teleconferencing can link individuals or groups. With small groups a

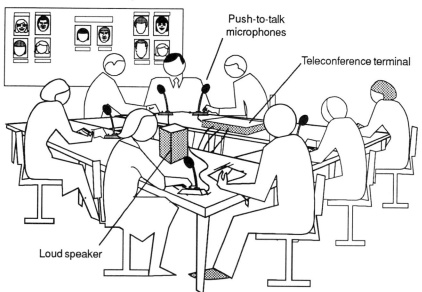

Figure 6.3 Audioconferencing

telephone with a speaker is adequate. With large groups linked push-to-talk microphones or voicepoints are used.

In the early days of a technology, people may be willing to persist despite manifest problems. The quality and reliability of the pictures in educational television in its early black-and-white stage was appalling. No two television receivers framed a picture the same. The variable capability of different receivers to show gradations of grey on the black-and-white scale meant that essential information had to be shown with great simplicity. Few antennas were correctly aligned and television images were seldom correctly adjusted (Tiffin 1976). In retrospect, it is surprising how long it took to realise that the real instructional message in educational television was in the sound and not in the pictures. The problem in audioconferencing, however, is in the sound. Telephone systems were not designed for more than two links. Echo formation and acoustic coupling in analogue telephone systems increases with the number of lines involved in an audioconferencing network. The trouble involves many variables, some of which may act in opposition to one another. For example, reducing ambient noise means closing windows, shutting off air conditioning and creating an electronic sauna. Seeing someone talk, as in a classroom, helps to decipher what they are saying. There are no visual cues in audioconferencing and the telephone system distorts the voice. Audioconferencing technology is improving. There are dedicated audioconferencing systems and techniques for coping with the limitations which, after years of tinkering, function well. A critical component of audioconferencing is some kind of 'cannot hear' button. When people participate in audioconferencing they learn how to talk into microphones and new protocols of speaking.

There are dangers in this situation. Learners can easily become frustrated. In audioconferencing, if the sound does not work there is little to fall back on. Audiocassette recordings that can be copied and sent to any centre that has poor sound reception are a limited solution.

Mutual intelligibility among all participants in an audioconference is only a first-level requirement. Students who use teleconferencing extensively want more than this. Since they cannot see the speaker, they want, as one telestudent put it, to 'hear the body language in a voice'. They want the subtleties of tone and inflection which provide the underlying affective message in verbal communication. Our telestudents said that it makes a difference when they have met other students and teachers because they can imagine what they are looking like as they are talking. It helps in audioconferencing to have photographs of the people at different sites where they can be seen on some noticeboard at each conference centre, and students at different centres sometimes make videos to introduce themselves and show what their centre and its environment look like.

Audioconferencing systems that are well established and have worked through their sound problems seem to function well. There is an imposed parsimony in the medium that may diminish the affective but augment the cognitive in learning. Audioconferencing systems mail materials out to centres for use as graphics during an audioconference. In this way slides or OHPs can be shown on cue when someone is talking, or people can look at handouts. Mailed materials can also include take-home work and exercises. Audioconferencing systems are sometimes linked with correspondence systems, a logical matching of synchronous and asynchronous instructional systems. Another integrating development has been the juxtaposition of audioconferencing with instructional television. Narrowcast transmission by satellite of an educational television programme is followed by an audioconference. This has become popular in business training in the United States, where it is sometimes called business television.

This is a virtual class where the telepresences have their eyes closed. Although such systems once established work well and are economical, the students seek to see.

Videoconferencing

As the name implies, this kind of conferencing uses video cameras and monitors at each centre so that participants can see as well as hear one another. It is also possible to show pictures of whatever is being discussed. The trouble is that video images need a lot of bandwidth and the super-highways are not yet completed. Videoconferencing has been expensive. This is changing with the application of compression techniques so that less bandwidth is needed. The amount of information in each frame of video and the number of frames per second can both be reduced though the results are low picture definition and motion that appears jerky. In this way it becomes possible to videoconference using the public telephone system. The cost of cheap, easily available videoconferencing is, therefore, low-quality pictures. This takes us back to the question addressed in the discussion on educational television. Why do we want the pictures?

Videoconferencing is mainly used to show people talking to one another. When it is used for instruction the tendency is to show pictures of students and teachers rather than explicit images of the subject that is being studied. Since images are of low quality, they need verbal explanation. In the interactive debating mode of teleconferencing the interest is in the affective aspect of seeing who you are talking to and how they are reacting to what is being said. We have argued the case for parsimony in presentation and that the simultaneous use of audio and video modes, unless they complement, can overload our capability to interpret information critically. The affective message contained in the visual image of the person talking can distract from the basic cognitive content in the audio channel. Yet, the assumption continues to be held, as it was with educational television, that

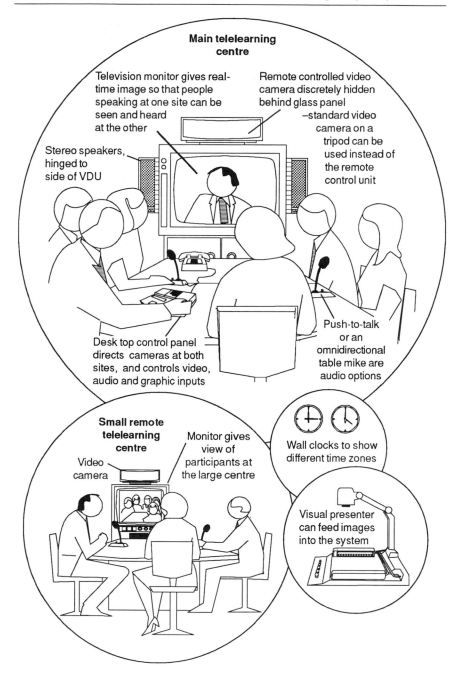

Figure 6.4 Videoconferencing

education with moving pictures, no matter what the quality, is better than education without.

Videoconferencing is primarily used to look at the people who are talking, but the more people who appear in a picture, the less clear is their image. The system is at its best when it uses the full screen to show the person who is talking in close-up – in other words, when it acts like a video phone. Voice-activated cameras are used that automatically get a shot of the person talking. Some systems use preset camera positions that make it possible for a conference convenor to select a shot of the person talking.

Videoconferencing has its own variety of problems. Cameras need light, but projected images need darkened rooms. Videoconference participants are not television talent. They look at the image of the person they are talking to on a monitor, not at the camera. The result is they appear to be looking off camera and they do not have the eye contact which gives conviction to what they are saying. Although most videoconferencing systems have a camera for showing objects or graphics, it is most likely to be used for showing text. Seldom are videoconferencing systems used to show visual phenomena with motion as the subject of instruction. When they do, someone with camera skills is needed. Videoconferencing centres do not normally employ people with artistic video production skills. Videoconferencing is where television was fifty years ago. This is a virtual class where the telepresences have their eyes open, but are myopic.

The answer to some of the problems of videoconferencing may lie in the advent of desktop video. By this is meant incorporating videoconferencing capability into a desktop computer. This represents the point in the mid-1990s when the development of the computer as a multimedia device converges with the development of telecommunications as a multimedia transmission system in a way that makes the technology easily accessible to many people. An individual can join a videoconference from a desk in their office or home and can see, hear and write to the other people in the conference. They can also send or present files of multimedia materials they have previously prepared. The synchronous and asynchronous modes mesh almost as easily as they do in a classroom. Slipping into this kind of telepresence could become as casual as telephoning. It brings the virtual class closer because it allows access by small groups and individuals to meet as telepresences.

Audiographic conferencing

An audiographic conferencing centre uses two telephone lines, one for sound and one for graphics, or, rather, for transmitting data between computers. The data appear on the computer screen as text or graphics. In other words, audiographic conferencing is audioconferencing with the addition of a computer link that provides a virtual whiteboard. Audiographic conferencing uses data bridges in parallel with audiobridges, and the bridging possibilities are the same as for audioconferencing except that the line costs are double.

Every audiographic centre not only provides the means to talk to and listen to every other centre, but it also has a video display unit (VDU) linked to a personal computer. This acts as the common whiteboard in the sense that every centre can add to it and every centre sees the same thing. It is possible to key in written messages with a graphics package and to draw pictures and diagrams. An electronic pen can make it possible to write directly on to the VDU screen. With an optical scanner it is possible to create files from existing documents. It is also possible to use a video camera to capture single frames that can be shown as still images.

Because of the bandwidth limitations of the conventional telephone line, a single frame of video could take several minutes to transmit. However, text, diagrams and video frames can be prepared as files and downloaded to the different centres before an audiographic conference begins. During a conference, files previously downloaded can be called up. The graphic itself does not have to be transmitted at that point because it is already stored in the memories of the different computers. This also means that any device linked to the computers at the different centres can also be activated. For example, if all the audiographic centres had a videodisk or a videocassette player and the appropriate software, video sequences could be triggered. In this way all the centres could watch the same video sequence at the same time. The same could be done for a CD player so that fixed pieces of music could be played at the same time. Inclusion of a CD-ROM player at each centre could mean that an encyclopaedic amount of information could be accessed in a conference.

In audiographic centres where there are ten or more people, large VDUs are necessary, and with twenty or more people, electronic whiteboards are used. A VDU image is projected on to the electronic whiteboard, and pressure on the electronic whiteboard simulates the effect of an electronic pen on a VDU screen. Although such systems are 'lash-ups' of bits and pieces of equipment, they are surprisingly effective and are leading to new modes of presentation.

Unlike videoconferencing where the different sites see reciprocal images because the purpose is to simulate a conference where everybody is looking at one another, in audiographic conferencing everybody is looking at the same picture. Although still images of the person speaking are sometimes shown, the pictures in audiographic conferencing tend to be more concerned with the subject that is being taught. Where videoconferencing appeals to the affective aspects of telelearning, audiographic conferencing focuses on the cognitive domain. It provides a virtual class where everyone can hear and speak to one another and can see and use the whiteboard. However, the telepresences cannot see one another.

Figure 6.5 Audiographic conferencing

ASYNCHRONOUS TELESERVICES FOR TELELEARNING

Facsimile is an adjunct of telelearning systems, not only for instruction but also for administration. It is a convenient way of sending pages of text and distributing timetables, brochures, lecture notes and assignments and last-minute materials. However, fax is not yet an easy way to transmit large amounts of text and, where long-distance calls are required, it is costly. Postal or courier services are better until the next generation of fax machines can deliver large quantities of text rapidly and inexpensively. It is, however, electronic mail (E-mail) and other network services that are proving the most powerful force in telelearning in the mid-1990s.

To access network services that offer E-mail, a user needs a computer with a modem. This is a piece of equipment which links a PC to the telephone system. As a telephone enables a human to use the telephone system by translating sound-waves into electronic signals, a modem translates the electronic signals from a computer into electronic signals that can carry over telephone lines. In this way, computers can 'talk' to one another by telephone. The user will also need a password and some software. With this they can log-on and use the system. If they use E-mail they can send mail or read mail that has been sent to them, print or file mail, reply to mail or forward it to someone else. If everybody in a telelearning system has a PC and access to an E-mail system, it can be used to distribute information to a class as a whole, to individuals or to groups, for tests and examinations and for readings and assignments. Students can do work on a word processor, then send it as a file to the teacher who can correct it and return it.

Bulletin boards systems (BBS) can be set up where messages can be posted for periods of time so that they can be read by anyone who is interested, and it is possible for readers to add their own messages. BBSs usually have some special theme and are a focus of debate. Computer conferencing is a form of BBS which restricts interaction to people in a special interest group (SIG). In this way it can provide a means for a class to interact on a subject asynchronously. Alex Romiszowski has run graduate courses since 1989 that linked people around the world through computer conferencing. He reports that the whole class would contribute to and develop the content of an assignment in a manner that would have been beyond any of them individually.

Another important area for education is online database services. These are collections of information stored in computers which can be accessed via a network. The information can be on current events, the stock market, agricultural prices, courses offered at colleges and so on. What is especially relevant to telelearning is access to libraries. At the moment the catalogues of many libraries can be accessed, but it is not normally possible to download the text of books once they are located. When this does become possible, the virtual class will have its virtual library.

THE EMERGING PATTERN

The three forms of teleconferencing are linked and converging. Any synchronous electronic meeting is an audioconference. Any teleconference in the future will have to include the computer-mediated communications, which is what is distinctive about audiographic teleconferencing, and computers will subsume video. Video images are appearing in windows in audiographic conferencing systems, blurring the distinction with videoconferencing.

Each of the different modes of teleconferencing has links with the earlier steps in using communications technology to seek an alternative to the classroom. Audioconferencing has developed links with correspondence education, videoconferencing links to educational television and audiographic conferencing to computers in education. As the three modes of teleconferencing draw together they also integrate much of what was learned previously about applying technologies to education. To add to all of this, audioconferencing and videoconferencing are also linked to developments of multimedia in computers.

The term 'multimedia' was originally used to describe media combinations such as sound/slide programmes, multi-image presentations and computer-interactive video. It involved 'integrating each medium and medium format into a structured systematic presentation' (Heinich *et al.* 1985: 172). The term has now been adopted to describe the computer-mediated integration of different media. What this means is that the various sound and image recording media can be digitised for use with a computer.

Audiographic conferencing is an example of multimedia in the original sense because it combines two media – the telephone and computer graphics. It is also multimedia in the new sense because the computer graphics can be derived from a video camera, an optical scanner or the computer itself. It is the way the computer screen has become a presentation system for sound and moving images as well as for text and graphics that is at the heart of the new multimedia movement. The computer has become a subsuming medium like television. Video shown via a computer is no more video than a film shown by television is a film. The video shown on a computer screen is digitised, and this means it can be changed and adjusted by the user. It can be windowed and the size, shape and position of the window can be changed, and the whole gambit of capabilities in whatever application package is being used can be applied to the subsumed media.

Computer-based multimedia systems that include video require a large amount of storage space. The development of compact discs using laser optic technology has provided this. CD-ROM is a multimedia technology with the kind of storage capacity we associate with sets of encyclopaedias. It stores sound, image and text in digital form and allows the user to access an individual item of information in seconds.

Television, like a book, presents information in a linear sequence. This is decided on by the producers of programmes. Computer-based multimedia systems are designed so that information can be accessed by the user in the sequence that the user wants. In educational terms, where ETV was teacher-driven, multimedia is learner-driven. What allows the user to navigate their way through all the information at their disposal in a multimedia system is a way of mapping information that was originally called 'hypertext'. It is now called 'hypermedia' in recognition of the fact that information could be in a whole variety of formats.

Multimedia systems can be networked. The World Wide Web (WWW) is a large-scale hypermedia network for textual information that has embedded pictures, moving images and audioclips. There are problems, however, in navigating large data sets in distributed hypermedia. Users become lost in hyperspace. A distributed hypermedia system called 'Hyper-G' is being developed at Graz University of Technology, Austria, to remedy this. It provides a variety of devices to help the user retain a sense of where they are in an information jungle. One is a 'local map' that shows the vicinity of a piece of information. Another is an 'information landscape' that the users can 'fly' over looking for salient information features (Maurer et al. 1994; Andrews and Kappe 1994).

A development that may be critical is 'bandwidth on demand'. What this means is that it will be possible to adjust bandwidth so that teleconferencing could use sound or video or computer graphics or text as they best fit the pedagogical needs of a teleclass. This would mean paying only for the bandwidth used rather than for the bandwidth that is made available as at present. It would encourage a rational, parsimonious approach to media selection. Video would be used when it was needed, not because it was there. Multimedia systems on computers make it possible to have variable video where image quality and frame speed are adjusted for transmission. We can accept low-definition images of people talking, but if too many frames of video are removed, the jerkiness of the image becomes distracting. By contrast, when the subject is a new surgical technique, high definition of the images may be critical, though what happens may be clearer when seen at only a few frames per second.

When the various aspects of telelearning are seen as a whole they have all the elements of a total educational system. Is this the emerging outline of a comprehensive telecommunications-based alternative to the transport-based classroom system of education? Does it have the communication capability to interlink the four basic ingredients of instruction at a variety of levels and allow for the shifts in fractal levels which are characteristic of the educational process? To test this we outline a total telelearning system for the telecommunications environment of the mid-1990s.[3]

DESIGN FOR A MULTI-LEVEL TELELEARNING SYSTEM

We have argued that there is a fractal dimension in learning. Learners need to be able to shift from trying to teach themselves to learning with other people. It was Lev Vygotsky's insight that, besides an ability to learn as individuals, we have the ability to learn with the help of others. We extend this to include people learning as part of small or large groups, or as a nation, or as a religion or a culture. However, at each level of learning there has to be a communication network that makes it possible for learners to interact with teachers, knowledge and problems. We looked at how this happened in classroom-based educational systems and how a student could study by themselves or call on the teacher or a peer for help, or learn as part of a class, or part of a school or part of a nation's educational system. For communication to take place in the conventional classroom, however, the four ingredients of learning have first to be brought together by transport systems. What we are looking at now is how a multi-level instructional system can be created when the basic ingredients of instruction are brought together by telecommunications.

In telelearning, four basic levels of communication appear to be emerging that learners can shift between with the same ease that they can shift fractal levels in a classroom. These levels are:

- the individual learner with PC and modem;
- small-group networks;
- course networks;
- virtual learning institutions.

It is the first three levels which form the virtual class. The fourth level can be thought of as constituting virtual kindergartens, virtual schools, virtual colleges, virtual universities and virtual training systems. The level of the virtual learning institution, as in conventional educational institutions, is concerned with the administration and support of telelearning systems, the design and development of courseware, the provision of telelibraries and telecounselling services and teleregistration. Keeping this in mind we will first look at the three levels of the virtual class and then at the level of the functions in the virtual school.

Level 1 – The individual and PC

We are fast approaching a point when to be a student will involve having some kind of personal computing device. It will take the place of biros and pencils and exercise books and texts. It will have to, if the student is

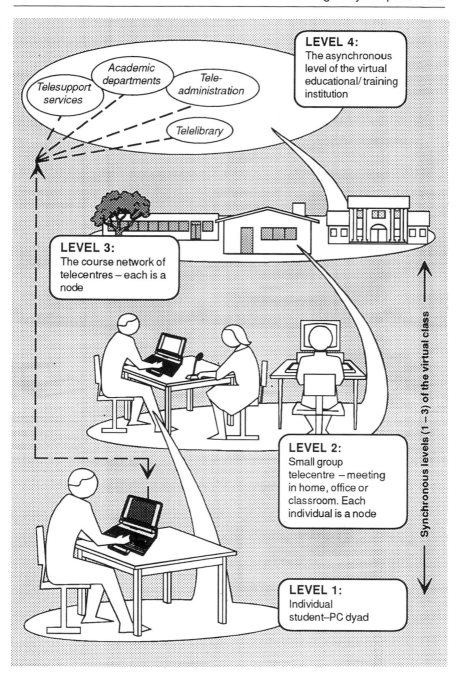

Figure 6.6 Design for a telelearning system

to be prepared for the real world. However, the PC device will do more than that. The kind of PC we can expect to see emerging for students will be a multimedia device with video and audio that will be able to link into telecommunications systems. In the next chapter, we look at how such devices will at some point acquire a capability for virtual reality. But for the moment we are looking at the kind of devices that are appearing on the market in the mid-1990s. Although at the moment such systems are expensive, we make the assumption that as they become standard equipment for students, prices will plummet.

'Self study' today calls up an image of a student at a desk or table struggling with an assignment which is written down in an exercise book or on a piece of paper (the problem). There are usually some textbooks (the knowledge). The student is both learner and teacher. The new image of self study is of a student and PC. Assignments can be E-mailed. Basic course texts will be on a disk, but books will be around for a long time and a student may still use a library, although increasingly students will look for the knowledge they need by accessing databases. Unlike the traditional student, the telestudent will be able to access knowledge that is in video or audio format and call up interactive teaching programmes. These will be intelligent, multimedia, computer-assisted instruction. The PC can take on the role of an automated teacher as well as being a source of knowledge and problems. One of our research students designed a computer coaching system for use with word processors that prompts students in business communications doing writing exercises (Waldvogel 1994). This kind of computer-assisted learning resembles Vygotsky's 'inner speech' in that it is a continuing echo of the teacher's advice and guidance.

The PC will be portable so that the student can work with it anywhere. The telestudent does not have to find a telecommunications outlet, provided there is a cellular system or proximity to a telephone outlet. The PC will automatically dial up the virtual educational network and identify itself. Once the system recognises that it is talking to the PC of a registered student, a menu will appear that allows the student to select from the different kinds of services available in the virtual school or college. For example, the student might want to do a library search, get some counselling, upload an assignment, get an extension on an overdue assignment, or voice mail a teacher.

These are asynchronous activities, so a student has flexibility of time as well as space. Electronic libraries and computer-assisted counselling services never close. It does not matter whether the student is at home, or at work, or moves to another town, or has to go into hospital, or lives in a lighthouse; they can still go to class. In other words, a student can use a PC (and modem) as an autonomous learner, or to take part in a virtual class. The device facilitates learning whether or not there is a ZPD.

Level 2 – small-group telecentre networks

Small groups of learners can get together using telecommunications, but a pattern that is emerging in telelearning is for small groups of learners to get together at teleconferencing centres where there are facilities for them to teleconference as part of a larger course network. These groups tend to be smaller than those who meet in conventional classrooms[4] (Rajasingham 1993). However, the logistics of the technology also encourage people to meet as small groups rather than as large groups. Four or five people can comfortably sit around a desktop PC in an office or a home. There is no need for any special arrangement, and both the room and the PC can be used for other purposes. With larger groups a large VDU is needed, or an electronic whiteboard and a projection system. This in turn means that sound, light and ventilation start to become problems and a dedicated room is needed, which creates issues of security and maintenance. The more people there are in a teleconferencing centre, the greater the problems and the expense.

Within a small group of people there is a variety of resources available for studying a particular problem. There is often someone who has some knowledge of the matter and someone who will emerge as a teacher in relation to that problem. The social dynamics of small groups are attractive to many people, but they are not something that conventional classrooms normally encourage.

Level 3 – course networks

A model that seems to work well in telelearning is where a number of teleconferencing centres are networked together for an organised course of study.

Telelearning seems to favour group communications, and some of the techniques that are developing involve deliberate shifts in the fractal levels of group interaction. For example, it is common in telelearning for each of the teleconferencing centres to be given a task which requires them to go out of teleconferencing mode for a few minutes. At this point, the fractal level shifts from the large course network to the small groups at each of the individual teleconferencing centres. Even here everybody might decide to take on a different part of the problem. In other words, activity shifts down to the level of the individual. When individuals have done their jobs, they come back together to synthesise their results, so shifting back to the small-group level. The teleconference reconvenes with all centres coming online together, so shifting to the fractal level of the course network. Each centre is called upon in turn to present the results of its work. One way of doing this is for each centre to type on the shared virtual whiteboard a bullet point that synthesises what they wish to say. This can then be discussed, defended and modified by the other centres. As each centre adds its points, the virtual whiteboard becomes a sequence of bullet points that represent the ideas of everyone in the network. It is then a simple matter for each centre to print off a copy for everyone present. Teleconferencing encourages a decentralised, learner-based, democratic approach to learning, in contrast to the traditional, centralised, hierachical approach that can still be found in traditional classrooms.

In a conventional class a teacher who is not holding attention well is conscious that groups of students are carrying on parallel conversations. In effect, they are shifting fractal levels. However, it is seen as a discipline problem. Teachers seek to gain the attention of the class as a whole and to keep them at that fractal level while they are talking. In teleteaching a teacher can be totally unaware that students have shifted fractal levels and are carrying on their own conversations. It is a startling experience for a conventional teacher to drop in on small-group telelearning centres and find that people are making cups of tea and conducting running critiques of any speaker they find dull, uninteresting or irrelevant.

Teachers in a conventional classroom will initiate a new topic in class and at the end give an assignment that tests whether students have understood what has been taught. A pattern in telelearning is for much of the teaching to be done asynchronously before a teleconference so that students have explored the subject and attempted problems before they come to teleclass, which is used, therefore, to summarise rather than to initiate, to draw a subject together rather than to open it up. In other words, there are tendencies in telelearning towards inverting the whole communication pattern of conventional classroom teaching.

Technical limitations to the number of teleconferencing centres that can be grouped together for a telecourse are disappearing. However, the essence of telelearning is interaction. If there are thirty people in a 1-hour teleclass, the average time for contributions from each person is only 2 minutes. There are ways to accommodate this. If these thirty people are distributed in six telecentres and the conference goes off-line from time to time, then individuals can interact at the small-group level and interaction at the course level can be between people representing the six telecentres. In other words, the telecentres shift between being networks of individuals to being nodes in the teleclass network.

This is the level of telecourses today. Theoretically, however, it is possible to imagine telecourses in which clusters of teleconferencing centres could choose one centre to represent them in a broader debate in a supra-course network at an international level. In this way, clusters of telecentres become nodes in large-course networks. Parker Rossman, in *The Emerging Worldwide Electronic University*, describes a number of formats that are being explored to create a global classroom. He looks at television classrooms where prominent authorities are interviewed by instructors on their work, and this is followed by a two-way audio interaction that allows students to call in and participate. He then looks at the concept of the virtual classroom developed by Murrey Turoff and Roxanne Hiltz, based on computer-mediated communications systems. He sees a third option in the teleclass which combines 'the best features of the computer network virtual classroom with interactive television using both a computer network and television', which he refers to as a 'global lecture hall'. He also notes the emergence of 'situation rooms' that bring together the technology, software and information needed for large-scale electronic instruction (Rossman 1992: 90–6).

Level 4 – the virtual learning institution

The levels of the virtual class operate synchronously, but interaction between a learner and a virtual educational institution is essentially asynchronous. The learner is a node in the network of the virtual institutions. The institution will also have an internal network in which the nodes are teleadministration, telesupport services, the telelibrary as well as its academic departments. Each of these departments in turn has its own hierarchy of fractal levels. The telelibrary can be thought of as a network of collections, a collection can be thought of as a network of books, a book can be thought of as a network of chapters, a chapter as a network of paragraphs and so on. A student seeking a unit of knowledge shifts through these different levels in a library. At the moment it is possible for a telestudent to search for information and knowledge primarily at the level of library catalogues in order to find the titles of books and articles. It is becoming possible to have articles downloaded to a learner. However, the point at which a telelearner can explore a telelibrary at all its fractal levels as they could in a conventional library is still to come.

Of course, other people can access the virtual educational institution besides its students. A course facilitator could access elements of an individual course design, and a prospective student could access the teleadministration services to get a catalogue of the courses offered to find information about a specific course down to the level of such things as individual prerequisites.

A comprehensive multi-level telelearning system that constitutes a virtual school, university, college, or some such educational institution, would exist, therefore, at synchronous and asynchronous levels. The asynchronous level would essentially amount to being able to access a complex system of integrated databases. This is the level of the knowledge–problem axis. Since accessing such a system is independent of time and space, there is no reason why, at the level of the virtual educational institutions, it should not be a global system. Moreover, by investing in collections of knowledge and courseware it becomes possible to attract large numbers of students.

The synchronous level is the level of the teacher–learner axis. It is a level that is developing with teleconferencing technology that allows learners and teachers to seek the fractal levels with which they are comfortable for dealing with different aspects of the problem–knowledge axis. The excitement at this level is in rediscovering the power of small-group dynamics in the learning process. And, interestingly, although individual learners can take part in a teleclass, the meeting of small groups of people in a teleconferencing centre in order to take part in a teleclass as a group is popular. It may be that this relates to the economy achieved by sharing a PC modem and line costs, but these meetings are also serving social needs in education. It will be a sad thing if learning and teaching become a solitary pursuit in real reality.

Whereas correspondence education, educational television and computer-assisted instruction in various ways sought to emulate, complement or supplement traditional teaching methods based on classroom communication, telelearning is emerging as a different way of learning. It empowers the learner, extends the range of fractal levels available to them and creates new social patterns for learning with others. This is not the application of pedagogical theory, but rather a process of self-organising for learning that is taking place in the new technological environment.

CYBERSPACE

In 1986 William Gibson wrote *Neuromancer*, a science fiction story in which the hero 'jacks in' to a global computer communications network of networks called 'cyberspace' (Gibson 1986). The idea of such a virtual teleworld has caught the imagination of millions of people around the world who are today using Internet. This is a real-world supernetwork which is growing with extraordinary speed and taking on some of the characteristics of Gibson's imagined network. Internet addicts see it as a protean form of cyberspace in which they are cybernauts exploring new worlds. Some of the developments in distributed multimedia systems such as the information landscape in Hyper-G, which has a graphical representation of data and allows a user to 'fly' over it looking for salient data structures, seem to approach Gibson's idea of cyberspace as a world of information in multimedia.

Internet is expanding so quickly that nobody knows how big it is. John Quarterman estimates that by the beginning of the 1990s there were approximately 100,000 users. By January 1992 Internet had 4 million users and they appear to be doubling every year (Quarterman 1993). Over 130 countries are using Internet. One of its architects, Vinton Cerf, predicts 100 million users by 1998, and says:

> The global Internet is only a sample of the potential for the real information infrastructure to come. Its shape may be only dimly

perceived and perhaps cannot be predicted clearly. It is almost certain, however, that it will be more complicated than anything we have now and perhaps more complicated than we are even capable of imagining.

(*Communications Week*, 21 February 1994: 29)

At the moment, people communicate on Internet by E-mail file transfer, bulletin boards and computer conferencing. They can access vast store-houses of information in databases and enter proto-virtual realities called 'Multi-user dungeons' (MUDs), 'MUD object-oriented' (MOOs), 'Multi-user Simulations Environments' (MUSEs) and 'Multi-user Adventures' (MUAs). These are:

> imaginary worlds in computer databases where people use words and programming languages to improvise melodramas, to build worlds and all the objects in them, solve puzzles, invent amusements and tools, compete for prestige and power, gain wisdom, seek revenge, indulge greed and lust and violent impulses. You can find disembodied sex in some MUDs. In the right kind of MUD you can even kill – or die.
>
> (Rheingold 1993: 145)

Internauts 'surf the net', catching the waves of thinking that interest them in an ocean of information. The Internet is anarchic and resists attempts to organise or control it. Howard Rheingold characterises it as an electronic frontier that people are homesteading and commerce is colonising (1993). In time, law and order will come and a more settled way of life, but in the meantime it provides a Darwinian environment for new ideas, new ways of doing things and for shaping and creating primitive text-based, computer-generated televirtual reality.

In this computer-mediated world of electronic communication, companies are already setting up stalls to sell software, publish electronic books and trade in sex, and it is here that virtual schools, colleges and universities are already being established (Rossman 1992). To begin with, they exist as written words keyed into the network. But networks as well as computers are becoming multimedia. It is now becoming possible to have video and audio as well as written words on the Internet. It can be used for videoconferencing and audioconferencing as well as for computer conferencing. This is peering into the Internet through the two-dimensional window of a VDU. When William Gibson's character jacked-in to cyberspace he found himself inside a three-dimensional visual graphic world composed of data that had shape, form and dimension with which he could interact. This kind of scenario will become possible when the multimedia computer and broadband telecommunications technology converge with computer-generated virtual reality. It is this that sets the scene for the virtual class in the fullest sense.

Chapter 7

Virtual reality

People say that life is the thing, but I prefer reading.
(Attributed to Logan Pearsall Smith)

. . . we are on the brink of having the power of creating any experience we desire.
(Rheingold 1991: 386)

Virtual = Being in essence or effect, not in fact.
(*New Webster's Dictionary* 1981: 1108)

In the last decade of the nineteenth century word began to spread about 'hertzian waves'. They could not be seen, needed no wires and could pass through solid objects yet they could be used for sending messages. The idea excited the popular imagination, in part because it seemed so bizarre, in part because it presented the possibility of an enormous advance in communications. In the twentieth century radio waves, as hertzian waves came to be called, are used by radio and television, technologies which have transformed the mindset of the world. The uses of the electromagnetic spectrum are still being extended. It becomes possible to make a telephone call from the top of Mount Everest, fax from the furthest regions of the Amazon forest, or link into Internet from an Inuit igloo. Exciting as these prospects are, radio waves and what they can do are no longer marvelled at. They are part of the environment.

In the last decade of the twentieth century, word is spreading of a strange new technology called 'virtual reality'. It seems set, in its turn, to become a defining technology for the century which follows. Perhaps in a hundred years time it too will be an accepted part of the environment. If it is, it will be a very different world from anything we can conceive of now.

At the moment most people associate virtual reality with some kind of helmet and glove which envelops the user in a fantasy world of computer graphics. This is, to what virtual reality will be capable of by the end of the next century, what experiments in hertzian waves a hundred years ago were to satellite technology today. Virtual reality as it is now does not constitute a serious alternative to the conventional classroom as a communication system for learning. It is what it could become in the next century as the technology matures that provides the challenge. We need, therefore, to try and understand virtual reality in terms of the future scenarios it presents for education. When we do that, we begin to see its implications for shifting the fundamental nature of the learning process.

Virtual reality is developing in conjunction with a cluster of other technologies, each of which also has the potential to transform the world in the next century. The virtual reality we are discussing is based on computer technology where the limits of development are yet to be projected. This fuels one of the great questions of our time. To what degree, and in what form can computer-processing technology produce artificial intelligence (AI)? Will virtual realities generated by computers have artificially intelligent creatures in them? Could they have artificial intelligence behind them, developing them, deciding what happens in them? We argue about the existence of an all-knowing God and whether there is intelligence behind the real world with responsibility for what occurs in it. Will there be non-human intelligence behind our virtual realities? Will we know if there is?

Virtual reality will be linked to broadcast and wired telecommunications technology. These technologies are undergoing major changes that will mature in the next century. The 'superhighways of information' are being built. They will soon be in use and will dramatically enhance the possibilities of telecommunications. At the moment they are seen as providing video on demand and access to new information services. In the future they will link people together in virtual realities.

Yet another technology in its infancy which will be related to virtual reality as it develops is nanotechnology. According to Eric Drexler (1990), this is not simply a trend towards miniaturisation of machines. A genuine technological revolution is involved when it becomes possible to build and control machines and computers at the molecular level.[1] This is when a total, realistic, virtual reality environment for all the senses becomes feasible.

Virtual reality is not something new. We have been seeking it down the ages. Looking back at the path we have taken in the search gives an idea of where we may be going. What we will call 'computer-generated virtual reality' (CGVR) is a new way of doing something that people have been doing for a long time. Experiencing a reality which seems real, but is not, is as old as dreaming, and humans have been using technology to induce it ever since they began to paint on cave walls[2] and use mind-altering drugs.

Language can evoke in the mind scenes that are not present in reality, as can the light waves emitted from a television screen or the dancing flames of a fire. What makes the new VR technology different is that the virtual realities are computer-generated, as distinct from the text-generated,

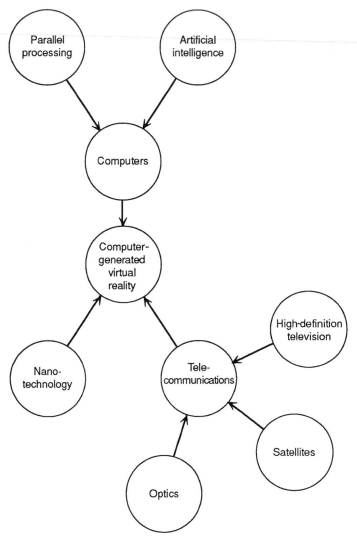

Figure 7.1 The technological convergence behind computer-generated virtual reality (CGVR)

film-generated or chemically generated virtual realities we are accustomed to. The question is whether CGVR can provide a better alternative for instruction to the old VR technology of the books and pictures used in conventional classrooms.

Computer-generated VR seeks to replace the proximal stimuli derived from the physical environment with proximal stimuli that have their distal origins in a computer. Thus the light reflected from the surfaces of real objects is replaced by patterns of light that carry computer-generated graphics; sound-waves from things in the real world are replaced by computer-generated sound; the touch of real objects is replaced by computer-generated stimulus of the skin's surface. The stimuli that the receptor nerves of the human nervous system receive come from virtual realities which are stored in software in a computer with which the person experiencing CGVR interacts.

INTERNAL AND EXTERNAL GENERATION OF VIRTUAL REALITY

What a learner brings to bear on a problem from memory, from the words and pictures that are evoked in their head is an internally generated virtual reality. It has no existence in the physical world other than as neural activity in the brain. As autonomous problem solvers, people have a choice between the reality in front of them, their internal virtual world or a mix of both. They can go into their mind to think through a problem, perhaps even closing their eyes to shut out the real world. They can solve problems apparently without thinking about them, by automatically reacting to them in the real world. When they are asked how they did it, they may say 'without thinking'. Some people mix remembered thoughts with their perception of the real world to solve a problem. An example of this is the use of rehearsal routines in motor skills. A diver, for example, will mentally rehearse a dive before doing it, a driver may do the same in working out how to back a car into a parking space. Vygotsky, in his concept of a zone of proximal development (ZPD), contrasted what a person could do as a result of their own internal capability with what they could do with external help. He was thinking of the external stimuli as coming from real people, in a real world. But proximal stimuli in a ZPD could be assistance from characters in a computer-generated virtual reality.

How different are externally generated virtual realities from the internally generated virtual realities that we initiate for ourselves? When people daydream, they initiate a self-controlled virtual reality which can be totally absorbing or projected on their perceptions of reality. On the other hand, as in the dreams that come in sleep, internally generated VR can be involuntary and fully immersive in the sense that it can place us in a total, credible, wrap-around, richly textured, high-definition, multi-sensory world that does not exist, yet with which it is possible to interact. Hallucinations, illusions and deliriums are terms given to classes of internally generated virtual realities where people confuse the real world with self-induced virtual realities. They believe they see and hear and even smell and touch things which cannot be physically verified as distal stimuli from the environment.

Memory is a storage system for states of consciousness of reality.

Memory of real events means that something that once happened in real reality is recorded for playback as a virtual reality. These kinds of memories are regarded as non-fiction virtual realities. Individuals may believe profoundly in the accuracy of their memories. Legal systems require people to take responsibility for the veracity of their memories. With their hand on a sacred book people swear that they will tell the truth, the whole truth and nothing but the truth. Yet memory plays tricks on us. We can record aspects of real reality by taking photographs or videoing and compare them to people's recollections and show that human memory is frequently far from accurate. A debate is taking place as to whether humans can manufacture wholly fictional virtual realities and be convinced that they are non-fiction. Freud developed a concept of repressed memory associated with traumatic events, and believed that recalling such memories was therapeutic in treating psychological problems. In recent years the acceptance of this concept has led to many adults and children in therapy recalling episodes of sexual abuse often associated with satanic rites. Consequent court cases in countries like the United States, the United Kingdom and New Zealand have led to a question as to whether these emergent memories were based on fact or induced by the therapy. Can we tell the difference between fictional and non-fictional realities, virtual or real? Think about the amount of time we spend conscious of the real world we are dealing with and how often and for how long we are 'on automatic' while thinking about something that has nothing to do with our surroundings. We can move back and forth between being a real presence in a real world to being a virtual presence in a virtual reality. Such a statement may puzzle someone who is strongly embedded in real life. Consciousness is a phenomenon that is unique to each individual, but many of us seem to live on a cusp between virtual and physical reality, between realities directly evoked by proximal stimuli or by internal neural events.

Animals learn from experience, from storing memories of real occasions and having some recall of these. As far as we can tell, however, humans are unique in that much of their learned experience comes not from physical reality but from virtual reality. So much of our learning is book-based, word-based or number-based that there is a danger that our problem-solving techniques relate more to virtual realities than to the real world. In a chapter entitled 'You guys really believe that?' in his book *Complexity*, Mitchell Waldrop (1992) describes a meeting between ten economists and ten physicists at the Santa Fe Institute. They wanted to see if they could find common ground in the study of complex systems in physics and in economics. The physicists were impressed by the mathematical models of the economists but shocked at the assumptions they were making. The economists argued that they had to make certain assumptions about reality in order to model an economy. However, the physicists pointed out that if the economists' assumptions about reality were wrong, the economists were solving the wrong problems. One aspect of the ZPD is that, in reaching out for assistance in problem solving, learners are adjusting their own internal version of problem solving to that of proficient problem solvers in a culture. What, however, if a socially accepted body of problem solvers (say, for example, the economists) are out of touch with real reality and are persuading newcomer problem solvers to join them in a virtual reality view of the world which does not correspond to the real world?

The bushmen of the Kalahari Desert say that 'There is a dream dreaming us' (Van der Post 1961: 137). The opposition of dreams and reality and the question as to which is most significant, physical or metaphysical reality, has haunted the human race since way back in what the Australian aborigines call the 'Dreamtime'. When we have difficulty believing in some good fortune in physical reality we say that it is a 'dream come true'. When the factual world becomes unbelievably unpleasant we say that it is a 'nightmare'. Martin Luther King said 'I have a dream' – and conjured up a vision that inspired a nation. People visualise better futures and then fight and die to try and make them reality. Societies cannot develop without some vision of what they want to be. It is hardly surprising that humans should be fascinated with dream-making machines. But CGVR is different. At a conference on the intelligent city in Singapore in 1991 there was a lot of interest in the applications of CGVR technology to architecture. In the final session a panel of experts was asked: 'Is there any special use for virtual reality in an intelligent city?' The answer was every builder's nightmare: 'If an intelligent city could be designed for a fully immersive, high-fidelity, multi-sensory virtual reality, then there would be no need to build it.' Intelligent cities of the future will need intelligent schools, but there may be no need to build them.

VIRTUAL REALITY GENERATORS

Words, whether they are spoken or written, are a way by which virtual realities can be generated and they are the principal way of generating virtual realities in conventional education. Here is a virtual reality programmed in words by Robert Graves:

> Beauty in trouble flees to the good angel
> On whom she can rely
> To pay her taxi cab-fare, run a steaming bath,
> Poultice her bruised eye.

(Graves 1959)

What images do these words evoke? Graves is a brilliant poet because with extraordinary economy of words he can generate very powerful virtual realities in many, though not all people. Reflected light carries a pattern of black and white from a book to the eyes of a reader and stimulates the

Figure 7.2 Jean-Léon Gérome, *The Bath*

proximal receptors at the back of the eye. Through a mechanism not properly understood, the pattern is perceived as words and pulls images and perhaps sound and even smell out of long-term memory and into conscious thought and sensation. This triggers the brain of the reader to generate a virtual reality.

Contrast the virtual reality Graves encoded in text with the virtual reality programmed by the nineteenth-century French painter Jean-Léon Gérome.

Figure 7.3 The child in toy-generated virtual reality

Again the mechanism is reflected light carrying a pattern of colours to the eye, but this time the virtual reality is more externally defined. You can enter Gérome's virtual reality and imagine what is happening, identify with the dramatis personae and think about what you would do; but the scene is set for you. Of course the limitations of this programme are that it is fixed in time and space. To extend it and continue the action and hear what is being said, you would have to fall back on your own VR generator. There is an area of overlap and interaction between the internally and externally derived virtual realities.

Television uses light and sound to transmit virtual realities that are even more explicit, because they have continuity and sound and replicate reality in a convincing manner. There is less call on the individual's imagination. He or she can identify with a character or a situation but there is no freedom of action. As in books, what happens is prescribed. Contrast this with the dynamic, interactive, fully immersive virtual realities that can be generated by toys, games and music.

THE EVOLUTION OF COMPUTER-GENERATED VIRTUAL REALITY

The origins of the computer lie in attempts to represent in numbers the reality of a country's population (Austin 1982). The example given previously of economists trying to model economies depends on the capability of computers to store and manipulate large bodies of data. Physicists use computers to model the physical world. Linguists use it to model languages quantitatively. Content analysis in communications studies uses computers to compare the virtual worlds of mass media with the real world. The computer is a virtual reality generator but with a difference. It is evolving.

Aeroplanes, motorcars and fridges are technologies that have developed, but have not evolved. There is a big difference between a modern airbus and the first flying machines, but they still do the same thing, only faster, further, higher and with more people. They have not evolved into devices that can turn into buses and do the difficult bit between the airport and the traveller's final destination. Nor have motorcars evolved so that they are also flying machines, or fridges so that they can alternate as stoves.

Computers, by contrast, have a historical evolution which seems almost biological in the sense that they acquire new functions but still retain older functions. Personal computers (PCs) have a numerical keypad and can be used as calculators, a link to their genesis as a device for doing sums. They have taken over the role of a typewriter and are beginning to subsume those of television and video. In doing this they have also absorbed associated technologies. The PC is doing to communication what the supermarket did to shopping. It is putting everything that is needed in one place, offering choice and making it easy to access. Word processors now have dictionaries and thesauri. Spell checkers are an adaptation of one of the functions of dictionaries, with the added benefit that they will check spelling mistakes the user was not aware of and build up a user's own list of words, acronyms and spellings. Pagemaker software and the new generation of printing machines subsume printing. Compact disc technologies are now incorporating library functions into PCs.

To begin with, computers were number crunchers, then they became devices for processing written words and diagrams. Now they are acquiring the ability to process images and sound and to recognise and synthesise speech. We can talk with them and link video cameras and microphones to them, scan in images and digitise them. Then we can manipulate the images. We have in the personal computer created an extraordinarily flexible multi-functional communication device which is now beginning to develop its own unique communications functions. The PC can be used for writing, painting or computing. It can also be used for the totally new forms of communications such as multimedia and virtual reality.

Besides the growing complexity of their communications capability, computers are also evolving ergonomically. They are shrinking and becoming more widely distributed and available. From being rare, remote, hugely expensive and inaccessible devices locked away in their own rooms, they became widely available on desktops. From the desktop, where they pretended to be a television set on top of a typewriter, they disguised themselves as briefcases called 'laptops'. Now they have shrunk to a point where the metaphor is a book. What will be the next metamorphosis of the personal computer? Will it take on and subsume the function of a pair of glasses? If so, this could be the point at which virtual reality is integrated into the PC. It could even become the basic default mode. Imagine booting up your PC and finding yourself in a virtual reality where you can ask for such functions as a word processor, paintbox, games and school. Just as 'windows' is a metaphor for paper on a desk, the default virtual reality could be a metaphor for a room in which you keep your shelves of books, where you can read or dictate a letter, send a fax, look at a video, paint a picture, listen to music . . . or decide you want to be in another scenario. At the moment CGVR is an experimental computer peripheral. Will it become a central function like the VDU and the keyboard in the current incarnation of the PC or will it hang around as an optional, dangling appurtenance as printers do at the moment?

Theoretically, miniaturisation can be continued to a molecular level. Will the functions of the PC disappear into the environment? Instead of intelligent, all-seeing and all-hearing spectacles, will we end up with an intelligent room that owes its inspiration to Plato's 'cave' – a cave whose walls can rearrange themselves to become libraries to browse through, books to read, multimedia screens, the balcony of a theatre, a classroom?

Film and theatre are immersive VR technologies. The purpose of darkening a theatre is to minimise the presence of physical reality. This is a direction that computer-generated virtual reality seems to be taking: to minimise, and ultimately to replace, stimuli from physical reality. It is as though previous VR technologies were gradually to combine and come closer and closer to a person's proximal sensory apparatus, until they overwhelm it and supply the totality of their perception. Think of how a television receiver stands in a room as part of the environment. Then think of how its sister device, the computer VDU, sits a foot or so from the person who uses it and dominates their vision. In today's computer-generated CGVR, the most common mode is a head-mounted display (HMD) unit which places two small VDUs directly in front of the user's eyes. These are designed to give a stereoscopic image and over 60 degrees of vision, so that what the person sees is three-dimensional and fills their total vision. What is visible in the real world is blocked out and replaced by what is visible in a virtual world. Of course the unwieldy HMD and the low-quality graphics remind the viewer that this is an artificial situation, but optical systems are becoming simpler and lighter and, if they take the form of spectacles, will be something that people are not conscious of wearing. The development of high-definition television is likely to impact on the quality of VR graphics, making the image more convincing. There is research into the possibility of retinal imaging, which uses lasers to stimulate the rods and cones of the foveal area of the eye to scan images directly into the visual proximal receptors of the human nervous system (Sherman and Judkins 1992: 52). In this case the images could be more intense and defined than those from the real world which have first to traverse and be adjusted by the lenticular system of the eyes with its various imperfections.

What is especially convincing in CGVR is the impression of being inside a virtual reality and being able to look around in it. This is achieved today by an HMD and a position-tracking system which provides information about head position to a reality engine in a computer. The reality engine relates the co-ordinates of the position of a person's head to a virtual reality so that it can generate an image that matches the point of view of the eyes and transmit this via a cable to the video screens in the HMD. This cybernetic reaction has to be done with a speed that deceives the human perception system into accepting the changed point of view as though it naturally followed from the head movement. The presentation of virtual reality as a wrap-around phenomenon depends for its detail and credibility on computer-processing speed and memory.

The first popular fully immersive sound virtual reality was the Walkman. It excludes and replaces sound from the real world. The information from the position tracking system to the reality engine in the computer that describes where the subject's head is, and how it is oriented, mean that it can also generate appropriate sounds for each ear as well as images for each eye. The principle is straightforward, but it is not easy to get precise and realistic synchronisation between sound and image in three dimensions. There are serious research issues to be resolved in developing credible virtual sound. Think of how quickly we notice if sound is out of sync in a film and how easy it is to tell the difference between natural sound and that coming from television or even from high-fi radio. Unnatural relationships between sound and image make it difficult to accept a virtual reality. This is provoking research into the nature of sound perception, which could lead to sound being adapted to each ear in each individual. This will make a difference for people who have hearing problems. As with CGVR vision, the research in CGVR sound is addressing perception not in terms of its distal source (for example, improving the quality of cameras and microphones), but in terms of proximal stimulus (how can sound be maximised for each ear and image for each eye?).

Bit by bit we enter the alternate world of CGVR. First we put our heads in so that we can see and hear virtual worlds. Then we put on a dataglove and waft it about in virtual reality as a disembodied token hand that can interact with the virtual environment. It can pick up virtual objects and move them and allow the user to navigate through the CGVR with special gestures. Next we give the hand feeling with force feedback so that it becomes a tactile glove. Soon there will be two touchy-feely hands and feet in VR. But what promises to make the biggest difference is the datasuit. Wearing one we will be able to venture our whole body into the worlds of CGVR.

Think of the datasuit as a second skin which eliminates the stimuli from the real world and replaces it by stimuli from a computer. What is felt and touched now corresponds to the computer-generated sounds and sights. Sherman and Judkins describe research to achieve this that uses compressed air pockets, crystals that vibrate with electric currents and banks of pins (1992: 55–6). Fibre optics that extend like a nervous system through the datasuit are joined together in a cable that links the suit and the HMD to a computer. One day in the future this umbilical cable will be cut. The growing miniaturisation of computer-processing capability, combined with the development of parallel processing, means that the computer generating the virtual reality will be part of the suit. Eric Drexler, in his book *Engines of Creation* (1990), describes how, with nanotechnology, a space suit could be designed in the future:

> The suit feels softer than the softest rubber, but it has a slick inner surface. It slips on easily and the seam seals at a touch. It provides a skin tight covering like a thin leather glove around your fingers thickening as it runs up your arm to become as thick as your hand in the region around your torso. Behind your shoulders, scarcely noticeable is a small backpack. Around your head almost invisible is the helmet. Below your neck the suit's inner surface hugs your skin with a light uniform touch that soon becomes almost imperceptible.
>
> You stand up and walk around experimenting. You bounce on your toes and feel no extra weight from the suit. You bend and stretch and feel no restraint, no wrinkling no pressure points. When you rub your fingers together they feel sensitive as if bare – but somehow slightly thicker . . .
>
> The suit manages to do all this and more by means of complex activity within a structure having a texture almost as intricate as that of a living tissue. A gloved finger a millimetre thick has room for a thousand micron-thick layers of active nanomachinery and nanoelectronics. A fingertip-sized patch has room for a billion mechanical nanocomputers with 99.9 per cent of the volume left over for other components.
>
> In particular, this leaves room for an active structure. The middle layer of the suit material holds a three dimensional weave of diamond-based fibres acting much like artificial muscle, but able to push as well as pull. These fibres take up much of the volume and make the suit as strong as steel. Powered by microscopic electric motors and controlled by nanocomputers they give the suit material its subtle strength, making it stretch, contract and bend as needed. When the suit felt soft earlier, this was because it had been programmed to act soft . . . it has no

difficulty supporting its own weight and moving to match your motions, quickly, smoothly and without resistance. This is one reason why it almost seems not to be there at all.

Your fingers feel almost bare because you feel the texture of what you touch. This happens because pressure sensors cover the suit's surface and active structure covers its lining: the glove feels the shape of whatever you touch and the detailed pattern of pressure it exerts and transmits the same texture pattern to your skin. It also reverses the process, transmitting to the outside the detailed pattern of forces exerted by your skin on the inside of the glove. Thus the glove pretends that it isn't there, and your skin feels almost bare.

The suit has the strength of steel and the flexibility of your own body. If you reset the suit's controls, the suit continues to match your motion but with a difference. Instead of just transmitting the forces you exert, it amplifies them by a factor of ten. Likewise when something brushes against you, the suit now transmits only a tenth of the force to the inside. You are now ready for a wrestling match with a gorilla.

(Drexler 1990: 90–1)

Drexler admits this sounds like science fiction, but goes on to say:

This is unfortunate. When engineers project future abilities they test their ideas, evolving them to fit our best understanding of the laws of nature. The resulting concepts must be distinguished from ideas evolved to fit the demands of paperback fiction. Our lives may depend upon it.

(1990: 93)

There is a foreword to *Engines of Creation* by Marvin Minsky, who, looking at the difficulties of predicting future technologies, says it is 'like building a very tall and slender tower of reasoning . . . the foundations must be very firm – and Drexler has built on the soundest of present day technical knowledge' (1990: vi). As Minsky also notes, 'Drexler has for many years courageously and openly exposed these ideas to both the most conservative sceptics and the most wishful-thinking dreamers among serious scientific communities' (1990: vi).

The ideas in this chapter may seem strange in the extreme to many educators. However, if we are to close the gulf between the scientific and technological world and its classrooms, we need to examine such radical notions as the adaptation of Drexler's space suit as the school uniform of the future.

If we accept the technological feasibility of Drexler's space suit, as something that allows a person to exist independently in space, dependent for all stimuli on a second artificial intelligent skin, then we have the perfect setting for virtual reality, because there would be almost no stimuli from the environment and no restraining tug from gravity to remind us of real reality.

Although Drexler postulates his suit as something that transmits information from the environment to the person inside it, it would as easily be able to transmit information that came via a telecommunications system from some other place.

TELEPRESENCE IN TELEVIRTUAL REALITIES

CGVR can be shared between two or more people and they can be linked by telecommunications. Besides developments in computing and nano-technology, there are developments in telecommunications that also impact on CGVR. Some 260 researchers are working on the telecommunications of the future at Advanced Telecommunication Research (ATR) in Kansai Science City, a Japanese high-tech park outside the old capital city of Kyoto. Under the direction of Nobuyoshi Terashima, President of the Communication System Research Laboratories, teleconferencing systems that use virtual reality are being developed. A prototype allows a person to sit at a table in front of a curved screen, put on a glove and a pair of glasses and find themselves in a virtual conference situation with other people with whom they can talk, shake hands and interact. The other people are not physically present any more than they would be if they were in a conventional teleconference. They are telepresences. And just as people's telephone voices are a modified version of their 'real' voices, so their visual telepresences are a computergraphic version of how they really look as they talk and gesticulate. It is like talking to an animated waxwork version of another person. The setting for the virtual teleconference can, like a set in a theatre, be changed. All that is required is a gesture with the gloved hand. What is being discussed – say, a statue, or a spacecraft or a model of a car – can be placed in the space between the people so that they can reach out and manipulate it.

Nobuyoshi Terashima uses the term 'telesensation' to describe the effect of virtual reality and telecommunications, and explains the principles of applying it to teleconferencing in this way:

> A teleconferencing system that imparts a sensation of realism is a concept introduced by ATR Communications Systems Research Laboratories. This system sends images of conference participants who are remote from one another to a conference hall via a high-speed telecommunications line. It then displays the images as 3D information on a screen, changes the images viewed by each observer according to their eye positions and allows participants to make eye contact with each other and to operate artificial objects using the movements of their hands/bodies.
>
> (Terashima 1993: 455)

He also points out the collaborative possibilities of telesensation:

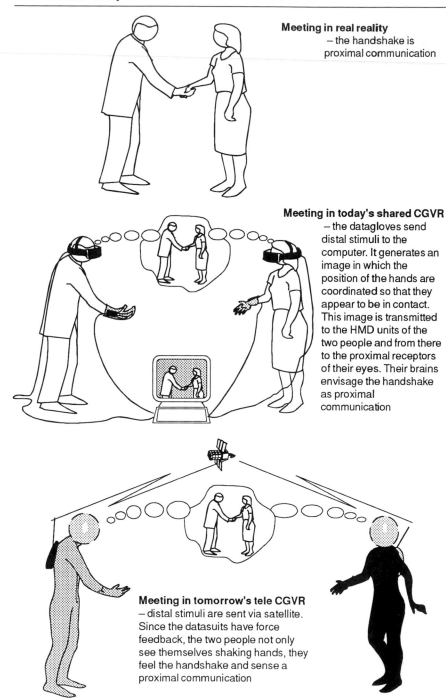

Meeting in real reality
— the handshake is
proximal communication

Meeting in today's shared CGVR
— the datagloves send
distal stimuli to the
computer. It generates an
image in which the
position of the hands are
coordinated so that they
appear to be in contact.
This image is transmitted
to the HMD units of the
two people and from there
to the proximal receptors
of their eyes. Their brains
envisage the handshake
as proximal
communication

Meeting in tomorrow's tele CGVR
— distal stimuli are sent via satellite.
Since the datasuits have force
feedback, the two people not only
see themselves shaking hands, they
feel the handshake and sense a
proximal communication

Figure 7.4 The changing nature of proximity

For instance, designers and clients can get together in a virtual meeting room to design a specific car, adjusting colour and shape to suit the client. In this way telesensation leads to the individualisation of manufacturing.

(Terashima, E-mail, 25 July 1994)

This is a focused use of CGVR and telecommunications technology. At the moment it involves a screen and projection system, a head-mounted unit and a glove, a PC and special software and video cameras. However, Terashima intends to make the technology simple and natural to use. He wants to make it possible to interface without the need for any kind of special apparatus.

Mass-produced, this need not be an expensive technology. It could be the basis of a multi-purpose home unit. It could serve as the virtual reality equivalent to the telephone allowing people to link as telepresences in groups as well as in dyads, in shared virtual realities that could be social, entertaining or informative. However, the screen could also serve as a surface for reading text, watching video or entering into private virtual realities. It could also be the point of entry into a televirtual class.

The transfer by telecommunications systems of coordinates relating to facial expression, head position, hand and finger movement and the movement of any virtual objects that are needed for the ATR system to work today requires the kind of bandwidth that will become available with broadband ISDN. It is, however, of a minor order compared to what will be needed in the future when the kind of telesensation Terashima envisages includes full body motion in detailed virtual realities along with information about tactile sensation, and relationships with shared virtual objects that have weight and texture and make sounds. What we are seeing in the coming 'superhighways' stage of telecommunications is a time of transition in telecommunications. The telecommunications technology that will allow full body, high-definition, total immersion CGVR will be in place when fibre optics have replaced copper as the distribution medium for terrestrial telecommunications. By this time we can also imagine improvements in satellite technology that will mean that the technology is not limited to the bounded medium of wires and cables. The backpack in the datasuit of the future will house a telecommunications transmitter and receiver that will make it possible for people to have the effect of meeting and communicating with one another in CGVR, no matter where they are. As time goes by, we can expect that the definition and coordination of such meetings will improve until the credibility and fidelity of such experience could rival that of real world experience. They may even be more focused and intense.

Chapter 8

The virtual class

In 1884 Samuel Morse sent a message from Washington to Baltimore asking 'What hath God wrought?'. The question remains unanswered.

(Edupage@ivory.educom.edu : 16 June 1994)

CGVR is part of a cluster of technologies that are drawing together to form the communications infrastructure of the information society. In so doing they will also form the infrastructure of education in the information society. Broadcasting and computers have been making an impact on education for some time. Telecommunications is having a growing impact in the 1990s. CGVR seems set to enter the field of education at the onset of the second millennium. At this point the combined effects of these technologies could acquire critical mass that would make possible virtual classes in virtual schools, colleges and universities in the fullest sense of the concept as an alternative to the classroom. The history of education in the second half of the nineteenth century shows that when new technologies are applied to education by themselves they are absorbed into the existing educational model. They do not change it. What we are looking at here is the possibility of radical change. Schools and classrooms are likely to continue providing community education for social and physical skills. The majority of academic study, however, will be conducted via an inter-face device that could look like a pair of spectacles to begin with, but may develop as a datasuit.

We make the assumption that it will be possible to co-mingle the communications functions already subsumed in multimedia PCs with virtual reality and with access to broadband telecommunications net-works, and we use the acronym CGVR to refer to this triple capability.

In Chapter 6 we studied the intermediate situation. Today, when some students may have their own PCs and modem and access to Internet, some may be able to access telelearning through a telecentre or some educational institution, but all students are still using pen, paper and texts. In this chapter we imagine the day when some students who can afford it may buy books and use paper and pen, but all students will use CGVR as a matter of course and have the kind of symbiotic relationship with it that they have with their clothes. They will wear the technology without thinking about it. The effect will be to make education available anywhere, anytime.

We argued that education in its many guises requires an intermeshing of four factors: learning, teaching, knowledge and problems. We also observed that there seemed to be a fractal dimension and that the intermeshing of these four factors took place at different levels. We looked at how this happened at the level of the individual learner, at the level of the group in a classroom and at the level of an organisation in a school. What we propose to do in this chapter is look at how these factors can be intermeshed at different levels when the communications system of education is based on CGVR. The levels addressed will be: the individual learner, the individual learner and teacher, the small group and the large institution.

LEVEL 1: THE AUTONOMOUS LEARNER

Learning, say those who are older – and they should know – is wasted on the young. If learning is to be lifelong then the needs of the elderly must be catered for. They represent a big market for education that can be delivered to them at their convenience. However, although they have the time, have acquired self-learning skills and have learned to enjoy learning, the senior third of any population have failing eyesight and increasing difficulty in finding printed material they can read. Many have arthritis and find holding a book and turning pages difficult. Walking to the library becomes harder. Having someone read to them may be difficult because hearing, too, declines.

The application of CGVR to this neglected sector of learners illustrates the possibilities of the symbiotic relationship of the technology with the individual. The possibilities of an electronic book become available with CGVR technology used as a reader. Gaze sensors which use a reflected infrared beam to detect exactly where a person is looking can register the word a person is reading, and the size of letters could be adjusted by the reader. Verbal commands such as 'Meaning', 'Pronounce', 'Encyclopaedia' would produce the information needed. If a person's eyes became tired they could simply say 'Read'. The infobahn technology that can download video programmes can deliver the full text of a book in seconds. Libraries will be able to make their collections available for immediate delivery as full text. The house-bound, bed-bound, institutionalised and imprisoned will only need to say 'Library', 'Catalogue', 'Subject', 'Browse', 'Download', to access the world of print. The same, of course, would apply to libraries of photographs, pictures, videos and films. Multimedia already does this and CGVR will subsume multimedia. In so doing it could improve them by adjusting the presentation to each ear and eye of the individual. Aside from providing lifelong learning opportunities, these technological advances could enrich the existence of people partially disadvantaged in hearing and sight.

Learners need to be able to access existing knowledge in conventional media in CGVR. However, CGVR as it develops also opens the prospect of being able to generate models of phenomena that are more explicit than anything we have had before. Such models could show movements and relationships that would be difficult to describe in words and numbers or with conventional diagrams and photographs. It would be possible to study models from any angle, from macro- and micro-perspectives, from within and without, in part and in whole. Such virtual reality models would seem particularly suitable to the representation of examples from a problem domain when these are real-life phenomena that are particularly difficult to demonstrate or show because of their size or the danger involved.

In real life, problems like soil erosion are not usually waiting in all their manifestations somewhere convenient to be studied. Their dynamics are difficult to study because they often take place in extreme weather conditions or are too slow for human perception. The creation of virtual landscapes from case studies of erosion would make it possible to analyse stages of erosion at macro- and micro-levels. A learner could ask to see the data from the case studies on which the simulacrum is based. It could appear as a window to one side of the virtual reality. The learner could vary the relationships between data from the original study on such aspects as slope angle, rain levels, wind speeds and directions and watch the virtual landscape change accordingly. It would be possible to take a distant macro-perspective while windowing aerial photos or a map or even a page of text to help interpret what is seen. Then the learner could zoom in to a micro-perspective of soil horizons exposed in gullies, asking at the same time to see diagrams and photographs of different kinds of soil and the changes that could take place in them. Conventional two-dimensional media could be expanded to fill the learner's vision, or they could appear in a two-dimensional window in a three-dimensional perspective. This is what we do when we hold a map while we orient it against a landscape or spread it out and bury ourselves in its detail. What would be different in CGVR is that when we see something of interest on the map we could then call it up and move through the map into a three-dimensional virtual reality.[1]

This pattern of slipping between two-dimensional conventional information and three dimensional CGVR is not dissimilar to the way our perception of the real world shifts subtly between two and three dimensions. The two-dimensional door of a classroom becomes three-dimensional when it is opened. Walk through it into the three-dimensional classroom where much of the instruction will be conducted on a two-dimensional whiteboard. Pick up a three-dimensional book, open it and read from the two-dimensional pages which become three-dimensional as you turn them and whose flat surface under a microscope may look like the Himalayas. CGVR has the capacity to serve as a conventional two-dimensional surface and mimic a page, screen or blackboard, but such a screen can also have the Alice-through-the-looking-glass quality of being a portal to a three-dimensional world. This attribute of CGVR has the potential for presenting information as a network in a way that is foreshadowed and experimented with in today's distributed multimedia systems.[2] It will allow a person to navigate knowledge and explore environments in a way that is unprecedented.

Shirley sat in her datasuit with her helmet on, watching Laurence Olivier as Hamlet in an old black-and-white movie. She was doing a course on 'Setting Shakespeare's Plays', and was comparing movie sets with theatrical sets when she wondered what the original setting was like. Where was Elsinore, anyway? 'Stop,' she said, and the movie held on a frame of the battlements at the opening of the ghost scene.

'Map,' she requested, then, 'Show Denmark', then 'Find Elsinore', and there it was, just where Denmark and Sweden faced each other across a thin strip of water. It must have been a very strategic position and she saw that its Danish name was Helsingor. With her finger she boxed Elsinore and then said 'Show', and there was the town with the ferry terminal and, on a peninsula that controlled the harbour, the castle itself. Next, she boxed the castle and got a plan which outlined the grounds and the buildings.

At this point, however, a window opened to the side of the plan which said: 'Helsingor Castle, Information Property of the Danish Government. Information services available. All major credit cards accepted.' Then followed a menu with accompanying prices. Shirley saw that there was a CGVR Shakespeare karaoke[3] of 'Hamlet in Elsinore' and selected it. A map appeared of the virtual reality, which was a reconstruction of the castle as it related to 'Hamlet'.

Each of the scenes from the play was marked at a place where they could have taken place. She chose Act 1 Scene 4, the gun platform where the ghost appears to Hamlet, and elected to be 'audience'. The way the VR scene manifested itself, slowly formulating from swirling mists to show Hamlet looking out into the dark was very different, she thought, from the opening of the curtains in a theatre. Maybe it owed something to the old movie she had been watching. An eerie lighting effect suggested the ghost about to emerge from the shadows. She admired the set for a moment and then said, 'Action', and the famous scene began. She watched it from the shadows at first and then using finger commands moved around and among the characters, thinking of the difference in the way a play is set and watched in virtual theatre compared to the communal, single perspective of film and theatre and the private keyhole vision of the old three-by-four television that used to be so popular.

As the scene came to a close she decided to see it again, this time from an actor's perspective, and said 'Act'. When the dramatis personae for the scene wind-owed, she elected to be the prince and, since she knew the part well, to do voice as well as motion. The virtual reality dissolved and then reformed around her and she was standing by the battlements in front of the castle in the vestments of Hamlet. Before she called 'Action' she looked down. It was odd to see herself as a tall, slim man and to look at things from a foot higher. She chuckled at the reverse idea of a tall man taking on the role of Ophelia and was startled at the deep masculine boom that came out.

CGVR as theatre attracts much interest. Brenda Laurel sees its use as a 'fantasy amplifier', a main driving force in CGVR development (Laurel 1991). Howard Rheingold (1991) looks at the work being done in Fujitsu and Carnegie Mellon to create artificial characters and at the possibility of 'plugging your whole sound-sight-touch telepresence system into the telephone network' in order to meet with telepresences which may or may not be based on real people. Lennart Fahlen and Charles Brown at the Swedish Institute of Computer Science work on 'aura collision', a way by which telepresences in virtual reality become aware of one another and orient towards one another.

In the scenario it was possible to get knowledge as and when it was needed – to see a particular film on demand, to find a fact when it was wanted, to chase information by bounding and leaping through it rather than scrounging around hour after hour for tiny morsels. At the moment we seem to be at the hunter and collector stage of information gathering, where we find the stuff by sniffing it out or tracking it down.[4]

Japanese manufacturing uses a system called 'Just in Time' (JIT). This refers to the way the materials, components and resources required to manufacture something are brought together when there is a demand for the product. Instruction needs a system that brings learner, teacher, knowledge and problems together just in time. It is what the classroom system tries to do by bringing learner, teacher, textbooks and problems together at one place for a period of about 40 minutes. It is what a good teacher seeks to do in that time. It is what a 'teach-yourself kit' is intended to provide.

To the extent that learning is 'closed', in the sense that the skills being taught are discrete, predictable and standardised, as in arithmetic, the resources needed to teach it can be standardised and kept to hand. But in more 'open' learning, such as how to express thoughts in prose or poetry, where a learner needs freedom to discover and construct what they learn, getting examples of the problems the learner wants to study and the knowledge needed to deal with the problems is difficult. This is especially so with autonomous learners who do not have an organising teacher to help them. Quite simply, it would be much easier to learn by yourself if you knew where to look for the problems and knowledge you wanted and if they were readily available when you wanted them. In supermarkets around

Figure 8.1 A platform in front of the castle at Elsinore (Helsingor)

the world, a credit card can be swiped and within seconds its validity checked and a purchase made. It is that kind of access to learning resources that is needed. Of course, accessing knowledge when you need it is at another level of complexity from accessing credit when you need it. But that is all it is – another level of complexity – to be breached by the development of computer and telecommunications capability.

If CGVR can provide instructional resources in two-dimensional as well as three-dimensional form, and can do this at the convenience of the learner, then it will make education available to many people for whom it is now inaccessible. Whatever shape the interface takes – a pair of spectacles, a head-mounted display unit or a datasuit – it should be like an automobile to the learner, giving them the kind of freedom that a car gives to the traveller: freedom from timetables, fixed ways of doing things and restrictions on destinations. They can go where they want, when they want, provided they can afford the costs.

LEVEL 2: LEARNER AND TEACHER

This is the dyadic teacher–learner situation, which is powerful because of the focused way it pulls together the four factors; learning, teaching, knowledge and problem. It is there in the classroom as everyone is working on a problem and a hand goes up, or when a teacher helps an individual in difficulties, or goes through an assignment with a student. The autonomous learner outside of a classroom manages, but there will often be a time when they want to put their hands up and get help. Most PC applications have an instructional manual and a help function that will provide computer-assisted instruction. The computer presents the problems, the help function provides the knowledge needed to solve them. Nine times out of ten it works. The tenth time, however, the autonomous learner pores over the manual and the help function in growing frustration. They need a teacher rather as they might need a doctor. Just as the autonomous learner wants just-in-time knowledge, they also need a teaching emergency service. CGVR should be able to offer two such services: one with human teachers and one with teaching entities derived from artificial intelligence (AI): virtual teachers.

Learning with virtual teachers

The term 'artificial intelligence' is loosely used about computer applications which in some way resemble the application of human intelligence. Here we examine the possibility of using as teachers expert systems that have the ability to learn.

We are not making the case that one day a computer will replace a teacher. We are simply looking at a trend that has been observable in the second half of this century. It began with the automation of some of the tasks done by teachers. This can be seen in 'teach-yourself' books, language labs, teaching machines and computer-assisted instruction. It is a trend that is typical of the development of an information society. Just as automatic telling machines automate some of the functions of a bank teller, so computers can automate some of the simple repetitive functions of a teacher. As students acquire their own personal computers there is no reason why these cannot be used to do simple instructional tasks. All teachers correct spellings and there can be few who enjoy the task. It has little effect as the feedback is too delayed. Doing this must cost millions of teaching hours per year. A word processor that questions dubious spellings as a student keys them in provides more effective feedback. This frees teachers to do the things that really do need human intelligence and compassion.

However, student PCs will not stay at the level of a word processor with a spell check. PCs are subsuming the media that are used for self-

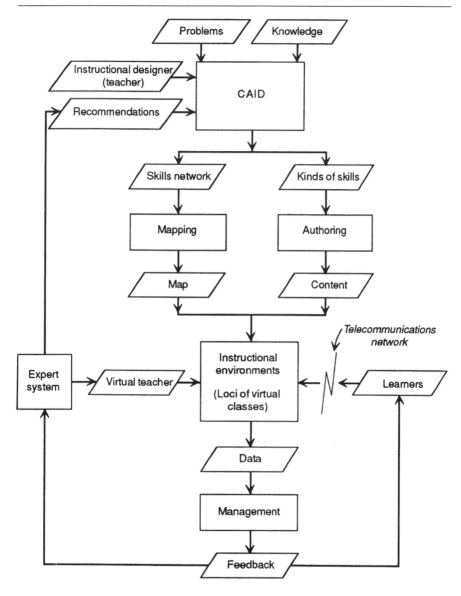

Figure 8.2 A computer-based instructional engine

instruction, such as interactive video. The various ways in which computers can be used for instruction steadily grow more sophisticated and begin to integrate. At some point students will interface with their PCs by speech. When the dimension of CGVR is added, a learner could get the assistance they need from a virtual teacher. This could be exactly the kind of teacher the learner always wanted – patient, caring and looking like Socrates or Madonna or a teddy bear.

To what extent would something of this nature be a form of mimicry with only the semblance of intelligence based on the expression of standardised responses derived from the statistical expression of standard situations? Is it possible that, one day, artificial intelligence could achieve sufficient complexity to breathe a kind of life into the virtual characters in a virtual reality and that some wise old owl in a learner's CGVR could act as a teacher in a way that owed nothing to human teachers? Figure 8.2 shows the design of a computer-based instructional engine. It is feasible now to drive conventional computer-based instruction.[5] However, it also contains the potential to develop instructional environments that could serve as the places where virtual classes meet and inhabit them with intelligent virtual teachers.

The elements of this engine for instruction fit together according to basic principles of instructional design. Logically the system begins with a *computer-assisted instructional design* (CAID) *function*. Into this is fed a class of problem and knowledge of how to solve it. The outcome is a design in the form of a network of all the minor skills needed to solve the class of problem that is being addressed. Each node in the network represents a skill that is either subsidiary to the problem-solving skill or a necessary prerequisite.

A skill, which is a node in a network of skills, can itself be seen as a network of more micro-skills. Learning can be seen as an alternating process of analysing and synthesising skills at different fractal levels.

The skills network is converted by a *mapping* function into a map of the instruction that a learner can use. The learner can select a skill node and receive instruction for that node. The map shows whatever hierarchical relations exist between the skills – in other words, where it is best to learn some skills before others. This is the basis for a recommended path for learning. However, a learner can use the map to navigate the instructional environment for themselves. Faced with such a choice, some learners start at the beginning and follow the recommended path, but others go straight to the main outcome skill and try to master it directly. Some, already having many of the subsidiary skills, succeed. For them the whole network was in fact a single node. Others who try this and fail will begin to backtrack through the subsidiary skills looking for what they needed to learn to accomplish the main skill. They create their own path through the network, missing out the nodes they feel they know. A system like this gives a learner the opportunity to work out what parts of a problem they can manage to deal with by themselves and what parts present a ZPD.

The CAID function also defines the kind of skill represented in each node. Behind this is the fact that different kinds of skills need to be taught in different ways. This information is fed into the *authoring* function, which could have templates for different types of skills and instructional environments. Today there could be screens of diagrams, pictures, animations and question formats in multimedia. Tomorrow they will include virtual realities.

When a learner selects a node in the map they are given a choice of ways to learn. For example, they can practise on a problem and see if they can work it out for themselves, or ask for an explanation of the knowledge that applies to the problem, or get a demonstration of how the knowledge can be applied to the problem.

In a system like this, the learner is receiving constant feedback on their progress, and there is a function that allows them to 'test' themselves (as distinct from practising problems) to see if they have mastered a particular skill. The results of such tests are fed into the *management* function, which is then able to organise information to show numerically or graphically the extent to which learners are successful in each skill they attempt and the extent to which the different skill nodes in a network are learned as part of learning the main outcome skill. The management function then provides feedback on the effectiveness and efficiency of the network as a whole and on the instructional effectiveness of each node in the network. It initiates an iterative process whereby the design is improved after each instructional cycle. It is in this way that it functions as an 'engine' of instruction.

This is a person–machine system like a motorcar which is driven by the learner. It is the way the learner uses the system that defines the shape it takes and what it does. The teaching function is programmed into the system by an instructional designer. Questioned by the software, the instructional designer provides the information from which the network is designed and later adapts the design in response to the feedback from the management function. This is done on the basis of professional expertise. Now let us take a system like this and add computer intelligence in the form of an expert system.

Expert systems are designed to address the relationship between knowledge and problems in a particular domain. They seek to 'capture' the expert knowledge of human specialists in the form of a chain of rules about the relationships between problems and the knowledge that can be applied to them. They also express the degree of confidence that can be given to their solutions. Expert systems can be designed so that, like any expert, they learn from their mistakes and grow more knowledgeable and more precise in their recommendations.

In the case of the instructional engine an expert system would be used to 'capture' the expertise of the instructional designer. The expertise in the form of facts and rules would be lodged in a knowledge base. An inference engine would apply this rule-based knowledge to the information from the management function in order to address questions as to how the design could be improved. Initially it could function at the level of '*if* a node is not used and *if* the final results show student results average above 90 per cent pass rate *then* remove the node from the network'. This kind of logical conclusion by the expert system, along with a statement of the degree of confidence in the advice, could be used by a human expert to support improvements in the instructional design. However, as the expert system became more expert it could take over more and more of the logic steps used in designing the instruction. It could begin to build up statistical pictures that allowed it to become increasingly precise in the way it adapted the instructional design to learner feedback.

As the expert system grew in complexity and capability there would be no reason for it to be limited to iterative designing after each cycle of instruction with each group of learners. It could begin to adjust designs to individuals as well as groups and at the level of nodes as well as networks. The ongoing adjustable design process could, therefore, be at the micro-level of the instructional node a learner is engaged in, or at the macro-level of the course as a whole. The network design of one course becomes a node in a larger network of a larger curriculum, which in turn is a node in the network of a whole subject area. Could we then think of interrelating expert systems at different fractal levels?[6]

A characteristic of expert systems is that they may not have much expertise to begin with but they have, theoretically, an infinite capacity for learning. An expert teaching system could grow up with a person, learning to adapt to the way they learn, becoming ever more expert on them and linking to and learning from other people's expert teaching systems.

All this is to view expert systems as being used to provide guidance in the development of the instruction. They could also be used to act as an 'expert' teacher to an individual learner. What would it be like to have an artificial intelligence as a teacher?

Shirley loved Woo, her wise old owl. He had been with her since she was a child. Of course in those days he looked like a cartoon. He would roost somewhere up in the right-hand corner of her CGVR and any time she raised her hand to him he would blink and look at her and be ready to help. He knew exactly where she was in her studies and that she hated to be told how to do things, preferring to try to work them out for herself, but he was so good at suggesting things she could try when she was really stuck. She got her first datasuit when she was in high school and then Woo became like a real owl. When she wanted him all she had to do was look at him and he would fly over and perch on her shoulder. His gentle whisper of encouragement and advice helped her through the bad patch when her parents divorced. It was through his guidance that she became a teacher herself. He was with her all through her time at the Trans-Pacific Teleteaching Training College. By that time she knew he was in touch with other virtual teachers. With them he organised the virtual classes, and it was through those links that he was able to advise her on how to relate to the other students with all their different cultures. Funny the shapes their virtual teachers took. The Thai student brought an elephant along with him and there was the girl from Peru with her virtual teacher as a snake coiled around her neck.

Now that she was a teacher herself old Woo was still there for her. He knew so much about her. All she had to do was whisper his name and she could feel his grip on the shoulder of her datasuit, ready to listen to the problems she was up against and look for the knowledge she needed. Trouble was when she had to lift her HMD unit off to deal with the real world. Because of the way she had distinguished herself in her finals (thanks to old Woo's wonderful coaching), she had got a very senior position teaching 3-year-olds while most of her friends from college were beginning with 17- and 18-year-olds. However, she was finding it hard going. Real reality never seemed to fit virtual reality. Take this group who had been in tears, listless and erupting into fights all morning, and refusing to dress in their datasuits. There was something she was missing. Pity Woo could not be with her in real reality. But she was sure it would work out. Woo had said he would have a word with each of their virtual teachers and pass on to them in the process some of his own experience.

Giving a virtual teacher a three-dimensional graphic and even tactile presence in this way is feasible. Bambi and Mickey Mouse are no more than animated drawings, yet children attribute human qualities to them. One of the authors designed a computer that looked like a teddy bear.[7] It could read stories and ask questions and teach children to read and write. Toys will acquire 'intelligence', and there is no reason why they cannot be used for teaching and be telepresent in CGVR. Or will the intelligence reside in the CGVR and the telepresence in the toy?

Nadia Magnenat-Thalmann, Professor of Computer Science at the University of Geneva, has been working on the development of what she calls 'virtual humanity'. Initially she was concerned with simulating virtual actors and modelling the surface appearance of the human body. She has developed a virtual Marilyn Monroe down to the detail of individual strands of hair, so that when Marilyn moves her virtual head the virtual hairs brush against one another. The virtual actress has a virtual wardrobe. When she dresses and moves, the virtual clothes swirl and fold and wrinkle of their own accord because of the properties they have. Now Nadia Magnenat-Thalmann and her researchers are modelling the behaviour as well as the appearance of virtual people. The virtual Marilyn Monroe is becoming autonomous and able to interact independently with other virtual Marilyn Monroes and a virtual Humphrey Bogard. She is ready to enter virtual reality and could, says Nadia Magnenat-Thalmann, 'be a teacher in the virtual class' (conversation July 1994).

The last part of the Shirley scenario relates to what Frederick Brooks of the University of North Carolina regards as one of the limitations of VR as an educational tool: 'Certain kinds of hyper-realistic simulations could be dangerously misleading' (Rheingold 1991: 45). There is also the danger of growing dependence on an artificial intelligence which becomes steadily more useful and knowledgeable. It is the opposite to the weaning from the teacher that takes place in traditional learning. A virtual teacher is helping learners to solve virtual problems in virtual reality. As we have seen, conventional classroom education is often guilty of divorcing the world of learning from the real world. There is a danger, as Shirley was discovering, that reliance on virtual teachers could further separate what is taught from real life. Bridging the gap between a protected learning environment like the classroom and the problems of the real world, it is preparing learners for has always been a function of the good human teacher. It is something a virtual teacher, in the last analysis, cannot really do.

The just-in-time teacher

It would be a boon to an autonomous learner if they could get a human teacher when they needed one. Increasingly that is likely to be when they are trying to solve a real-life problem with what they have learned and find it is not as straightforward as the instruction implied. One of the great strengths of the classroom system is that a learner has only to put their hand up to get a teacher's attention. The trouble is that this is only possible during class time. There is also the simple fact that some learners are uncomfortable with some teachers and do not in consequence learn from them. The focused dyadic teacher–learner relationship has affective overtones that are not dissimilar from doctor–patient relationships. Respect, trust, sincerity, confidence are important, as well as the 'treatment'.

What is needed is a network of teachers that makes it possible for learners to find the teachers they need when they need them. Instead of having to sign on for a course that approximates to what the learner wants to learn and travel to be taught in a classroom by somebody nominated by an institution, the learner can select the teacher they want, meet with them in telepresence and focus the instruction on their specific needs. There need be no restrictions on the distance to be travelled to meet a teacher. A learner can have a teacher in telepresence from anywhere in the world. Just as learners can be anywhere, so too can teleteachers. They can live where they want without the pressures of travelling to work or of conforming to the ideas, methods and timetable of an institution. Teleteachers can advertise as part of an IVANS (international value-added network service). They would make their living by virtue of their professional skills, with the world their market. We could imagine some of them as general teaching practitioners ready to diagnose basic learning needs and help where these were within their competency, but also being able to guide people to more specialist teachers when that was appropriate. The Advanced Telecommunication Research (ATR) virtual teleconferencing system could be used for this so that learner and teacher meet as telepresences in a televirtual reality with the problem under study lying in the space between them. Anybody who has ever acquired a computer knows the need they have at times to get on the telephone to someone and ask how something is done and the difficulty they then have in not being able to show the problem or see the solution.

LEVEL 3: THE SMALL GROUP

Sometime in the first decade of the next millennium it will be possible to generate a virtual version of the kind of classroom we are all familiar with. Students and teachers will be able to sit and talk with each other in telepresence and use a whiteboard or watch slides or films or read books and write as they do today in conventional classrooms. Nobuyoshi Terashima believes that the ATR virtual teleconferencing system could be adapted to this. If the classroom as we know it is the best locus for learning that we can think of, then we will be able to re-create it, endlessly, without a building programme. Nobody has to travel to get to it, and when it is not in use, it can be turned off. This, in itself, means that the idea of a computer-generated virtual class represents a solution in the near future to the problem of finding classrooms to accommodate the gigantic expansion of education predicted for the next century.

Will we really use CGVR simply to replicate the existing learning system that the conventional classroom supports, or will we use it as an opportunity for a paradigm shift in education where we re-think and re-design learning systems in their entirety? New technologies often begin by imitating the appearance of the technology they seek to supplant. The shape of things to come is in the popular imagination seen in terms of the existing way of doing things. Educational television in its early days essentially took the form of a televised teacher giving a lecture. The presentation part of a lesson was enlivened with smart graphics and film or video inserts, while the untidy interactions of a classroom were left out. ETV mistook form for function. Will a televirtual classroom simply be an electronically generated simulation of what we have now?

Conventional classrooms are built to last and are not easily changed. Creating a room with four walls and a whiteboard and some desks is an elementary exercise for a CGVR authoring system. It is difficult to think that, when teachers and learners can select and adjust the place where they learn, they will remain with images that evoke the classic classroom. Form in CGVR is infinitely malleable. The real challenge to the instructional designer of the future will be in adapting the functionality of CGVR to the functionality of instruction without the mindset of the conventional classroom.

The ATR prototype can accommodate three people at the time of writing, but Nobuyoshi Terashima says that in the future there will be no limits to the numbers who can meet in telepresence. A successful tele-teacher who has a number of telelearners might suggest that they meet synchronously as a small group for a teletutorial, or as a slightly larger group for a teleseminar or an even larger group for a teleclass.

The teachers and the other students a learner meets as telepresences in CGVR are unlikely to be the same people as those a learner meets in a conventional school. What draws them together is that they have a common interest in a subject rather than the accident of living in the same schooling zone. Rheingold argues that virtual communities develop their own cultures (1993). They could be very different people from very different backgrounds and places, but this does not have to be apparent because they meet as telepresences. They can choose to be who or what they want other people to think they are. A paper on virtual communities in Japan reported on the habit of cross-dressing, where community members might represent themselves as someone of the opposite sex or of a different age (Aoki 1994: 202–20). Perhaps in a virtual orchestral class learners will present themselves as their musical instruments or in a virtual history seminar as personages from the time under study.

There is no need for learners to be together through the day in a CGVR class. The system is flexible. Learners can study autonomously, they can study with a virtual teacher, they can study together as pairs or in small groups. Teachers can join them as telepresences for one-on-one tuition or teachers and learners can meet as a group in a virtual class. What we see here is a technology that can address the fractal levels in learning. A learner can use the technology to slip between levels. They can act as their own teacher or they can get help from an artificial teaching entity. If this is not working or if they prefer to learn with other people, then the learner can shift levels and work with a peer or teacher to intermesh the four factors of instruction. Or they can move up to yet another level of complexity and try to intermesh the four factors with a large group of learners and teachers. In a televirtual class this may mean trying to intermesh the learner, teacher, knowledge and problem factors with a variety of people from different places, different countries, different cultures who have in common an interest in learning how to apply knowledge to a particular problem domain, but approach it from different perspectives.[8] We could at this level be looking at very large numbers of people indeed and an intermesh-ing of learners, teachers, knowledge and problems at levels of complexity beyond anything that currently exists in conventional educational and training systems.

LEVEL 4: THE LARGE INSTITUTION

Carl Eugene Loeffler is Project Director of Telecommunications and Virtual Reality at the Studio for Creative Inquiry in Carnegie Mellon University. He is building a virtual city on Internet. He calls it the Virtual Polis.[9] To access it from Internet will require an HMD unit and some special software. Theoretically it could be a virtual mega-city accessible to millions of people. It is a three-dimensional networked virtual reality with high-rise buildings, private domiciles and a park. You can move about in it as a telepresence and meet with the telepresences of other people. You can buy a plot and build a virtual house or rent or purchase existing virtual houses, apartments or shops. You can set up your own business and advertise it – on virtual billboards. Shopping and entertainment, as in any metropolis, are seen as major functions that will attract a lot of people. Carl Loeffler is a visionary who sees his Polis as having many aspects. It could be viewed, he believes, as a graphic user interface (GUI) for home-based electronic shopping and entertainment. He also sees it as an experiment in tele-existence. If so, then it will need a university to research and teach what is learned in tele-existence about tele-existence. Beside the park at one side of downtown Polis there could be spires and a clock tower indicating that there is a university.

Shirley had just joined UTE, the University of Tele-existence (see cover illustration). There were no conditions, other than the fee which allowed her to use the facilities. Getting on to courses was another matter. It all depended on the professors, how many students they accepted, what they expected in a student, how much they charged and of course whether you really wanted to study with them. After all, just as anyone could be a student, anyone could offer a course and run it any way they wanted and charge what they wanted. She had heard that some courses were really Mickey Mouse and was surprised the university let teachers get away with it. But then again it was up to the learner to choose what was worth doing, and the open policy of letting learners and teachers find their own levels had, everyone agreed, resulted in some brilliant innovations in teaching. One thing about surfing the net. Word always got out about the courses. There was a system she had heard about where groups of students who really wanted to study a particular topic or learn about the ideas of a particular person would hire someone to teach them, paying whatever they needed to.

She stood in the quad watching the patterns the telepresences made with the colours of their gowns. Each colour signified a field of interest, so there would be clusters of people with the same colour all arguing with one another, and blinking on and off as they came and went. Of course you did not have to use a gown and a lot of the students did not when they were downtown, but the tradition was that if you were in the quad in your colours you were ready to debate with anyone.

Whoever designed the VR for the quad had poetic vision. She loved the way the fractal trees would take on the colour of the group near them and begin to rustle their dimensions with the heat of an argument.

There was a reassuring link with tradition in the shapes of the four towering buildings on each side of the quad. Each one was dedicated to the founding factors on which the university was based; learners, teachers, knowledge and problems.

Pointing at the Building of Knowledge, she flew up to its great rotunda and looked around at the giant mappa mundi *of knowledge about tele-existence and virtual reality. UTE was there in the centre with the world's biggest collection of virtual realities. Some benefactor had had the wisdom to foresee the need to begin collecting from the beginning. The other parts of the map showed the known territory of other collections of information and knowledge in different media that were allied or related to the field of tele-existence and virtual reality. Most of them could be accessed through Internet, but these days networking knowledge was like using the underground. You were always having to change networks and it was expensive. What was really fascinating was the* terra incognita *at the periphery of the map which was continuously updated as rumours came in of new developments in CGVR. Then there was the land claimed by researchers as they opened up new territory and staked their claims. To see the whole domain of a subject laid out on a 'live' map that was endlessly developing was exciting, and all she had to do to find out more about something was to box it with her finger and, like a Mandelbrot set, it would show another knowledge map at another level of detail. You could search and explore until you found the knowledge you wanted and downloaded it for study.*

It was also possible to use the system to find an expert in a field, or someone who shared your interests. There was always a group of people in the rotunda looking at the mappa *and gossiping about the rumours and who was doing what. You could tell from the colours they wore and the direction of their gaze what interested them. Soon she was talking to what she knew from the shape of his gown was a second-year student who shared her interest in the effects of tele-existence on children. Before long the conversation switched to what was happening in the Place of Problems.*

The Place of Problems was where research was done. The special methodology for which UTE was famous was the designing and developing of virtual reality case studies of problems. Of course the University of North Carolina at Chapel Hill had been one of the first with their VR simulacra of molecules, but it was the success of the UTE soil erosion virtual reality that had really started the ball rolling. It had been adopted by so many different fields of study from geography to agriculture, earth sciences to ecological studies. What had really legitimised it as a research technique in universities was the way new research results and data could be integrated to make the virtual reality more detailed, realistic and accurate. When someone tried to incorporate discordant data, the anomaly it presented showed up at once. On one famous occasion this had led to tremendous debate. As a result there had been a fundamental revision of the conventional model of soil erosion.

Shirley found it difficult to understand the relation between the Place of Problems and the Building of Knowledge. The second-year student explained that the construction of a simulacrum of a problem generated a field of study of the problem. Because it was often a new way of looking at the problem, it led to new ideas as to how to deal with the problem. So the study of problems led to new knowledge and the CGVRs developed in the Place of Problems finished up in the Building of Knowledge. A lot of the virtual realities that were created to study problems, the student said, were now being used as settings for virtual classes. In some cases the virtual realities incorporated instructional assistance. He described a language lab VR he had used for learning Japanese where you could be in a room, shop or street in Japan. If you pointed at an object you would hear its name spoken and virtual people would speak a few lines if you looked at them.

It would be more fun, thought Shirley, to do that in telepresence with someone of her own age from Japan. She recalled the time she had played Hamlet and wondered about doing drama with students in telepresence. Then she thought of being a medical student and having a class inside a virtual reality of a human heart or skull. That in turn brought to mind what she had heard about the research and teaching in telerobo-presence. Apparently it was possible to telepresence in micro-robotic devices using the kind of conventional interface system that got you into Polis. When she asked the other student about this he said that he was doing a course in marine biology and driving micro-subs. It went back to the old PC flight simulators. After they filmed Gibson's story 'Dogfight' everyone was into robo-flying tiny drones, which were replicas of vintage aircraft. The technique had been adapted to other fields. In biology they were using robo-ants to observe micro-ecologies and robo-owls to study nightlife. He did not notice that Shirley had suddenly become lost in thought and carried on. His teacher had just arranged for him to access a micro-sub at the Australian Institution of Marine Science in Queensland so that he could do a paper on the Great Barrier Reef. Would she like to tele-experience with him when he took it out to see the coral spawn at full moon in November?

Entry to the Place of Problems was restricted. Shirley learned she needed to be registered with the human ethics committee and be part of a research programme before she could get a password that would let her access any of the research in progress. She moved with her new friend to the Learners' Locus. As they drifted through its peculiar portals Shirley was startled to find herself looking into something like an atrium without any top or bottom to it. Around the sides were corridors and stairs that reminded her of an Escher picture (probably where the idea comes from, said her friend) and rooms from which came music and shouts of welcome. Telepresences were floating up or sinking down the atrium, and Shirley and her companion joined them and tried to make sense of all the flags and banners and strange creatures which hung around the rooms they drifted past. It was open day for student societies, special interest groups, protest groups and trend-setters. Her friend explained that they could as easily find out about the different groups from a conventional bulletin board. 'But,' he smiled, 'students go to a university to meet students as well as study, even if we are all telepresences.' And he nodded to what appeared to be Napoleon standing on a balcony and frowning at the shapes that drifted past. 'This place,' he said, watching her, 'is also for showing off simulacra designed and authored by students.' At that moment Napoleon took his hand out of his jacket and the arm suddenly became 5 metres long as it reached out to her. She laughed and shook it, at which the hand detached itself and politely said: 'Here's a helping hand to join the History Society.'

Shirley enjoyed herself in the atrium, joined a couple of societies, and then said goodbye to her new friend. As they swapped E-mail addresses she was fascinated to find that he lived in Bolivia.

Before she left the campus, Shirley wanted to visit the Towers of Teaching. She moved back into the quad first and was delighted to find that the VR was programmed to have a day. It was now early evening and there seemed as many people as ever, but then she remembered UTE stayed open all the time and was available to anybody from any country. Lights were coming on and the last of the sun was touching the tops of the towers. Was it true, she wondered, that the taller the tower in which the great teaching dons had their chambers, the higher the esteem in which they were held? Anybody could teach at UTE, but few survived for long if they did not establish a reputation. The ones who had the rights to rooms in those towers were legends. They did not have to worry about fancy new teaching techniques. Some of them preferred to hold old-fashioned lectures. Well, she supposed, they were not just passing on knowledge like junior lecturers. They had something to say, so perhaps they should say it in the way that they wanted. She pointed at the imposing entrance to the towers and triggered herself into a VR that was, with its oak walls and balustraded staircase and the faintest of choral renderings of 'Gaudeamus igitur', the very epitome of a grand old university. She entered the great lecture theatre – a masterpiece of CGVR authoring; so detailed it seemed more real than the real thing. Yet it could never be filled, there was never a shortage of seats with a clear view and the sound was always crystal clear, however feeble the speaker's real voice. Even the great screen, which could be for a film or a portal to another virtual reality, when not in use looked just like an old blackboard.

She moved back to the quad where there was a large crowd of telepresences watching a performance of virtual music. A full moon ivoried the towers of teaching. It was the balance, she mused as she lifted off her HMD unit and savoured the heat of the midday sun. It was the special balance of the traditional and the new that made for a great university. That and keeping up appearances.

Chapter 9

Think global

. . . to seek, receive and impart information and ideas through any media and regardless of any frontier.
>Article 19 of the Universal Declaration of Human Rights, 1948

. . . signs point to the emergence of a worldwide electronic university.
>(Rossman 1992: 1)

It is technically feasible to have a virtual learning environment created by computer-mediated communications where learners can exist as tele-presences. In Chapter 6, we saw that a protean environment for virtual classes is already beginning to emerge. In Chapter 8 we looked at some of the forms the virtual class could take in the near and distant future. The question this chapter addresses is, what are the factors that are likely to determine the development and adoption of the virtual class as industrial societies become information societies?

TELECOMMUNICATIONS VERSUS TRANSPORT

The virtual class uses telecommunications instead of transport to bring the four factors of instruction together. There are some obvious advantages to this. Telecommunications do not contribute to traffic jams or cause pollution. Telestudents do not have to wait for buses or strap-hang in metros, nor do they need cars and car parks. However, there is a difference between commuting across a city and a healthy 20-minute walk. Many tertiary-level students live on a campus and many schoolchildren are within easy walking distance of their schools. Travelling to a classroom is not necessarily a problem.

The catchment areas of primary schools are usually small and the distance their students travel to school may not be a problem. Secondary schools have larger catchment areas and transport problems for their students are more likely. However, it is at a tertiary level that the distance between where people live and work and where they go to study may become a serious matter for many students. Universities offer a wide variety of specialist subjects which attract people from around the world. Of course, students who travel long distances to study on a campus will normally live on or close to the campus during their course of study, but this means they have residential as well as travel costs. It is people seeking tertiary education who are most likely to have travel problems, but students of any age group can have travel problems if they live in remote places or are disabled, house-bound or incarcerated. Therefore, it is in distance education and tertiary education that the development of the virtual class-room is likely to make its first advances. However, in time it will affect everyone's way of learning.

Even if going to a school is only a 5-minute walk, it does not mean that the school can teach all the subjects and skills that an individual learner wants. Today, people accept limitations on what they learn because of where they live. The virtual class opens the possibility that any learner, no matter where they are, could be put in touch with any teacher, in any area of knowledge, that addresses any problem domain. Although conven-tional classes will continue for some things, they will co-exist with virtual classes.

Are telecommunications costs really becoming less than those of trans-port? Today telecommunications costs tend to be artificially high and transport costs artificially low. Governments subsidise transport systems and perpetuate an industrial society, while telecommunications companies which often have a monopoly, make handsome profits, as the user pays. Moreover, telecommunications costs are distorted. Long-distance calls cost considerably more than local calls. To a transport-based mindset this makes sense. The greater the distance, the more we expect to pay for using telecommunications. However, this may not reflect the cost to the tele-phone company. The cost of a satellite link on an international call that spans the world is a tiny fraction of the actual cost of an international call, and if a satellite is used it does not matter whether the transmitting and receiving dishes are 10 metres or 10,000 kilometres apart. It is the ground system at the local level that is expensive. Many countries enhance the distortion by subsidising free local calls from long-distance charges. If there were to be a genuine level playing-field for transport to compete with telecommunications then it would be relatively expensive to use tele-communications over short distances, but relatively inexpensive over long distances. The greater the distance, the greater the economy of using telecommunications.

In the long term, fibre optics will reach most of the homes in an information society and accessing satellite communications could continue to become increasingly simple and inexpensive. The difference between local and international calls is diminishing as competition grows and as satellite technology presents an alternative to terrestrial systems where distance will not matter. As this happens it becomes of little concern where a person is when they are using telecommunications. This makes possible what could well be the biggest difference between the conventional classroom and the virtual class. Transport systems such as roads, railways, shipping and airways respect national boundaries. Immigration and customs barriers can be erected across roads and railways and at airports and wharf sides. Information does not need customs or passport formalities to cross borders. Transport-based conventional classes are organised nationally. The virtual class, because it uses telecommunications, can be global.

THE GLOBAL EDUCATIONAL UTILITY

Denis Gooler described the National Utilities Corporation's concept of an educational utility thus:

> The education utility consists of a massive and dynamic reservoir of information and educational programming, from which individual teachers and learners can select the information and education resources they wish to work with, and when. The appropriate information can be transmitted via a state network in an economical manner to the school or site requesting the information.
>
> (Gooler 1986: 18)

There are echoes of educational television in the idea that providing information is the answer and that such technologies are levers to get schools back on their feet. However, Gooler looks beyond schools to the way such a network can provide knowledge in homes and become international. What is interesting is the way he uses a water utility as a metaphor for an educational utility, with the idea of some reservoir from which knowledge flows that can be turned on like a tap as a basic part of civilised life.

We prefer the metaphor of the electrical utility. This was first developed to bring electric lighting. Then it became a universal source of power for such things as heaters, fridges, stoves and radios. It became a norm to put plugs in homes so that people could plug in any device that worked with electricity. Because of this, more and more devices were powered by electricity. Part of the basic infrastructure of an industrial society is its power grid. Progress, as a civilised society, is having electricity available anywhere, any time and at reasonable cost for all citizens.

Telecommunications were first set up to provide telephone and telegraph services, but they have now begun to serve other information needs. It is becoming standard to put jackpoints in rooms so that people can jack-in information devices such as computer modems, fax machines and security systems as well as telephones. In the future, in an information society, information will be available anywhere, any time, like electricity. It will be possible to telephone microwave units to have a meal ready by a certain time. Fridges will be able to telephone a store when they are short of butter or bacon. A crib will get in touch with a parent to say the baby is awake or not well. The plain old telephone system is becoming an information utility. But there is something further. It is possible for a third party to use a telecommunications system to provide some special service that adds to the value of the basic telecommunications service. Examples of these are E-mail services and telebanking. They are called 'Value-Added Network Services' (VANS). Education could be a VANS.

VANS can operate at international levels when they are called an 'international value-added network service' (IVANS). If a point is reached where there is little difference between international and national tele-communications costs, then the way is open for global competition between providers of network services. The issue of free trade in informa-tion services is of growing concern in discussions on General Agreements on Tariffs and Trade (GATT) and in the newly formed World Trade Organisation (WTO). The superhighway telecommunications systems of the future could allow free international trade in telebanking, telemedicine or teletranslation services. It could also mean free trade in telelearning as an IVANS.

THE COMMERCIALISATION OF EDUCATION

Who will pay for a virtual educational system, the state or the user? The neo-liberal economics that have become the dominant paradigm for so much of the world over the last decades of this century has meant that the provision of education as a 'public good' paid for through taxation is challenged. There is an argument for placing education on a user-pays basis and deregulating educational institutions so that they can vie for the educational dollar of students who then become their clients. This trend is especially manifest in tertiary education, which is also the level at which the virtual class makes most sense.

Advances in science and technology mean that, increasingly, industrial processes are knowledge-based and -driven (Renwick 1984, cited in Bigum and Green 1992: 213). Workers have to maintain their employability by constantly renewing their knowledge and skills. Human resources develop-ment is coming to be regarded as a political imperative for national economic survival. In many parts of the world governments find them-selves facing two contending trends as to how to be competitive in a global economy while at the same time ensuring the social and cultural well-being of the people who vote for them. Where economies are market-driven, anything that cannot be measured in terms of profit and loss tends to be marginalised or discounted. But much about education does not lend itself to measurement in quantifiable terms (Marginson 1993). Economists and policy makers have as much difficulty conceptualising the cost benefits of an educated citizenry as they have the cost benefits of a healthy citizenry.

In the current environment this means pitching technological visions against educational Utopias. Education as a branch of economic policy, driven by the profit motive, subject to open market competition and paid for by a demanding user is placed against education as a mix of social and cultural policy, concerned with equal opportunity and the preservation of national culture and local ways of life. The titles of this chapter and the next one are taken from Buckminster Fuller's challenge to think globally and act locally. It implies that the two perspectives are not inconsistent with each other and can be complementary. As economies increasingly become global, issues such as environmental destruction require global collaboration.

In an information society there is a demand for knowledge workers with internationally competitive skills. There is a rapidly expanding market of people around the world who want tertiary-level education that gives them an economic edge. This is a market of people who are prepared to pay for an education that is convenient to access and want qualifications that will make them professionals in an international sense. It is this end of the educational spectrum that conventional classroom-based education is failing. It is here that the global utilities based on the virtual class would seem to have most to offer. However, if educational purposes are too tightly linked to economic policies and market forces they will become narrowly utilitarian. Countries will lose the goals of education to develop citizens with social and cultural skills as well as work skills.

As Strike, the American philosopher of education, points out, in a society which distributes its goods by a free market system, fairness in competition consists in part in ensuring that the opportunity to acquire a marketable talent is not achieved by social rank. Fair competition requires equal opportunity to acquire the means of competition (Strike 1982: 184). Without cultural and social skills, community life would become barbaric; without sports and the arts, life would be uncivilised. These are areas which may be better taught in community classrooms that bring together people who live in the same locality.

There has to be a balance. Parker Rossman compares the development of global educational utilities at the university level with the international concept of the university that existed in the Middle Ages (1992: xii). We need to remember that for the vast majority of the people who lived in Europe in the Middle Ages and could not afford an education, life was nasty, short and brutish. The commercialisation of education needs to be a way of reducing educational costs so that educational utilities are within the reach of 'anyone, anywhere'.

ECONOMIES OF SCALE

Adding more classrooms and adding teachers to an educational system does not achieve economies of scale. Because of this, governments look in dismay at growing demands for education. By contrast, the virtual class scenario makes economies of scale possible. There are no limits to the size of virtual lecture theatres, no costs for building, maintaining, cleaning, lighting and ventilating virtual class spaces. However, this has to be compared to the costs of an interface device so that teachers and learners can access virtual classes. As we have seen, this could take several shapes such as a PC, a head-mounted display unit in the form of a pair of spectacles or a datasuit. Whatever it is, the costs of computer-based equipment, like the costs of software and courseware, is volume-dependent. As long as the numbers of people using virtual classes are small the costs will be high, but when millions of students around the world are using the technology, the costs per capita will be low. The way the prices of PCs and their software drops as the market for them grows world-wide is an indication of what could happen.

Getting the mass markets in education that will bring about economies of scale will depend upon the quality of instruction being better than that which is possible in classrooms. With millions of paying students it becomes possible to invest in courseware development, hunt out the latest research, find the best authorities on a subject, contract top instructional designers and create imaginative virtual realities of the phenomena under study. With the incentive of global markets, we could imagine knowledge-based companies investing in the design, development and marketing of virtual environments for education in an information society in the way that the giants of the automotive industry now invest in motorcar manufacturing for the industrial society. How could a conventional teacher with conventional resources compete?

There is no evidence that, as the years go by, the quality of what happens in classrooms progressively improves. Teachers can learn from experience and improve their performance, but when they retire there is no process of osmosis whereby they can pass on their experience so that new teachers can begin where their predecessors left off. By contrast, the iterative principles of instructional design do permit progressive improvement of instruction. The feedback from one cycle of instruction can be built into the design for the next, and the design can be held in a computer memory and endlessly improved in the manner described in Chapter 8.

Is this to do to learning what McDonald's did to eating? Are we talking about 'hamburgerising' how we teach and franchising the facilitation of education? Where skills and knowledge are not embedded in a cultural matrix, as for example in mathematics and science, why not develop instruction as a product that is easy to deliver and digest and appeals to the taste of learners around the world? So far the goal has proved elusive. Attempts to globalise instruction such as Plato, the computer-based learning system, and *Sesame Street*, the educational television system, have had some success but not the kind of take-off that we see on the Internet.

There are other economies of scale. Teachers are the biggest single item of expenditure in any conventional educational systems. However, in the virtual class a teacher is not responsible for looking after children as well as teaching them. The principle of a teacher acting *in loco parentis* which ties teachers to being present with their charges even when they are not involved in instruction does not apply in the virtual class. By contrast, we look at the idea of JIT teachers, who are only involved when they are needed. Many of the tedious automatic functions such as taking registers or correcting spellings and sums can be automated. Some of the lower-level functions in instruction will become computer functions. Such factors as these and the development of virtual teachers could mean a progressive reduction in the proportion of time a learner is in need of a human teacher.

Another major expense in conventional classroom learning is its dependence on paper as a storage medium. The cost of paper is going up. The cost of computer-based storage is going down. Books are already being published on the Internet. CGVR can subsume text and has the potential to improve on the page format of books just as the codex improved on scrolls. People have a deep affection for paper pages, but the barbaric habit of felling forests to feed our reading habits is a luxury that the planet may not be able to sustain for much longer.

Large groups of people in conventional classrooms require toilets, recreation space, somewhere to eat, health facilities, emergency facilities, places to leave their clothes, bicycles and cars. The idea of an educational utility will have much appeal at the tertiary level, where people can substitute study at home or at their workplace for the classroom. This may reduce the cost of instruction at a tertiary level, but at secondary and primary levels, where parents are likely to be at work, the need for the custodial function in education remains.

Schools and colleges have sports fields, theatres, gardens and buildings. These contribute to a sense of community. They also cost money. How can a spirit of collegiality be engendered in a virtual educational institution? Chapter 8 suggested that it will be possible to create educational institutions as elaborate virtual realities in which imagination can be set loose to shape an educational environment that is a dynamic manifestation of the mind and the creativity of the people who inhabit it in telepresence rather than a static legacy of the past.

Whether an educational institution exists in the real world or in cyberspace, it needs management and an administration. This is especially the case in tertiary education. Virtual educational institutions will still need management and administration for overall planning, policy development, curriculum concerns and responding to feedback from teachers and learners. There may be some new functions, such as marketing, cultural issues and technology design and implementation. However, many of the current administrative functions would vanish. There would be no need to manage and administer the use of space. The buildings committee, the garden committee, the parking committee, the people responsible for fires and emergencies could all go. In a networked environment many basic administrative acts, such as registration, are automated. There is no need to worry about returning electronic library books on time, no giant timetable problem finding classrooms for classes. A virtual educational entity could have as many virtual classes as anybody could ever need and they could take any shape, size or form the teacher or the student wants.

TEACHERS AND THE VIRTUAL CLASS

Stewart Brand describes how, when he was writing his book on the media lab at MIT, he E-mailed its director, Nicholas Negroponte, to ask, 'When you are on the road, who runs the Lab?' Three hours later he got an answer: 'The fact that I am replying to you from Japan two hours after your question from California, somewhat begs the question. The lab doesn't know I am gone' (Brand 1988: 24).

University professors are already becoming teleworkers in some countries. They cluster their face-to-face activities such as teaching, tutorials and attending committees so that they have time to themselves for marking, preparing lectures and doing research. Increasingly they are doing this from home. All they need is a telephone, fax machine and a PC with a modem. What is triggering this trend is Internet and the new generation of portable PCs which allow work to be picked up and taken anywhere. As yet universities do not quite know how to react to this. Most universities and colleges are creatures of the industrial revolution and see work as what is done at a workplace during work hours. In consequence, the advantages of teachers teleworking, like the advantages of students tele-learning, are yet to be widely perceived. It is a brave educational institution that solves its space problems by giving its academics a portable PC with modem and telling them to double up on offices and parking lots by time sharing and teleworking.

The application of information technology in many fields has led to unemployment. Will this happen to teaching? If the educational process becomes a commercial one there will be pressure to down-size the number of teachers. Such pressures exist in countries adopting New Right economics and seeking ways to reduce the budget for education. On the other hand, there is a growing market for education, and the custodial function of schools will mean that primary and secondary teachers will work in a conventional manner for a long time. It is at the tertiary level and in distance-independent education that the demand for teleteachers seems likely to expand at first.

The pattern of work for teleteachers and the way they are remunerated could be very different from those of traditional teachers. We have suggested that teleteachers could be more like doctors, available when needed and selected by learners because of the quality of their teaching. Market forces would be at play. Good teachers in high demand could charge accordingly. Poor teachers would lack business. The pressure would be heightened by trends towards intelligent, computer-based instruction. We have already formulated the logic by which this could develop and suggested the idea of virtual teachers in virtual learning institutions. For many years there has been a shibboleth when speaking of the application of information technology to education that says the teacher can never be replaced by a machine. We hope that will prove true for many years to come, but the application of artificial intelligence to computer-based instruction will mean that much of what teachers do will be replaced by information technology. Hopefully, this means that the boring, mundane aspects of teaching, such as marking, spelling, checking sums and registers, will be done by technology, freeing teachers to deal with the subtleties and nuances of their professional transactions. However, there is a disturbing trend in the applications of information technology for any resulting growth in employment to be at the lower levels of activity. It has been suggested that there is only one aspect of a supermarket that still defeats attempts at automation, and that is bagging the goods bought. Will the future for the teacher be as the ultimate source of knowledge and wisdom or as wetware devices that help children blow their noses and tie their shoelaces?

THE FLOW OF NEW KNOWLEDGE

Coombs saw the biggest problem in education as the slow trickle down of new knowledge through the system. If the virtual class can resolve this problem it will have an enormous advantage, especially at the tertiary level. We had an insight into this issue in one of our experimental telelearning projects which linked three telecentres for a graduate diploma course.[1]

We had intended to link centres that were similar. Instead we got three very different centres; our university, a rural community polytechnic college whose principal[2] wanted it included because of a belief in rural equity of access to education, and an intermediate school whose headmaster[3] wanted his staff to be prepared for the future. This headmaster explained that teachers could not take time off to travel to attend classes, but he could organise the timetable so that they could leave their classes and slip down the corridor to become students in their turn, using the school's teleconferencing facilities. In the second year of the project, the University of Hawaii's Department of Communications also joined the project and seminars became rich with the tele-involvement of researchers at an international level. Teleseminars on the applications of CGVR to education would include people like Meredith Bricken and John Bowes of Washington State University discussing their state-of-the-art research on virtual reality to students who, at the University of Hawaii, were from six different countries and in New Zealand from remote rural communities or straight out of a class of primary-school children.

It was here that we made a serendipitous discovery. We found that our students were walking out of their teleclasses into their own classes and directly applying what they themselves had learned. In the space of a few minutes learners became teachers. We had short-circuited the slow trickle down of knowledge. Obviously, the primary school teachers did not go back to their classrooms and start to use virtual reality. What was more important was that, in their words, they looked at their classroom with different eyes. They began to think of what effect CGVR would have on primary education, how their role would change, what it would mean to go to school in the future, and they began to talk to their students about virtual reality. They were mediating what they were learning for their students and beginning to think through a technological change before the technology arrived. Contrast this to the incitement to Luddism that goes with the arbitrary introduction of new technology in schools when staff are expected to adapt after its arrival. The bureaucracies of educational systems may impose, but in the classroom the teacher still rules, and if the teacher's mind and heart is not in an innovation, it will not work. One of the most exciting things about teleteaching is that it gives a sense of participation, it allows group involvement and discussion. We found that it was not just our students (the primary teachers) who were attending at the primary-school centre. The subject matter was discussed in homes and parents began to sit in on our teleclasses. Knowledge was also being rapidly devolved to the community the school served.

TECTONIC SHIFT

Arthur Brian examines a new economic theory which describes mechanisms whereby small chance events early in the history of an industry or technology can tilt the competitive balance. He argues against conventional economic theory which is built on the assumption of diminishing returns where negative feedback tends to stabilise the economy, achieve equilibrium and make the most efficient use and allocation of resources. Brian suggests that in many parts of an economy stabilising forces may not always operate. Instead, positive feedback magnifies the effects of small economic shifts. Increasing returns economics, as it is called, has strong parallels with modern nonlinear physics as described in chaos theory which, Brian suggests, could be the appropriate theory for understanding modern high-technology economies. He argues that while resource-based economies such as agriculture, bulk-goods production and mining are subject to diminishing returns and hence to conventional economics, economies that are knowledge-based are subject to increasing returns. This is because, unlike material resources, information is infinitely renewable (Brian 1990). Could it then be argued that the virtual class, because it offers positive feedback in the economy, would generate increasing returns?

To extrapolate from Brian's argument, if the virtual class is considered as an increasing returns economy then the measurement of its cost-effectiveness should be modelled on dynamic processes based on non-linear, random-process theory. This seems to make sense, because the use of the new technologies in education is neither predictable nor mechanistic. It is process-driven, dynamic and evolving, and it may take a relatively trivial unpredictable event that would seem to have little direct bearing on the matter to precipitate exponential expansion.

In January 1994 a non-trivial earthquake hit Los Angeles. Angelenos are famous for their car culture. They are locked into a pattern of behaviour where they even use the car for taking the dog for a walk. But after the earthquake, people living in LA were no longer anxious to hit the freeways. A surge in teleworking was reported (Bonfante 1994: 31) and, as we have seen, teleworking and telelearning are closely related. Angelenos by all accounts are drifting back to their old habits, but one day an event like this could trigger the tectonic forces that are mounting in education.

Chapter 10

Act local

. . . To make of learning the joy of discovery.

(School prayer)

When the technology itself grows powerful enough to make the illusions increasingly realistic . . . the necessity for continuing to question reality grows more acute.

(Rheingold 1993: 229)

The serpent speaks . . .
'She did not know then that imagination is the beginning of creation. You imagine what you desire; you will what you imagine; and at last you create what you will.'

(G. B. Shaw, *Back to Methuselah*, Part I, Act I)

The ancient Sumerians did not build schools to teach people to read and write just so that they could tally sacks of grain. They have left ample evidence in the form of stories and poems that education was entry to virtual worlds of the mind. Since they first began to paint on cave walls, people have been able to switch their state of consciousness from real reality to virtual reality. Education has been a way of initiating the young into the virtual realities of their culture and helping them understand its relationship to real reality.

The extent to which people live in virtual reality could be increasing. Anybody who spends 3 to 4 hours a day in front of television is spending a quarter of their waking lives in that virtual reality. To this, add the time spent reading newspapers, magazines and books, listening to the radio, trips to the cinema and theatre, talking about things that are not present and plain old-fashioned day dreaming, and it is not difficult to accept that many people spend most of the time they are conscious in virtual reality. And then, of course, there are the dream worlds of sleep. The question addressed in this chapter concerns the time we spend in real reality. How is it affected by the kind of virtual realities we experience?

We may learn to think at a global level, but how does that affect the way we act in the locality in which we live?

Harold Innis argued that the media that people used determined the kind of society they live in. That medium, such as stone or clay or wood, was 'time-binding'. Because it was heavy and difficult to move it held people in one place and encouraged traditions of preserving and passing down knowledge in a culture that was locked into a location by its media. By contrast, paper – which he called a space-binding medium, because it could be easily transported – facilitated communication across distance and encouraged societies to expand territorially (Innis 1950). Innis was mentor to Marshall McLuhan, who foresaw that the expansion of telecommunications technology would create a world-wide network of information which would lead to a global village. McLuhan argued that the dominant media affect the way people see the world. Therefore, oral cultures are different from print cultures and radio cultures from television cultures. This was one reason for his idea of the global village because he saw telecommunications as oral and as bringing back the traditions of the oral culture of the village on a world scale (McLuhan and Fiore 1967). What he did not foresee was that telecommunications would also create a world-wide net of the written word, the spoken word, the visual world and a world in which people could meet in a telepresence. This he would have perceived as crucial, because he believed that media were extensions of the senses. So the book was an extension of the eye, clothing an extension of the skin and electric circuitry an extension of the central nervous system (McLuhan 1964). The idea is strangely prescient of virtual reality.

McLuhan argued that the dominant media profoundly affected people's perception of reality (1964). In other words, we interpret real reality in terms of our virtual realities, and our virtual realities are constrained by the media in which they are generated. In this sense, McLuhan draws an important distinction between 'hot' and 'cool' media (1964). Hot media are those that make it possible to spell out a message in a very complete way. A film is a hot medium because it is explicit, and shows in sound and image exactly what is taking place. It is a virtual reality that requires little imaginative participation by the perceiver. McLuhan believed that 'hot media' led to passivity in people. Cool media, by contrast, leaves a lot to the imagination. Radio is a cool medium, it requires people to make their own pictures. Cool media provide cues that enable people to generate their own virtual realities. Marshall McLuhan would have regarded virtual reality as a hot medium, becoming hotter as it becomes more immersive, more comprehensive and more detailed. George Gerbner and his research associates argued that heavy viewing of television distorts people's view of reality so that they are more likely to see the real world in terms of the values and events of television (1986). What will heavy use of virtual reality do to our view of the world? What will we do when we use it, not just for entertainment or information, but for learning?

In this chapter, we are looking at the balance between virtual reality and real reality in a world which may not be too far away where the dominant medium could be teleCGVR reality. In doing this we take the perspective of Innis and McLuhan that there is a profound relationship between the media of virtual reality and real reality. However, we go a step further because we are looking at the part played by education in this balance between the two realities. Education is a process where learners are taught to apply knowledge to problems in virtual reality as well as in real reality. In addition, education is a process of ensuring that such learned capabilities are retained. It is not a flow of information the user can take or leave as they please. Societies seek through education to ensure that its members see the real world in terms of its virtual realities. In the future this moulding will not be something that takes place in childhood and earlier adolescence to prepare people for a relatively static society. It will be a lifelong process in which people are expected to be plastic, moulded and remoulded many times to adjust to the quickening pace of change.

In 1987 one of the authors was doing a case study of a technical correspondence institution to look at how in the future it could change from being based primarily on print and postal services to being based primarily on computers and telecommunications services. While she was struggling with evidence that suggested that postal services might diminish in the future, a large number of post offices in rural areas which the institutions served were closed down. The transfer from a transport system to a telecommunications system become inevitable even while the possibility was being studied. In the year in which this book was written, the Internet doubled the number of its users, twice. Al Gore made the idea of superhighways of information something that everyone could see, and the development of telecommuting, telebanking and teleshopping began to accelerate. Things that we described as possibilities when we started writing were realities by the time we came to this chapter. The pace of change is accelerating. The information society comes on apace. Computers are beginning to enter people's homes at the rate that telephones, radios and televisions did in the past and they are acquiring sound and video. They can be used to fax as well as E-mail, to videophone and videoconference. We no longer need to communicate with them by typing; we are starting to talk to them and listen to them. It is not just the computer that is becoming multimedia, so too are the telecommunications networks. The race is on for the magic device that pulls all the elements together and puts them in the hands of the general public.

It becomes hard to imagine the kind of world 5-year-olds entering school today will find when they leave it ten or fifteen years from now.

Shirley lifted her helmet off and took a deep breath. She felt a bit hot and sticky and desperately needed to go to the bathroom. There were some things, she thought, you still couldn't do in virtual reality. She decided to have a shower at the same time. 'Needlespray,' she said to the shower, which, recognising her voice, switched itself on to the temperature she liked best. As she was drying off, the bathroom told her that there was a message from her mother to say she was on standby with Teletourism, one of the companies for which she did part-time work. The bathroom also added that her urine analysis showed her consumption of sugar was up and this corresponded to a rapid increase in weight over the last week. 'Oh, shut up,' she said crossly, and the bathroom meekly said, 'Yes Shirley' and shut itself off. She put on a tracksuit and her helmet, and left the house just as a hover carrier drew up. It gave a sigh as it lost air pressure and sank down while it deposited some groceries that the fridge had ordered. Then with a hiss, the carrier picked up pressure, lifted itself and moved off. Shirley picked up the cases it had left and carried them into the house. It was all very well for the smart fridge to tell the house's tele-agent to do the teleshopping, but somebody still had to do the dumb things like carrying in the groceries.

Mum and Dad were always telling her of the days when they had a car and used to go into town to shop. It sounded like fun, but they would have a job doing that now. The roads were in such an appalling condition that only heavy-duty buggies could handle them. That was why hovercraft had become so important. Surfaces didn't matter to them and they were automated to make deliveries or pickups at places marked on their maps.

Being now late for her class, Shirley ran through the gardens. They looked good at this time of year and there was so much activity in them. This was her community and these were her people. But when she arrived at the community centre her mood changed. There was a large group of people arguing. She slipped quietly past them, took her shoes and helmet off and entered the great classroom of the community centre. Her group was waiting, but they were all subdued. They were conscious of the troubles outside and that they were part of them. She looked up at the great wooden beams and the rich carvings. She loved the echo they gave when everybody was singing. That reminded her. She glanced at the back of the hall where the community cybersuits hung idle. They were used for virtual classes and mind-work by people in the community who could not afford to buy their own.

The problem had come two months ago when the community had put on a teleperformance as part of the international telefestival of folk dancing. They had been successful and won a prize, but they had also caught the attention of an info-agent who had reported them for infringement of copyright. Infringement of copyright! It was their community hall, their songs and their dances. But in the teleconference with the company lawyers, they had been shown documents signed ten years before by the Community Committee, which gave a company the electronic rights in perpetuity to the traditional dances and songs of the village. There were some elders around who remembered it. The money they had received helped repair the roof of the centre and to buy some urgently needed VR equipment so the village could get info-work. They hadn't really realised what it meant. Nobody had even thought of it when they put on their show. Now there was this huge fine to pay and until it was paid the community was cut off from telecommunications services. There was no info-work and no one they could be angry with, or argue with, except themselves. There was no national telecommunications company to complain about to the government. Nearly all the world's telecommunications was in the hands of a dozen giant companies whose corporate existence seemed to be in a CGVR rather than any particular country. The only way of communicating with the companies was by telecommunications, and if they chose to cut people off because they lived within the boundaries of a local community there was nothing anybody could do about it.

There was a beep from Shirley's helmet. She glanced at the group guiltily. 'Go on Shirl', said the class leader, 'we know you live outside the community.'

Shirley picked up her helmet and went to the back of the hall to put it on. She dropped the visor and there was her mother. 'Where is the rest of you, Shirley?' she snapped. 'You know what it is like in the community at the moment, mother,' said Shirley. 'I didn't want to put my suit on.' 'Then get yourself back to the house fast and get your suit on,' said her mother. 'I need you to help me. There is a Japanese family flying in this evening. They want to go down to the Franz Josef glacier tomorrow and I want you telepresencing with them.' 'The Franz Josef!' Shirley was startled. 'Why would they be going there?' 'Well, I suggested it to them,' said her mother. 'You've been working on that project for weeks so I told them you were a teleguide.' 'But mother', Shirley was now really concerned, 'I've never been to the Franz Josef, I only know it in VR.' 'So what's the difference?' said her mother. 'I'm not sure,' said Shirley. 'It looks so beautiful in the CGVR, but some of the old books describe it as though it is dangerous and the weather is not something that can be controlled.'

'Books!' snorted her mother with scorn. 'Now you listen, girl. We are still paying for your Japanese classes. If they like you, this could mean a whole week's work. They are expecting you to presence with them as a Japanese woman, so you need to work up an identity. I've booked you in to Telepersons' for a fitting. It's in half an hour so. So get back fast.'

Just at that moment the group went into the chant. Some of their pent-up anger came through. Their eyes flashed, their feet stamped. The shadows in the carvings remembered an older reality. Shirley moved to the door mouthing her apologies, but her friends were lost in the magic they were making. So she left them, put on her shoes and jogged home, the sun on her face and the wind in her hair and the smell of the blossoms in her nostrils. 'This', she thought, as she did some fancy footwork and spun around so that the densely settled countryside swung around her, 'this is what it's really all about. This is where I belong. This is my world. These are my people and this', she decided then, 'is where I am going to have my babies.'

> *Three hours later a smart young Japanese woman was introducing herself to Mr Koji Matsumoto and his family, on the edge of a great crevasse on the upper slopes of the Franz Josef glacier. To their ears her Japanese sounded odd and there was something strange in the way she moved and said things, but she fitted comfortably into their party and she certainly knew a lot about the glacier. They felt sure they would be in safe hands when they took the helicopter out to the real Franz Josef the following day. A window opened in the VR to say that their international flight was landing. So they arranged to meet the telepresence the following day and slipped off their helmets as they touched down after the two-hour flight from Japan to New Zealand.*

The map is not the territory. A CGVR of a real reality is only a model. 'What aspects of reality are and what are not embodied in a model is entirely a function of the model builders' purpose' (Weizenbaum 1984). We may choose to spend much of our life in virtual reality rather than in real reality, but we do not in reality thereby replace real reality. The Franz Josef glacier still exists despite all the books, photos and films about it. And it will exist, however detailed are the virtual realities that may be made of it. People may work in virtual reality, but they still have to do physical tasks in real reality. They may have heroic personae in virtual reality, but they will still suffer from acne in the real world. It may be possible to have masturbatory sex in virtual reality, but babies are born in real reality and that is where people eat and defecate and grow up and grow old, and we will always need to learn to relate physically to real reality *in* real reality.

Classrooms will continue to exist so that learners can switch between a virtual class and a real class. What will change is the function of the conventional classroom and its centrality to education. The virtual class is a meeting place for virtual communities of learners with a shared interest in the same subject. The conventional classroom of the future will be a community classroom, a meeting place for people who live in the same locality and have interests in common because they are neighbours. They may well share the same culture because they live in the same area. In the virtual class, culture, like presence, is something that can be selected, not something that one is born into. In the conventional classroom, distance matters, and catchment areas may well be smaller than they are now as populations increase and become more distributed, less urbanised and less dependent on transport systems. The education that takes place in them will be more a manifestation of community needs than national needs. It will be a place where people learn social and interpersonal communication skills, to express themselves in song and dance, to take part in sports and team activities, to learn arts and crafts, cooking and woodwork, gardening and pottery and skills of doing that involve touch and taste and smell. The custodial function of the conventional classroom will still be there. Some-one will have to look after the community's children. It may be that the conventional classroom becomes a community classroom centre where young and old gather for learning in a more informal group-centred, nurturing environment than today's school-based classrooms.

We come back to the experiment described in the first chapter which sought to find a balance between learning with a computer and learning as part of a group. We will need to find a balance between learning in a virtual class and learning in a community class, between thinking globally and acting locally. The impact of the Internet is already creating this duality in universities. Academics and students with access to the Internet find that they spend more and more of their time linking with people around the world who are interested in the same things and think in the same way. By contrast, their links with people on campus are more in terms of social and cultural activities and issues to do with parking and fire drills.

Whether people bring their own interface systems, or are provided with them as part of the classroom, they will need to find some way they can alternate between being jacked-in to a virtual class and being in group mode with their community peers. It will be more complex than the shift that takes place in a conventional classroom when a teacher moves from a classroom discussion to a book-based exercise. There will be different schedules and timetables in the virtual class and the community class. However, it will not matter where the learner is when they want to jack-in to an educational utility, any more than it matters where somebody is now when they want to read a book.

CGVR technology had its origin in the need for simulations in workplace training, and a strong argument for the development of the telelearning aspect of the virtual class is the expected expansion of teleworking. Teleworking, like telelearning, means switching between the virtual and the real, the global and the local. The two must necessarily mimic each other, because one is a preparation for the other. The equipment that is needed for teleworking is also the equipment needed for telelearning. To be successful as a teleworker means a habit of lifelong learning, such as is expected of the medical, legal and teaching professions. This suggests the re-emergence of the home as a centre of learning as well as a centre of work, but not just for preschool years; telelearning would become a lifetime survival service for teleworkers and their families.

The idea of teleworking in a telecottage sounds idyllic. Instead of grinding into the office through the rush hour, to stay at home in some pleasant suburban or rural setting enjoying a richer and less stressful life seems ideal. There is, indeed, an elite of teleworkers who live in beautiful places and conduct much of their business by telecommunications, but there could be a downside for teleworkers in developed countries. The steady decline in the cost of long distance and international calls means that a global workforce of info-workers is emerging. Businesses can go looking for cheap, international information workers. If the information worker does not have to be physically present in an office, then a company is no longer bound to find workers who live within commuting range of its offices, workers who may be bonded in a union and subject to the salary standards and legal conditions of a particular country. Increasingly it is becoming the practice of companies to contract workers part-time for a particular purpose, rather than taking on people on stringent contractual obligations which can be upheld by the laws of a country. A global information-based company has the whole world from which to choose its workers. Already, American companies off-load information work to Barbados and Santa Domingo, to Ireland and the Philippines, because wages there are so low that it more than compensates for the long-distance telecommunications costs. The artificially high costs of international tele-communications will come down. The development of a new generation of satellite technology could bypass existing terrestrial telecommunications systems. Access to some kind of PC/communications device could mean access from the most remote village to the global workforce and to global learning systems that enable a person to succeed in that workforce. No longer will remote villages in developing countries need to wait for the slow growth of conventional national telecommunications and educational systems that cannot keep pace with the population expansion. The tele-worker of the future in developed countries could find life harder, with living standards having to adapt to global rather than national standards. But for people in the developing countries the new technical environment holds promise when it means that the locality they live in no longer prevents them from competing for a place in the sun.

Shirley's story imagines a return to the days of cottage industries when the whole family needed to work. Although the telecottage is seen as a 'smart cottage' with labour-saving gadgetry and little need for transport, the family is locked in to long hours of low-paid info-work. The 'gardens' have a subsistence as well as decorative purpose. They provide food when times are hard. The telecottages house telecrofters[1] who struggle to survive.

As the information society infrastructure slips into place, the population of the world is doubling. Pressure on the world's finite resources, such as land and extractive fuels, will increase. So too will pressure to expand educational opportunity. The very survival of the human species depends upon this, and there is no way that education as we know it today could expand proportionately.

The virtual class is needed because it mimics the way of working in the information society. But something in the nature of a community class-room will also be needed because it mimics the way people physically live. Classrooms are rooms, and rooms are still the critical subsystems in which people perform most of their activities and there are no signs that this will change. We shall still use bedrooms and bathrooms and living rooms and there will still be offices, shops and theatres and we will still need classrooms.

Rooms cut out the natural reality of the outdoor world where we are at the mercy of the elements and accidental happenings, and need to focus on physical facts in order to navigate them; where absent-minded excursions into virtual reality can be dangerous and survival depends upon awareness to the distal stimuli of real reality. Rooms create a protected artificial reality in which people can live on the cusp of virtual and real reality. They reduce the amount of energy needed to keep warm and dry. They provide shelter and security and make it easy to put more energy into communications.

Enter a cinema or a theatre and you change natural light and climate for artificial conditions adapted to human comfort. Although the cinema or theatre is an artificial reality it is still part of physical reality. Then the lights dim and the show begins and the audience slips into a virtual world. Think of drawing the curtains, turning on the light and sitting in front of a fire and letting yourself day-dream, or switching on the radio or television and letting the virtual realities of mass media wash over you. Rooms are the basic communication systems of civilisation and have been for as far back as we can trace cities. We will need them to protect our bodies while our minds are in CGVR.

Buildings are clusters of rooms and cities are clusters of buildings. They are an amalgam of artificial realities, and while one view of the future is of a return to the countryside and rural development, another is of the creation of a new kind of city, an intelligent city.

High on the list of what most people perceive as intelligent in a city is safety. A striking thing about the design of intelligent cities is how clearly they are protected from presumably unintelligent areas around them. There is an emphasis on sophisticated security systems based on plastic cards that provide an open-sesame not just to the city, its buildings and its rooms but also to its services. They are passport and identity cards, credit and banking cards, permit to park and log-on cards. No need for money in this Eftpos (Electronic Funds Transfer Point of Sale) environment and no need to wonder where anybody is and what they are doing. Every transaction a citizen makes with their smart card makes it possible to monitor their movements and activities, and to measure and analyse their behaviour. It is then possible to learn about their habits and predict and anticipate their needs.

In the conventional city the environment between buildings is dominated by traffic and pollution. Within the buildings endlessly recycled sick air freezes people in the summer and gives them a sauna in the winter. Intelligent cities are green cities. Indeed, some of them are grafted on to technology parks. They are designed to be aesthetically pleasing, with a harmonious relationship between natural vegetation and buildings, and to

Figure 10.1 Suntech City is an intelligent city which is being built in Singapore. It has the shape of a hand that is envisaged in the model (the tall buildings are the fingers, the short building is the thumb). Singapore seeks to be the world's first 'intelligent country'

minimise motorised traffic in favour of pedestrian walkways. Some intelligent cities will have residential sectors with intelligent houses from which intelligent citizens can stroll to their intelligent schools, shops and offices. Motorised transport, therefore, is mainly used for moving to and from the intelligent city and so only pollutes the less fortunate surroundings. The city itself can be free of the private vehicle and thus preserve its own environment.

Intelligent climate control within buildings and the intelligent management of facilities has as an objective, besides comfort and convenience: the reduction of energy costs. This is important because, with all their gismos, intelligent cities use a lot of energy. It makes sense that a really intelligent city will be an economical city.

An interesting aspect of the drive toward intelligent cities is the need to rationalise the cost of information technology. Paradoxically, the more companies strive for a competitive edge through buying expensive new technology, the more it costs them to run their business. It is the cost of office automation that has led to intelligent buildings where facilities can be shared. It is the extension of this trend that has led to the super block, the clustering of intelligent buildings round a plaza that allows a centralised facilities management system. And it is the merging of super blocks that leads to the idea of the intelligent city.

Of course, all of this implies an intelligent communications infrastructure that is broadband and multimedia. Could intelligent cities be the first islands of the information society communicating with one another directly across the intervening seas of pre-information societies? Will they be to the information revolution what Leeds and Manchester, Pittsburgh and Osaka were to the industrial revolution? Will they bring in the millennium, create harmony between people and environment, or will they provoke social upheaval and new classes of haves and have-nots?

In Germany, Japan, Singapore and Indonesia, intelligent cities are now taking shape. They could prove to be blind alleys of development and monuments to technological madness, but their emergence is significant.

The designers of intelligent cities place much emphasis on the need to develop community values and community centres. The idea for an intelligent classroom in an intelligent city is not much dissimilar to a community classroom in a televillage.

It is easy to see evil shapes in the information shadows of the virtual class. Already there is deep concern about the way in which the information we inadvertently provide when we shop with credit cards, or fill in forms and questionnaires, is used to create data profiles of our habits and circumstances, and how this information is increasingly coordinated and sold to companies so that they can better target us for sales and predict what we will do. Imagine if all the data on what we learned, how we learned it and all the foibles we showed in the process were also to be made commercially available. This would provide a much more profound insight into our nature than information about our shopping habits. The idea of software information agents who can travel networks looking for information on our behalf as to the cheapest prices on commodities we want to buy sounds a delightful idea. In education they could also be used to find the courses we want or nuggets of information in subjects we are studying. But what if information agents were used as data detectives to look for copyright infringement or to find people who are studying or teaching subjects that had come to be regarded as undesirable or subversive?

On the other hand, there are some exciting promises in the virtual class. Nation-based educational systems are imposed. Everybody has to go to school. Curricula are prescribed and choice of subject or methodology is restricted. For many, schools are a tedious time of waiting. By contrast, the virtual class lets the learner decide what they want to study, when they want to study it and how they want to study. It empowers the learner to go and look for the learning that has meaning for them. It motivates the learner to strive to learn. The quality of striving in learning is known as 'conation'. Surprisingly little attention is paid to it in education, yet Kathryn Atman argues that it is one of the principal factors that determines success in distance learners (Atman 1987: 14), and who would doubt its potency in any kind of learning?

FRACTAL LEVELS

In this book we have argued that learning takes place through communication systems that bring together learning, teaching, knowledge and problem in such a way that, from the learner's point of view, everything clicks into place. Light dawns, the student's face clears. Got it! This is the reward of study. The reason people become teachers. But it is not necessarily easy to bring the four factors together in a way that produces this result, and what works for one learner may not work for another.

Communications can be seen as a networking of information at levels that vary from that of the neurological network of a human brain to the telecommunications network of the global village. We have suggested that there could be a fractal dimension to this and since education is communication, that it will have networks at different fractal levels. However, education is a special case of communications that needs to network its four fundamental factors at each level. What could be critical in education is for a learner to be able to shift between levels as they seek the point where the learner–teacher and knowledge–problem axes lock into place and they *understand*. Even if they do understand at one level, learners may seek verification that they understand at other fractal levels. In this way they come to see the kind of problem domain they are studying from different perspectives, their understanding is holistic, and there is feedback at each level to reassure them that their new problem-solving capability is culturally and socially acceptable. This view of education suggests that the greater the number of fractal levels, the greater the potential of an effective educational system. If this is so, then the virtual class scenario for education in the future information society will benefit to the extent that it retains the existing fractal levels in conventional educational systems and adds to them by providing a global level.

Table 10.1 takes communication levels that are recognised in communication studies as being broadly applicable to societies around the world, and relates these to the levels of communication found in the educational systems of industrial and information societies.

There is the level of the learner alone, which is present in all educational systems. Then there is the shift in level that Vygotsky defined in the ZPD from the learner alone to the learner with a teacher or peer to help them. A dyadic level can be traced across the three traditional educational systems. In the emergent telelearning phase of the kind of educational system that will exist in an information society, the dyadic relation can be made via telecommunications as well as in person. However, there is likely to be a growing dyadic relationship with computerised instructional systems. Of

Table 10.1 Fractal levels in the educational systems of industrial and information societies

Recognised levels of communication across cultures	Educational system of industrial societies			Educational system of information society	
				Emergent	Future
Society	Home	Workplace	Classroom	Telelearning	Virtual Class
Mass national & international	Culture	Profession	National Educational System	Regional consortia	Global utility
Organisation	Community	Business organisation	School	Telecourse	Virtual learning communities
Group	Family	Work team	Class	Telecentre	Virtual class + community class
Dyad	Parent + child	Apprentice + worker	Teacher + student	Telelearner + PC	Learner + CGVR virtual teacher
Intrapersonal	Child	Apprentice	Student	Telelearner	Learner

course, textbooks have always provided an alternative dyadic relationship to a teacher in traditional classrooms, but computer-based instructional systems will develop in capability. In a future virtual class situation where the PC has been subsumed into a CGVR interface, we can see the emergence of virtual teachers based on artificial intelligence. The learner will have a choice of linking by telecommunications with a peer or a human teacher or, in a way that Vygotsky did not envisage, calling on a virtual teaching entity.

The small-group level of communication that we can see at work in the family or the work team was never really catered for in conventional classrooms where numbers tended to be above the level at which small-group dynamics operate. In today's telelearning systems, small groups in telecentres redress this tendency. In the experience of the authors, the greater the reliance on information technology, the more important the social aspects of education become and it is likely that something in the nature of community classrooms, where small groups of people can meet in face-to-face situations in real reality will be needed in the future to complement the virtual class.

The virtual class in Table 10.1 is placed at the small-group level on the assumption that small-group dynamics will operate in virtual reality as they do in real reality. Initially, the technology will limit the numbers who can meet in a virtual class; however, in the long-term there are no limits to the numbers of people who can meet in a televirtual reality. Large groups of people may want to come together in a virtual class because they have the same conative drive in a particular area of study. With large numbers, the level shifts to that of a large group or organisation. At this level there is a greater emphasis on support services and administration, and much of the communication will be asynchronous. Rheingold's idea of a virtual community seems relevant. He describes supportive learning in virtual communities where a member can raise a problem they cannot handle alone and have the knowledge and teaching resources of the whole group brought to bear on the problem (Rheingold 1993). This is the ZPD on Internet. By a 'virtual learning community', however, we mean something more complex that provides support services, libraries and administration. An idea of the shape a virtual learning community could take is the scenario for the University of Tele-existence which is described at the end of Chapter 8.

At a mass level, the learner could today, in a telelearning system find themselves as part of a consortium of schools or universities. The Network College of Communications in the Pacific makes it possible for graduate research students to link on Internet with other graduate students in eight other universities, tap the resources of more than 100 academics, look into the libraries of fourteen institutions and access the case studies of problems in eight research institutions. Such initiatives are pioneering. They point towards the development of global educational utilities, giant educational consortia that make education available as international, value-added services to anyone, anywhere who can afford them.

At the organisational and mass levels of communications we see the possibility that a disjunction could develop between the educational system of the industrial society and the educational system of the information society. There are not the same parallels that exist at the intrapersonal, interpersonal and group levels. At the local level we can see continuation and coexistence of the educational systems that exist in industrial societies with the virtual class system of the information society, albeit with major modifications. We have suggested that with teleworking the home could become a more important base for education than it is now and that it could be the location for access to the virtual class as could the classroom – which might become a community centre for a locality. But what would happen to schools and national educational systems as the regional and global levels of education come into place? The issue is critical if Robert Reich's view of the future of the nation state in a global information society is valid:

> There will be no *national* products or technologies, no national corporations, no national industries. There will no longer be national economies, at least as we have come to understand that concept. All that will remain rooted within national borders are the people who comprise a nation. Each nation's primary assets will be its citizen's skills and insights. Each nation's primary political task will be to cope with the centrifugal forces of the global economy which tear at the ties binding citizens together – bestowing even greater wealth on the most skilled and insightful, while consigning the less skilled to a declining standard of living.
>
> (Reich 1991:3)

The only thing we can be sure of in forecasting the future is that whatever happens will not be what is forecast – which, of course, leaves one saying, 'But why bother?' The answer is that by attempting to visualise the shape we would like the future to have we can influence the shape it actually takes. At the beginning of this book we wrote that our purpose was to enjoin debate about future scenarios for education in an information society. We feel that it is especially at the national level that such debate is needed, and would hope that the development of global education means the metamorphosis, not the demise, of schools and national educational systems so that educational systems in an information society acquire global levels as well as, rather than instead of, national levels. In this way evolution from today's classroom educational system to tomorrow's system, based on the virtual class, could also be progress.

Graham Chapman argues that,

> If the population of the world doubles in the next thirty years, the most important fact will be that the number of brains has doubled, and these brains are more and more interconnected because of the communica-

tions explosion. In crude terms the mental power of the earth will go up by far more than four times for every doubling of the population because of this interconnectedness.

(Chapman 1993: 31)

From being ourselves, conscious of the touch of the wind, the smell of the earth, the cry of a gull and the ache of a distant view, we could one day jack-in to the cyberspace of a virtual class and shift through fractal levels to be part of a global consciousness.

A reason for shifting up the scale of fractal levels in learning is to learn what cannot be learned at lower levels. Throughout history there has been some kind of classroom. First it was a place where people learned to apply the knowledge of the local community to the problems of the community. Then it became a place where they learned to apply the knowledge of a nation to the problems of a nation. Now we are recognising that we live in a global village, where what we do in the place where we live creates or solves global problems. We need a place where we can learn to think globally and act locally. We believe it can be found in the virtual class. The search goes on.

A posse ad esse (From the possible to the actual)

(Medieval Latin proverb)

You have control over action alone, never over its fruits.

(Bhagavad Gita)

Notes

1 THE VISION

1 Progeni, Wellington, New Zealand, 1984–85.
2 Carlos Fuentes, founder of the Telesecundaria Educational Television System in Mexico.
3 An airplane/train race was scheduled in New York State on 29 May 1910, but the train really served as an observation platform (Kane 1981: 88). What seems to have made an impression is that the airplane actually managed to complete the course.
4   God guard me from those thoughts men think.
    In the mind alone
    He that sings a lasting song
    Thinks in a marrow bone.
                W. B. Yeats, 'A Prayer for Old Age', verse 1 (Finneran 1983: 287)

2 EDUCATION IS COMMUNICATION

1   The Zone of Proximal Development defines those functions that have not yet matured, but are in a process of maturation, functions that will mature tomorrow but are currently in an embryonic state. These functions could be termed the 'buds' or 'flowers' of development rather than the 'fruits' of development. The actual developmental level characterises mental development retrospectively, while the zone of proximal development characterises mental development prospectively.
                (Vygotsky 1978: 86–7)
2 Tharp and Gallimore derive a general definition of teaching from Vygotsky: 'Teaching consists in assisting performance through the ZPD. Teaching can be said to occur when assistance is offered at points in the ZPD at which performance requires assistance' (1988: 31).
3 In our research, audio noise was the single biggest problem in telelearning systems. For some years we thought that the problem was peculiar to us. There was no literature on the subject. It was mainly through conversation at conferences that we began to realise how common the trouble was. Now advertisements for audio systems for education are claiming to have solved the problem.
4 De Angelis finds that the neural patterns of the brain suggest a fractal dimension (1993).

3 IN A CLASS OF ITS OWN

1 Thomas Hughes (1822–96), who wrote the classic story *Tom Brown's Schooldays* describing life in an English public school in the nineteenth century, was himself a headmaster. As many similar stories attest, beatings were a common matter and regarded in much the same way as the following inscriptions on Sumerian tablets of the same period as Mari: ' "I must not be late or my teacher will cane me." "Why when I was not here did you talk?" Caned me. "Why when I was not here did you go out?" Caned me' (Bowen 1972: 15).
2 Regional distribution of aid to education by multilateral banks and funds between 1986 and 1990 amounted to US $6,594 million. This is mainly for buildings and equipment (UNESCO 1993: 43–5).
3 This was the 'Anatomy Project' conducted by the Multinational Project in Educational Technology of the Organisation of American States in conjunction with the Anatomy department of the Federal University of Pernambuco in Recife in 1973–76.

4 THE WRITING ON THE WALL

1 The Dunedin Multidisciplinary Health and Development Study is a twenty-one-year longitudinal study of 1,661 children. There are over 500 publications and reports (Silva 1994).
2 *Sesame Street* was based on research that suggested pre-schoolers would pay attention for short periods. Research in Brazil that used video to record attention patterns of university entrance students showed students paying attention to subject content for times that averaged eight minutes across subjects. They would then break concentration in some way (chat with a neighbour, light a cigarette, leave the room) before paying attention again. (Unpublished report Fundacão Brasiliero de TVE 1973, Rio de Janeiro)
3 Personal conversation with Professor Hartshorne, 1967, Madison, Wisconsin.

5 ROADS TO THE VIRTUAL CLASS

1 J. Tiffin produced a documentary film which involved shots of a wide variety of television classrooms and conventional classrooms. There was a manifest difference in the way the children behaved.
2 For advice to producers on how to adapt phenomena for the camera in educational television, see Combes and Tiffin (1978).

6 TELELEARNING IN CYBERSPACE

1 The Interactive Instructional Television Systems in Alabama (IITS) uses telephone lines to transmit digitally compressed video, allowing courses to be taught simultaneously on three campuses.
2 Motorola's IRIDIUM is the best known LEO system with a total of sixty-six satellites arranged in six orbits of eleven satellites, but there are others such as Globalstar and Orbcomm (Conte 1994: 598–602). The Teledesk Corporation, which includes Bill Gates of Microsoft, proposes a LEO network of 840 satellites to deliver global multi-media Internet services.
3 The description is based on the design scenario John Tiffin did for the Telecommunications Corporation of New Zealand (1992) which serves as the

basis for the development of the New Zealand Telelearning Network, and also on the design of a telelearning system commissioned by the Ministry of Maori Development for New Zealand Maori from Lalita Rajasingham.

4 There are variations in this pattern. For example, on the rural east coast of New Zealand, Maori use *Maraes* (meeting houses) for their teleclasses because the community sits in on these classes to add support to the learners (Rajasingham 1993).

7 VIRTUAL REALITY

1 Drexler (1992) summarises fifteen years of research in molecular manufacturing, which is 'the use of nanoscale mechanical systems to guide the placement of reactive molecules , building complex structures with atom by atom control'. Drexler argues that 'It has become clear that this degree of control can be achieved' (1992: xvii).

2 Howard Rheingold describes how cave paintings were used to generate VR (1991: 375–85).

8 THE VIRTUAL CLASS

1 All these features are possible with multimedia, and ATR and SICS (Swedish Institute of Computer Science), among others, are developing CGVR systems in which it is possible to access other media. Professor Milton Petruk of the University of Alberta is project manager of a Canadian consortium that has produced a series of CD-ROM courses in high-school mathematics which allows students to visualise equations.

2 An example of this is Hyper-G, a world-wide networked hypermedia system.

3 The authors understand that the idea is being worked on.

4 Despite the awesome capabilities of the Internet to find out about Elsinore Castle, one of the authors had to visit it. Surprisingly, the link with the play was denied or played down. 'There was no Hamlet here.' 'Maybe Shakespeare visited as a travelling actor and got an idea for a set.' Maybe this explains the lack of information.

5 This is a simplified version of a design created by John Tiffin in 1980 when he was a director of Aries International in Washington, DC. He was invited by Pierce Harpham to join Progeni in New Zealand and develop it. A version first appeared in 1984 and was sold in Australia, New Zealand and China as Forge. Training Solutions of Wellington, New Zealand, continue to develop and sell the system. John Tiffin has continued to work on the idea independently as a framework for the development of the virtual class.

6 For the moment the scale-up problem exists in AI. A 'small knowledge system cannot extend to a large knowledge system because the knowledge is specified for a narrow domain' (Makino 1992: 339).

7 Invented in 1981 by John Tiffin EdWARD (Educational Writing and Reading Device) 'read' bar codes placed under text or embedded in pictures and 'spoke' words keyed into his keyboard. He was, however, too expensive to manufacture in the times he was born into.

8 The value of this is becoming apparent in the NCCP (Network College of Communications in the Pacific), where the problems graduate students are researching receive comment via the Internet from contrasting cultures. The

richness of this kind of interchange is something commented on by students and academics.

9 The description of Polis is based on an E-mail from Carl Loeffler. Carl Loeffler encouraged the authors to design a university for his city and the imaginative exercise is based on this.

9 THINK GLOBAL

1 Known as the Tri-Centre Project (1991–92). It linked Victoria University of Wellington to Evans Bay Intermediate School and the Wairarapa Community Polytechnic. Its success led to the development of the New Zealand Telelearning Network, which was established in 1994.
2 Nick Zepke.
3 The late Tony Stanley.

10 ACT LOCAL

1 Crofters are Scottish smallholders who combine subsistence farming with a cottage industry.

Bibliography

Allen, D. W. (1992) *Schools for a New Century*, New York, Praeger.

Altbach, P. G. (1985). 'The great education crisis', P. G. Altbach, G. P. Kelly and L. Weis (eds), *Excellence in Education: Perspectives on Policy and Practice*, Buffalo, NY: Prometheus Books.

Andrews, K. and Kappe, F. (1994) *Soaring through Hyperspace – A Snapshot of Hyper-G and its Harmony Client*, Eurographics Symposium and Workshop on Multimedia, Graz, Eurographics Symposium and workshop on multimedia (June).

Aoki, K. (1994) *Virtual Communities in Japan*, Pacific Telecommunications Council, Sixteenth Annual Conference, Hawaii (16–20 Jan.).

Aquinas, S. T. (1975) *Summa Theologiae*, vol. 32, *Consequences of Faith*, London: Blackfriar.

Arthur, W. B. (1990). 'Positive feedbacks in the economy', *Scientific American* (Feb.): 80–5.

Atman, K. S. (1987) 'The role of conation (striving) in the distance education enterprise', *The American Journal of Distance Education* 1(1): 14.

Austin, G. D. (1982) *Herman Hollerith: Forgotten Giant of Information Processing*, New York: Columbia University Press.

Australian Telecottage Conference, v. a. (1993) *Proceedings of Australian Telecottage Conference*, Australian Telecottage Conference, 29 Nov.–1 Dec., Gold Coast.

Averch, H. A., Carroll, S. J. (1972) *How effective is schooling? A critical review and synthesis of research findings. Prepared for the President's Commission on School Finance*, Santa Monica, CA: Rand.

Barcan, A. (1993) *Sociological Theory and Educational Reality: Education and Society in Australia since 1949*, Kensington, NSW: New South Wales University Press.

Baudrillard, J. (1983) *Simulations*, New York: Semiotext(e).

Beare, H. and Boyd, W. L. (eds) (1993) *Restructuring Schools: An International Perspective on the Movement to Transform the Control and Performance of Schools*, Philadelphia: Falmer Press.

Becker, G. S. (1964) *Human Capital: A Theoretical and Empirical Analysis with Special Reference to Education*, New York: Columbia University Press.

Beeby, C. (ed.) (1969) *Qualitative Aspects of Educational Planning*, Paris: UNESCO International Institute for Educational Planning.

Bell, D. (1973) *The Coming of Post-Industrial Society: A Venture in Social Forecasting*, New York: Basic Books.

Best, J. B. (1992) *Cognitive Psychology*, St Paul, MN: West Publishing Co.

Bigum, C. and Green, B. (eds) (1992) *Understanding the New Information Technologies in Education: A Resource for Teachers*, Geelong, Vic.: Centre for Studies in Information Technologies and Education, Deakin University.

Bloom, B. S. (ed.) (1956) *Taxonomy of Educational Objectives Handbook: Cognitive Domains*, New York: David McKay.

Bonfante, J. (1994) 'Visions for a shattered city', *Time Magazine* (14 Feb.): 31.

Botkin, J., Elmandjra, M. and Malitza, M. (1979). *No Limits to Learning: Bridging the Human Gap: A Report to the Club of Rome*, Oxford: Pergamon Press.

Bowen, J. (1972) *A History of Western Education*, vol. 1, *The Ancient World*, London: Methuen.

Brand, S. (1988) *The Media Lab: Inventing the Future at MIT*, New York: Penguin Books.

Brian, A. (1990) 'Positive feedbacks in the economy', *Scientific American* 262(2): 80–5.

Butler, M. and Paisley, W. (1980) *Women and the Mass Media: Source Book for Research and Action*, New York: Human Sciences Press.

Chapman, G. (1993) 'What do communications flows actually mean?' *Pacific Telecommunications Review* 15(2): 27.

Chomsky, N. (1972) *Language and Mind*, New York: Harcourt Brace Jovanovich.

Chu, G. W. and Schramm, W. (1968) *Learning from Television: What the Research Says*, Washington, DC: National Association of Educational Broadcasters.

Clavell, J. (1975) *Shogun*, London: Hodder & Stoughton.

Combes, P. and Tiffin, J. (1978) *Television Production for Education*, London: Focal Press.

Conte, R. (1994) 'Rural telephony: a new approach using mobile satellite communications', Pacific Telecommunications Conference Proceedings, Hawaii, PTC.

Coombs, P. H. (1968) *The World Educational Crisis: A Systems Analysis*, New York: Oxford University Press.

Coombs, P. H. and Tiffin, J. (1978) *Television for Education*, London: Focal Press.

Coombs, P. W. (1985) *The World Crisis in Education: The View from the Eighties*, New York: Oxford University Press.

Cubberly, E. P. (1948) *The History of Education*, Cambridge, MA.: The Riverside Press.

De Angelis, T. (1993) 'Chaos, chaos everywhere is what the theorists think', *The American Psychological Association Monitor* 24(1): 1.

Denison, E. F. (1962) *The Sources of Economic Growth in the US and the Alternatives Before Us*, New York: Committee for Economic Development.

Dordick, H. S. (1987) *Information Technology and Economic Growth in New Zealand*, Wellington, NZ: Victoria University Press for the Institute of Policy Studies.

Drexler, E. K. (1990) *Engines of Creation*, London: Fourth Estate.

—— (1992) *Nanosystems: Molecular Machinery, Manufacturing and Computation*, New York: John Wiley & Sons.

Drucker, P. F. (1986) *The Frontiers of Management: Where Tomorrow's Decisions are being Shaped Today*, New York: Truman Talley Books.

Ebbinghaus, H. (1964, 1st edn 1885) *Memory: A Contribution to Experimental Psychology*, New York: Dover.

Eco, U. (1983) *The Name of the Rose*, London: Secker & Warburg.

Edelman, G. M. (1992) *Bright Air, Brilliant Fire: On the Matter of the Mind*, New York: Basic Books.

Edwards, E. (1968, 1st edn 1865) *Libraries and Founders of Libraries, From Ancient Times to the Beginning of the Nineteenth Century*, Amsterdam (1st edn London): Gerard Th. van Heusden.

Elton, B. (1991) *Gridlock*, London: Sphere Books Ltd.

Finn, C. E. (1991) *We Must Take Charge*, New York: The Free Press.

Finneran, R. J. (ed.) (1983) *W. B. Yeats, the Poems: A New Edition*, London: Macmillan.

Freeman, K. J. (1922) *Schools of Hellas: An Essay on the Practice and Theory of Ancient Greek Education from 600–300 BC*, London: Macmillan.

Gabriel, L. L. (1994) 'VSAT service in the Pacific: the next trend', Pacific Telecommunications Conference Proceedings, Hawaii, PTC.

Gadd, C. J. (1956) *Teachers and Students in the Oldest Schools*, London: London School of Oriental and African Studies, University of London.

Gagné, R. M. (1970, 2nd edn; 1965, 1st edn) *Conditions of Learning*, Holt, Rinehart & Winston Inc.

Gagné, R. M. and Briggs, L. J. (1974) *Principles of Instructional Design*, Holt, Rinehart & Winston Inc.

Gerbner, G. and Gross, L. (1986) 'Living with television: the dynamics of the cultivation process', *Perspectives on Media Effects*, Hillsdale, NJ: Erlbaum.

Gibson, W. (1984) *Neuromancer*, New York: Ace Books.

Gooler, D. D. (1986) *The Education Utility: The Power to Revitalize Education and Society*, Englewood Cliffs, NJ: Educational Technology Publications.

Graves, R. (1959) *Collected Poems*, London: Cassell.

Halliday, M. A. K. (1978) *Language as Social Semiotic*, London: Edward Arnold.

Hansford, B. (1988) *Teachers and Classroom Communication*, London: Harcourt Brace Jovanovich.

Harasim, L. M. (ed.) (1993) *Global Networks: Computers and International Communication*, Cambridge, MA: The MIT Press.

Harris, M. H. (1984) *History of Libraries in the Western World*, Metuchen, NJ: Scarecrow Press.

Heinich, R. (1970) *Technology and the Management of Instruction: Monograph 4*, Washington DC: Association for Educational Communications and Technology.

Heinich, R., Molenda, M. and Russell, J. D. (1985) *Instructional Media*, New York: Macmillan.

Hibler, R. W. (1988) *Life and Learning in Ancient Athens*, Lanham, MD: University Press of America.

Hiltz, S. R. (1986) 'The virtual classroom: using computer mediated communications for university teaching', *Journal of Communications* 36(2): 95.

Hughes, T. (1974, 1st edn 1857) *Tom Brown's Schooldays*, London: Dent.

Illich, I. D. (1971a) *Deschooling Society*, London: Calder & Boyars.

——— (1971b) *Celebration of Awareness: A Call for Institutional Revolution*, London: Calder & Boyars.

Innis, H. A. (1950) *Empire and Communications*, Oxford: Clarendon Press.

Jackson, P. (1990) *Presidential Address*, Annual Meeting of the American Educational Research Association, Boston.

James, W. (1890) *Principles of Psychology*, London: Macmillan.

JANCPEC (Triple-T Subcommittee) (1992) *The Triple-T Revolution and Economic Development*, Japan (Sept.).

Jürgens, H. and Peitgen, H-O. (1990) 'The language of fractals', *Scientific American* (Aug.): 60.

Kane, J. N. (1981) *Famous First Facts: A Record of First Happenings, Discoveries, and Inventions in American History*, New York: H. W. Wilson Co.

Kramer, S. N. (1959) *History Begins at Sumer*, Garden City, NY: Doubleday.

——— (1963) *The Sumerians at Sumer*, Chicago: University of Chicago.

Kuhn, T. S. (1962) *The Structure of Scientific Revolutions*, Chicago: University of Chicago Press.

Kurtzman, J. (1993) *The Death of Money*, New York: Simon & Schuster.

Lacayo, R. (1993) 'School's Out – of Cash', *Time* 141(14) (5 April): 38.

Laurel, B. (1991) *Computers as Theatre*, Menlo Park, CA: Addison-Wesley.

Lave, J. and Wenger, E. (1991) *Situated Learning*, Cambridge: Cambridge University Press.

Lewin, R. (1992) *Complexity: Life at the Edge of Chaos*, New York: Maxwell Macmillan International.

McLuhan, M. (1964) *Understanding Media: The Extensions of Man*, New York: McGraw-Hill.

McLuhan, M. and Fiore, Q. (1967) *The Medium is the Massage*, New York: Random House.

Mahesh Yogi, M. (1969) *Maharishi Mahesh Yogi on the Bhagavad-Gita: A New Translation and Commentary with Sanskrit Text, Chapters 1 to 6*, Harmondsworth: Penguin Books.

Makino, T. (1992) 'Editor's message to special session on ontological knowledge base', *Journal of Information Processing* 15(3): 339.

Malamah-Thomas, A. (1987) *Classroom Interaction*, Oxford: Oxford University Press.

Mandelbrot, B. B. (1983) *The Fractal Geometry of Nature*, New York: W.H. Freeman.

Marginson, S. (1993) *Education and Public Policy in Australia* Cambridge: Cambridge University Press.

Marryat, C. (1929) *Mr Midshipman Easy*, London: Phoenix.

Maurer, H. (1994) 'Advancing the ideas of the World Wide Web', Hypermedia Conference, Auckland, NZ (July).

Maurer, H., Rajasingham, L. and Tiffin, J. (1994) 'New Zealand heritage sold', *NZ Science Monthly* (March): 6.

Minsky, M. (1986) *The Society of Mind*, New York: Simon & Schuster.

Moll, L. C. (ed.) (1990) *Vygotsky and Education: Instructional Implications and Applications of Sociohistorical Psychology*, Cambridge and New York: Cambridge University Press.

Moore, M. G. (1993) 'Editorial: is teaching like flying? A total systems view of education', *The American Journal of Distance Education* 7(1): 1.

Morita, A. and Reingold, E. M. (1987) *Made in Japan: Akio Morita and Sony*, London: William Collins.

Murdock, G. P. (1949) *Social Structure*, New York: Macmillan.

NCOEIE (1983) *A Nation at Risk: The Imperative for Educational Reform: A Report to the Nation and the Secretary of Education*, Washington, DC: The National Commission on Excellence in Education.

Nicolopoulou, A. and Cole, M. (1993) 'Generation and transmission of shared knowledge in the culture of collaborative learning: the Fifth Dimension, its play world, and its institutional contexts', *Contexts for Learning*, New York: Oxford University Press.

Papert, S. (1980) *Mindstorms: Children, Computers and Powerful Ideas*, New York: Basic Books.

Penrose, R. (1989) *The Emperor's New Mind: Concerning Computers, Minds, and the Laws of Physics*, New York: Oxford University Press.

Peters, O. (1973) *Die didaktische Structur des Fernunterrichts unter suchungen zu einer industrialisierten Form des Lehrens und Lernens*, Weinhen: Beltz.

Pfeiffer, J. E. (1982) *The Creative Explosion of Enquiry in the Origins of Art and Religion*, Ithaca, NY: Cornell University Press.

Picot, B. (1988) *Administering for Excellence: Effective Administration in Education: Report of the Taskforce to Review Education Administration*, Wellington, NZ: The Taskforce to Review Education Administration.

Postman, N. (1985) *Amusing Ourselves to Death: Public Discourse in the Age of Show Business*, New York: Viking.

Presseisen, B. Z. (1985) *Unlearned Lessons*, Basingstoke: Falmer.

Probine, M. S. and Fargher, R. W. S. (1987) *The Report of a Ministerial Working Party:*

The Management, Funding and Organization of Continuing Education and Training, Wellington, NZ: Office of the Minister of Education.

Progrow, S. (1983) *Education in the Computer Age*, Beverly Hills, CA: Sage.

Quarterman, J. S. (1993) 'The global matrix of minds', *Global Networks: Computers and International Communication*, Cambridge, MA and London: The MIT Press.

Rajasingham, L. (1988a) 'The coadunation of distance education and new communication technologies: the New Zealand Technical Correspondence Institute: a case study', Victoria University of Wellington.

———— (1988b) *Distance Education and New Communications Technologies*, Wellington, NZ: Telecom Corporation of New Zealand.

———— (1993) *Shaping the Future in Ruatoria: The Role of Information Technology*, Ngata Memorial College, Te Puni Kokiri (Ministry of Maori Development).

Reich, R. (1991) *The Work of Nations: A Blueprint for the Future*, London: Simon & Schuster.

Renwick, W. L. (1984) *Proposal for a Board of Studies: Report of the Working Party on the Board of Studies*, Wellington, NZ: Department of Education.

Rheingold, H. (1991) *Virtual Reality*, New York: Simon & Schuster.

———— (1993) *The Virtual Community*, Reading, MA: Addison-Wesley.

Rogoff, B. (1990) *Apprenticeship in Thinking*, New York: Oxford University Press.

Romiszowski, A. J. (1976) 'A study of individualized systems for mathematics instruction at the post-secondary levels', Loughborough: University of Technology.

———— (1981) *Designing Instructional Systems: Decision Making in Course Planning and Curriculum Design*, London and New York: Kogan Page, Nichols Publishing.

———— (1986) *Developing Auto-instructional Materials: From Programmed Texts to CAL and Interactive Video*, London and New York: Kogan Page, Nichols Publishing.

Rose, S. (1992) *The Making of Memory*, London: Transworld Publishers Ltd.

Rossman, P. (1992) *The Emerging Worldwide Electronic University: Information Age Global Higher Education*, Westport, CT: Greenwood Press.

Rudy, W. (1984) *The universities of Europe, 1100–1914*, Cranbury, NJ: Associated University Press.

Rumble, G. and Oliveira, J. (1992) *Vocational Education at a Distance: International Perspectives*, London: Kogan Page, in association with the International Labour Office.

Salomon, G. (1990) 'Cognitive effects with and of computer technology', *Communication Research* 17(1 Feb.): 26.

Salomon, G. and Globerson, T. (1989) 'The computer as a zone of proximal development: internalizing reading-related metacognitions from a reading partner', *Journal of Educational Psychology* 81(4): 620.

Schultz, T. W. (1961) 'Education and economic growth', *Social Forces Influencing American Education*, Chicago, University of Chicago Press.

Searle, J. R. (1992) *The Rediscovery of the Mind*, Cambridge, MA and London: Bradford.

Sendov, B. (1986) 'The second wave: problems of computer education', *Information Technology and Education*, Chichester: Ellis Hall Ltd.

Shannon, C. E. and Weaver, W. (1949) *The Mathematical Theory of Communication*, Urbana: University of Illinois Press.

Shaw, B. (1922) *Back to Methuselah*, London: Constable & Co.

Sherman, B. and Judkins, P. (1992) *Glimpses of Heaven, Visions of Hell*, London: Hodder & Stoughton.

Silva, P. A. and McCann, M. (1994) *Annotated Bibliography of 500 Publications and Reports from the Dunedin Multidisciplinary Health and Development Research Unit, 1975 to 1994*, Dunedin: Dunedin Multidisciplinary Health and Development Research Unit, University of Otago Medical School (Feb.).

Sinclair, J. M. and Coulthard, R. M. (1975) *Towards an Analysis of Discourse*, Oxford: Oxford University Press.

Singh, J. (1994) 'INMARSAT and personal mobile satellite services', Pacific Telecommunications Conference Proceedings, Hawaii, PTC.

Singh, J. A. L. and Zingg, R. M. (1939) *Wolf-children and Feral Man*, New York: Harper.

Skeat, R. W. W. (1924) *An Etymological Dictionary of the English Language*, Oxford: Oxford University Press.

Stonier, T. (1983) *The Wealth of Information: A Profile of the Post-industrial Economy*, London: Thames Methuen.

Strike, K. A. (1982) *Liberty and Learning*, Oxford: Robertson.

Sutton, C. (ed.) (1981) *Communication in the Classroom*, London: Hodder & Stoughton.

Taylor, F. W. (1947) *Scientific Management: Comprising Shop Management, the Principles of Scientific Management: Testimony before the Special House Committee*, New York: Harper.

Terashima, N. (1993) *Telesensation – A New Concept for Future Telecommunications*, TAO First International Symposium, Japan, TAO International Symposium 6–7 Dec.

Tharp, R. G. and Gallimore, R. (1988) *Rousing Minds to Life: Teaching, Learning, and Schooling in Social Context*, Cambridge and New York: Cambridge University Press.

Tiffin, J. (1976) *Problem Structures in ITV Systems in Latin America*, Pd.D. thesis, Florida State University.

——— (1978) 'Problems in instructional television in Latin America', *Revista de Tecnologia Educativa* 4(2).

——— (1979) *Problema de Televisão Educcativa*, Rio de Janeiro, PRONTEL.

——— (1980) 'Educational television – a phoenix in Latin America?' *PLET* 17(3)(Nov.): 257.

——— (1989) 'The failure of success and the success of failure', *Educational Training Technology International* 26(2) (May): 136.

UNESCO (1993) *World Education Report 1992*, Paris, UNESCO.

Van der Post, L. (1961) *The Heart of the Hunter*, Harmondsworth: Penguin Books.

von Weizsacker, C. F. (1980) *The Unity of Nature*, New York: Farrar Straus Giroux.

Vygotsky, L. S. (1962) *Thought and Language*, Cambridge, MA: MIT Press.

——— (1978) *Mind in Society: The Development of the Higher Psychological Processes*, Cambridge, MA: Harvard University Press.

Waldrop, M. M. (1992) *Complexity: The Emerging Science at the Edge of Chaos*, New York: Simon & Schuster.

Waldvogel, J. A. (1994) 'A case study in the development of a computer support writing program for post-teaching reinforcement at tertiary level', MA thesis, Victoria University of Wellington.

Weizenbaum, J. (1976) *Computer Power and Human Reason, From Judgement to Calculation*, San Francisco: W. H. Freeman.

Wertsch, J. V. (ed.) (1985) *Culture Communication and Cognition: Vygotskian Perspectives*, Cambridge and New York: Cambridge University Press.

Wilkinson, L. C. (ed.) (1982) *Communicating in the Classroom*, New York: Academic Press.

Williams, F. (1992) *The New Communications*, Belmont, CA: Wadsworth.

Woods, B. (1993) *Communication, Technology, and the Development of People*, London: Routledge.

Index

adult education 75
Advanced Telecommunication
   Research (ATR) Communication
   Systems Laboratories 7, 139, 155–6,
   190
Allen, Dwight 9
Altbach, Philip 9
Anatomy Project 189
Andrews, K. and Kappe, F. 117
Aoki, K. 156
apprenticeships 52–3, 56
Aquinas, Thomas 40
artificial intelligence (AI) 35–6, 101,
   127, 148, 185, 190
asynchronous, communications 104,
   110, 112, 185; instructional activities
   16; systems 120, 122, 123;
   teleservices 115–16
Atman, Kathryn 182
ATR see Advanced Telecommunication
   Research (ATR) Communication
   Systems
audiocassettes 109
audioconferencing 5, *108*–10
audiographic conferencing 6, 112–13,
   114, 116
aura collision 146
Austin, G.D. 133
authoring function 150–1
autonomous learner 143–7
Averch, H.A. *et al.* 9, 11

bandwith 102–3, 117, 141
bandwith on demand 117
banks/banking 20, 79, 101, 164, 180, *see
   also* telebanking
BBS *see* bulletin board systems
Becker, G.S. 58

Bell, Daniel 48
Best, J.B. 41, 93
Bigum, C. and Green, B. 164
blackboard/whiteboard, conventional
   61–3; electronic 112–13, 121
Bonfante, J. 171
books *see* written text
Botkin, J. *et al.* 71, 72, 83
Bowen, J. 189
brain, as communication-processing
   system 32, *34*
Brand, Stewart 87, 168
Brian, Arthur 170–1
Bricken, Meredith 170
Brooks, Frederick 154
Brown, Charles 146
buildings, intelligent 181
bulletin board systems (BBS) 107, 115
business television 110

CAI *see* computer-assisted instruction
cameras 112
CD-ROM 43, 113, 117, 190
cellular telecommunications 15, 17
Cerf, Vinton 124
CGVR *see* computer-generated virtual
   reality
chaos theory 170–1
Chapman, Graham 186
Chomsky, Noam 11
cities, intelligent 131, 180–2
classroom/s 10; as broadband
   environment 41; and communication
   19, 57–63; control in 68, 70;
   conventional 155, 177–8; as
   dominant form of education 87;
   function 58–63, 177–8; mixed ability
   in 78; physical qualities of 19–20;

purpose of 57–8; space problem 74–6; storage problem 76–7; teaching in 12; time problem 77–9; use of desks and blackboard/whiteboard in 61–3
climate control 181
Club of Rome 83
coaxial cable 103
Cole, Michael 23
Combes, P. and Tiffin, John 189
communication, defined 26; and education **26–39**; fractal dimension in 36–9; functions of system *21*; levels of 183, *184*, 185–7; mathematical theory of 27–9; (non)verbal 19; patterns of in the classroom 20–2, *60–1*; storage of 30–6; in telelearning 118–24; transmission of 26–30
compact discs 116
computer assisted counselling (CAC) 14
computer conferencing 107
computer-assisted instruction (CAI) 5, 35, *98–101*
computer-assisted instructional design (CAID) function 150
computer-generated virtual reality (CGVR) 127–9, *128*, 131, 139, 141, 167, 170, 177, 178, 185, 190; application of 143–7; attributes of 144–5; defined 142–3; and the elderly 143; evolution of 133–9; and virtual teacher 149–53, *see also* futures scenario; virtual reality
computer-managed instruction (CMI) 99–101, *100*
computers 87, 89, 99, 103, 134, 174; applied to learning 97–101; as communication-processing system 32, 34, *35*; introduction of 81; learning to use 82; use of in multimedia systems 116–17
conation 182
consciousness 130
Conte, R. 189
control, in the classroom 68, 70; in education 45–7
Coombs, Philip H. 9, 169
Coombs, Philip W. 80
correspondence systems 87, 88–9, 110, 116, 124
Cubberly, E.P. 67
cybernetic process 45

cyberspace 101, 124–6

datasuit 15, 137
DBS *see* direct broadcast satellite
De Angelis, T. 188
Denison, E.F. 58
design *see* instructional design
desktop computers 56, 112
desktop video 112
digital transmission 103
direct broadcast satellite (DBS) 104
distance education 15, 87, 169, *see also* education
dreams 131
Drexler, Eric 6, 127, 137–9, 190
Dunedin Multidisciplinary Health and Development Study 189
dyads 28, 37, 42, 43, 183

E-mail *see* electronic mail
Ebbinghaus, Herman 30
economies of scale 166–8
Edelman, Gerald 36
education, back to basics 9; classroom for 57–63; commercialisation of 164–6; as communication **19–47**; communication systems needed for 39–47; conventional 35; conventional balanced with telelearning 3–5; declining standards in 9; defined 22–6; eras of 48–9; as form of programming 34; four factors of 24–6; home as 49–52; as lifelong activity 23, 73; need for planning horizon 17–18; paradigm of 11–12; primary, secondary and tertiary education in 66–8; two by four by six 87; use of term 19; workplace as 52–6
education systems 10; changes in 183, 185–7; as distance-independent 15, 87, 169; failure to adapt 71–3, 80–4; national 81; removal of obstacles 84–6; size of problem 73–4
educational television (ETV) 5, 87, 90–7, *95*, 96, 109, 110, 155, 163, 167; (dis)advantages 94–5
EdWARD (Educational Writing and Reading Device) 190
Electronic Funds Transfer Point of Sale (Eftpos) 180
electronic mail (E-mail) 79, 82, 89, 107, 115, 120, 164, 174, 191; 'flaming' 17

Elton, Ben 1
ETV *see* educational television
experience 130
expert systems 151–2

Fahlen, Lennart 146
family, defined 49
fax 89, 163, 174
fibre optics 17, 103, 137, 141, 162
Fifth Dimension Project 23
film 135
Finn, Chester 9
Finneran, R.J. 188
fractal geometry 37
fractal levels 45, 49, 63, 99, 117, 122,
    123, 156, 183, *184*, 185–7; in
    apprenticeship training *55*; in the
    classroom 64, *65*, 66; in
    communication 36–9; in family
    educational network *51*
Franklin, Benjamin 84
Freud, Sigmund 130
Fuentes, Carlos 90, 188
Fuller, Buckminster 165
futures scenarios, the 'Shirley' vision
    13–15, 145–6, 152–3, 154, 157–60,
    175–7, 179

Gabriel, L.L. 104
Gadd, C.J. 48
Gagne, R.M. and Briggs, L.J. 23
General Agreement on Tariffs and
    Trade (GATT) 164
GEOs *see* telecommunications satellites
Gerbner, G. 173
Gérome, Jean-Léon 132–3
Gibson, William 124, 125
global, classroom 122; education utility
    163–4; lecture hall 123; thinking **161–
    71**
Globalstar 189
Gooler, Denis 163
graphic user interface (GUI) 157
Graves, Robert 131–2
GUI *see* graphic user interface

Halliday, M.A.K. 49
Hansford, B. 19
Harpham, Pierce 190
Hartshorne, Richard 81, 189
HDTV *see* high-definition television

head-mounted display (HMD) 135–7,
    157
Heinrich, R. 11; *et al.* 116
hertzian waves 126
high-definition television (HDTV) 97,
    103
Hiltz, Roxanne 10, 123
HMD *see* head-mounted display
home, as communication system for
    education 49–52
Hughes, Thomas 189
Hyper-G 117, 190
hypermedia 117
hypertext 117

ID *see* instructional design images, full-
    motion and stepped 93–5
information society 48, 183;
    transformation to 2
information technology, as alternative
    system for education 6; application of
    168–9; defined 5; potential of 20
initiate, response and follow-up (IRF)
    64
Innis, Harold 173, 174
instructional design (ID) 47
instructional television *see* educational
    television
Integrated Services Digital Network
    (ISDN) 103, 141
Interactive Instructional Television
    Systems (IITS) 189
international value-added network
    service (IVANS) 154, 164
Internet 16, 37, 124–5, 157, 167, 174,
    185, 189
IRF *see* initiate, response and follow-up
IRIDIUM system 189
ISDN *see* Integrated Services Digital
    Network
IVANS *see* international value-added
    network service

Jackson, Philip 12
Johnson, Lyndon 8
Jürgens, H. *et al.* 37
Just in Time (JIT) 146
just-in-time teacher 154–5, 167

Kane, J.N. 188
King, Martin Luther 131
knowledge 62–3, 77, 99; access to 146–

7; flow of new 169–70; movement in the family 50; transmission of 43–4, *see also* learner-teacher-problem-knowledge
knowledge-problem 123
Kramer, S.N. 48
Kuhn, T. 10–11, 12

Lacayo, R. 74
laser optics 116–17
Laurel, Brenda 146
Lave, J. and Wenger, E. 54
learner-teacher 54, 64, 148–55
learner–teacher–knowledge–problem 24–6, 39, 41, 42–3, 44–5, 62–3, 64, 66, 98, 124, 143, 146, 156, 183
learners 46, 59; and personal computers 118, 120–1
learning 40; closed and open 146; social embeddedness of 23
lecture 67
LEOs *see* Low Earth Orbiting Satellites
libraries 76–7, 123, 143; access to 115–16; electronic 120
links 37
literacy, decline 40–1
Loeffler, Carl Eugene 157, 191
Low Earth Orbiting Satellites (LEOs) 104, *106*, 189

McLuhan, Marshall 173, 174; and Fiore, Q. 173
Magenat-Thalmann, Nadia 153
maintenance learning 83
Makino, T. 190
Malamah-Thomas, A. 19
management function 151
Mandelbrot, Benoit 37
mapping function 150
Marginson, S. 164
Maurer, H. *et al.* 117
media, hot and cool 173; two-dimensional/three-dimensional 144–5, 147
memory 129–30; artificial 31, 43; auxiliary 35; biological 31, 43; collective 31; computer-based 31; eidetic (photographic) 30–1; individual 31
Menem, Carlos 73
Minsky, Marvin 36, 138
Moll, L.C. 22

Moore, Michael 13
Morita, Akiru 76
MUD object-oriented (MOOs) 125
multi-purpose home unit 141
Multi-user Adventures (MUAs) 125
Multi-user dungeons (MUDs) 125
Multi-user Simulations Environments (MUSEs) 125
multichannel learning 41
multimedia systems 40, 52, 101, 116–17, 124, 142, 143, 145

nanotechnology 7, 127, 137, 139
narrowcast transmission 110
National Commission on Excellence in Education (NCOEIE) 9
Network College of Communications in the Pacific (NCCP) 185, 190
networks 150–2; in communication 37–9; course 121–3; educational 29–30, 50; family 29, 50; fully meshed 59; interconnectibility of 29; learning 42; N-adic social 29; political 29; telephone 29; transport 29; triadic 37
Nicolopoulou, A. and Cole, M. 23
nodes 37–8, 40, 59, 66, 123, 150, 151
noise 27
non-linear random process theory 171

online database services 115–16
oral skills 82–3
Orbcomm 189
Organisation of American States (OAS) 90

Papert, Seymour 74, 87
paradigm, use of term 10–11
PC *see* personal computer
Penrose, Roger 36
personal computers (PCs) 52, 81, 87, 113, 120, 142, 179, 185; advances in 148–9; development of 134–5; and individual learner 118, 120–1
Peters, O. 88
Petruk, Milton 190
plain old telephone system (POTS) 102, 103
planning horizons 17–18
Plato computer-based learning system 167
portable computers 56, 168
post-industrial society 48

postal services 89
Postman, Neil 40–1
pre-industrial society 48
pre-school education 74, *see also*
    education
Presseisen, Barbara 9
primary education 66, 73, 167, *see also*
    education
problem-solving 23–4, 42, 62–3, 64, 99,
    see also learner–teacher–knowledge–
    problem
processing, in communication 32–6; for
    education 44–5
Progrow, Stanley 9
proximal stimuli 40

Quarterman, John 124

Rajasingham, L. 6, 121, 190
Rand Corporation 8, 11
real reality, time spent in 172–4, 177–82
Reich, Robert 186
Renwick, W.L. 164
research, action 12–13; futures
    scenarios 13, 15, 145–6, 152–3, 154,
    157–60, 175–7, 179; quantitative and
    qualitative 11–12
Rheingold, Howard 7, 78, 125, 146,
    156, 172, 185, 190
Rogoff, Barbara 22, 23, 50
Romiszowski, Alex 77, 115
Rose, Steven 30–1, 49
Rossman, Parker 122, 123, 125, 161,
    165
rote learning 31
Rudy, W. 83
Rumble, G. and Oliveira, J. 6

Saloman, Gabriel 97
school/s, unable to respond 71–3
Schultz, T.W. 58
Searle, John 36
secondary education 66, 167, *see also*
    education
self-study 120
Sendov, Blagovest 99, 100, 101
senses 92–3; use of in learning 40–3
Shannon, Claude 35; and Weaver,
    Warren 19, 27–9
Sherman, Barry and Judkins, Phil 16–
    17, 137
SIG *see* special interest group

Silva, P.A. 189
simulations, use of 52–3
Sinclair, J.M. and Coulthard, R.M. 64
Singh, J.A.L. 104
skills 150
small-group, dynamics 155–6, 185;
    telecentre networks 121, 124
space, as classroom problem 74–6
special interest group (SIG) 115
speech recognition systems 15
Stanley, Tony 191
storage, as classroom problem 76–7; in
    communication 30–2; for education
    43–4
Strike, K.A. 165
Studio for Creative Inquiry 157
sundial, as communication-processing
    system 32–*3*
superhighways 102–4, 107, 127, 141,
    164, 174
Sutton, C. 19
synchronous, communications 104,
    107, 110, 112; systems 123;
    teleconferencing 107–13
systems analysis 21–2, 59

Taylor, Frederick 56
Taylorism 56
teacher–learner interaction 89
teacher-to-learner ratios 79–80
teachers 122; changing role 168–9, *see
    also* learner–teacher–knowledge–
    problem
tectonic shift 170–1
tele-existence 157
teleactivities 2
telebanking 76, 164, *see also* banks/
    banking
telecentres 185
teleCGVR 174
telecommunications 2–3, 5, 43, 84, 139;
    current applications 102; versus
    transport 161–3
telecommunications satellites (GEOs)
    103, *105*
teleconferencing 6, 107, 155; emerging
    patterns 116–18
telecottages 2, 178, 179
Teledesk Corporation 189
telelearning 17, 78, 104, 171, 178, 183,
    185; asynchronous teleservices for
    115–16; balanced with conventional

learning 3–5; design for multi-level system 118–24, *119*
telelibrary 123
telemedicine 164
telephones 20, 76, 110, 115, 163, 164
teleport 104
telepresence 112, 113, 139, 141
teleschools 3
telescuela (television schools) 90–2
Telescundaria system 90–2
teleseminars 78
telesensation 139, 141
teleservices 115–16
teleshopping 2, 76
teleteachers 169
teletranslation 164
teletutorial 156
televirtual class 141
televirtual realities 3, 139, 141
television 8, 20, 76, 103, 133, 173; as surrogate child-minder 52, *see also* educational television
teleworking 2, 56, 168, 171, 178–9, 186
Terashima, Nobuyoshi 7, 139, 141, 155
tertiary education 66–8, 78, 167; use of blackboard/whiteboard in 67, *see also* education
Tharp, R.G. and Gallimore, R. 22, 23, 188
theatre 135, 180
Tiffin, John 96, 109, 189, 190
time, as classroom problem 77–9
Time magazine 84
training 44
transmission, in communication 26–30; for education 40–3
transport systems 1–2; problems of 107; versus telecommunications 161–3
transport-based classroom model 75–6, 77, 117
Tri-Centre Project 191
Triple-T (Tourism, Transport and Telecommunications) 38
Turoff, Murrey 123

UNESCO 74, 189

Value-Added Network Service (VANS) 164
Van der Post, Laurens 131

VANS *see* Value-Added Network Service
VDU *see* video display unit
very small aperture terminal (VSAT) 104
video 96, 109, 110, 117; interactive 149
video display unit (VDU) 6, 113, 125, 135
videoconferencing 3, 110, *111*, 112, 116, 174
videophone 3, 174
virtual class 8, 10, 11, 84, 85, 110, 112, 116, 118, 123, 125, **142–57**, 168, 178, 179, 185, 187; in the future 6–8; as it is now 5–6; and teachers 168–9
virtual communities 156
virtual educational institution 167–8
virtual humanity 153
virtual learning environment 16, 17
virtual learning institute (VLI) 10, 123–4
virtual learning space (VLS) 10
virtual objects 136
Virtual Polis 157, 191
virtual reality (VR) 97, 99, 125, **126–41**; application 7; development 127; explained 6–7; generators 131–3; internal/external 129–31; telepresence in 139, 141; time spent in 172–4, 177–82
virtual school 15–16
virtual teachers 148–54
VLI *see* virtual learning institute
VLS *see* virtual learning space
Von Weizsacker, C.F. 32
VR *see* virtual reality
VSAT *see* very small aperture terminal
Vygotsky, Lev 22–3, 27, 49, 64, 66, 118, 120, 183, 185, 188

Waldrop, Mitchell 130
Waldvogel, J.A. 120
Walkman 76, 136
Weizenbaum, J. 177
Wilkinson, L.C. 19
Williams, F. 38
Woods, Bernard 17
word processors 134
workplace, as educational system 52–6
World Trade Organisation (WTO) 164
World Wide Web (WWW) 117

written, skills 80–1, 82; text 43–4, 56, 167

WWW *see* World Wide Web

Zepke, Nick 191
zone of proximal development (ZPD) 22–4, 49, 52, 54, 66, 73, 80, 99, 100, 120, 131, 150, 183; defined 188; examples of 25–6

ZPD *see* zone of proximal development